AMERICAN BUILDING

2: The Environmental Forces

That Shape It

Also by James Marston Fitch

WALTER GROPIUS

ARCHITECTURE AND THE ESTHETICS OF PLENTY

AMERICAN BUILDING 1: THE HISTORICAL FORCES THAT SHAPED IT

AMERICAN BUILDING

2: The Environmental Forces That Shape It

BY JAMES MARSTON FITCH

SECOND EDITION REVISED AND ENLARGED
ILLUSTRATED

HOUGHTON MIFFLIN COMPANY BOSTON

ISBN: 0-395-12667-3
Library of Congress Catalog Card Number: 65-10689
Printed in the United States of America

Some of the material in this book has appeared in various forms in the
following publications. All articles are by James Marston Fitch unless otherwise noted.
Chapter 1
1. *Annals of the New York Academy of Sciences,* vol. 128 (September 27,
    1965), pp. 706–714.
2. *Journal of Aesthetic Education,* vol. 4 (January 1970).
3. *Environmental Psychology: Man and His Physical Setting,* by Prohan-
    sky, Ittleson and Rivlin (New York: Holt, Rinehart and Winston, 1971).
4. *Architecture, Environment and Behavior* by Robert Gutmann (New
    York: Basic Books, 1971).
Chapter 5
1. "Control of the Luminous Environment," in *Scientific American,* vol. 219
    (September 1968), pp. 190–203.
2. *Lasers and Light: Readings from the Scientific American* (San Fran-
    cisco: W. H. Freeman and Company, 1969).
Chapter 6
1. "For the Theatral Experience, an Architecture of Truth," in *Arts in
    Society,* vol. 4, no. 3, 1968.
Chapter 7
1. "The Manipulation of Space, Time and Gravity," *Proceedings of En-
    vironmental Design Research Association,* University of North Caro-
    lina, Chapel Hill, 1969.
Chapter 11
1. Section entitled "Training Tomorrow's Architects" appeared in "The
    Profession of Architecture" in *Professions in America* (Boston: Hough-
    ton Mifflin, 1965).

To C. R. and J. D.
who at different levels
made it possible

PREFACE TO THE SECOND VOLUME

This volume, the second of two, deals with the same subject matter that was covered in the latter half of the first edition published in 1948. That earlier version sought to establish a holistic concept of man/environment relationships — a necessary frame of reference within which building could be fruitfully analyzed and viable goals for its future established. Unfortunately, it cannot be claimed that either the building field, or the professions which guide it, have found it worthwhile to pursue this theoretical line. Indeed, in many respects, it must be admitted that American architecture today pays less attention to ecological, microclimatic and psychosomatic considerations than it did a quarter of a century ago. Despite its visual novelty and purported modernity, our architecture is on the whole as formalistic in its main configurations — and hence as unsatisfactory in its overall performance — as it was half a century ago, before the appearance of the Bauhaus and the International Style.

Ironically, this failure to achieve experientially acceptable levels of performance takes place at the center of the world's most developed technology. It might almost be said, in fact, that the failure is *made possible* precisely by the overwhelming presence of that technology. The sheer ubiquity of equipment for the manipulation of the natural environment — heating, cooling and ventilating; artificial illumination; acoustics and electronic communications; rapid transport — has led architects, engineers and planners to behave as if this circumambient environment could be ignored as a factor in design.

Paradoxically, however, this same technology has made possible advances of profound significance in an altogether different sphere of human activity — that of space exploration. Aerospace medicine, in its effort to take man safely into outer space, has had to carry on an examination of man/environment relations which are unprecedented in both scope and precision. Directly or indirectly, this program has mobilized the talents of thousands of ecologists, environmentalists, anthropologists, physiologists and psychologists. And, whatever light they may have been able to throw on the problems of man in space, their work has enormous significance for the fate of man on earth. Even if unwittingly, they now have created for architects, landscape designers and city planners the conceptual basis for a wholly new approach to the design of human settlements.

This great and growing corpus of environmental studies has proved to be of inestimable value in the preparation of this volume, as a comparison with the earlier volume will quickly reveal. It has enormously widened and enriched my own understanding of this, the most important facet of man's existence. At the same time, it has been the source of satisfaction to find that my original hypothesis (reformulated in Fig. 3) has been substantially confirmed. If this book helps to convince the design professions of the urgency of adopting these new perspectives of our biosphere as guides to our interventions in it, it will have more than served its modest purpose.

JAMES MARSTON FITCH

Columbia University in the City of New York
September 1971

CONTENTS

AMERICAN BUILDING

2: The Environmental Forces
That Shape It

1.
EXPERIENTIAL BASES FOR
ESTHETIC DECISION

The fundamental thesis of this book is that the ultimate task of architecture is to act in favor of man: to interpose itself between man and the natural environment in which he finds himself, in such a way as to remove the gross environmental load from his shoulders. The central function of architecture is thus to lighten the very stress of life. Its purpose is to maximize man's capacities by permitting him to focus his limited energies upon those tasks and activities which are the essence of the human experience.

This successful interposition between man and his natural environment furnishes the material basis of all great architecture. To wrest the objective conditions for man's optimal development and well-being from a Nature which only seldom provides it, to satisfy his physiological and psychological requirements at optimal levels — this beyond question is the objective basis of any architecture which is both beautiful and good. To design such a building, as Gropius once so movingly put it, is an authentic act of love.

It goes without saying that all architects aspire to the creation of beautiful buildings. But a fundamental weakness in most discussions of architectural esthetics is a failure to relate it to its matrix of experiential reality. Our whole literature suffers from this conceptual limitation since it tends to divorce the esthetic process from the rest of experience, as though it were an abstract problem in pure logic. Thus we persist in discussing buildings as though their esthetic impact upon us were an exclusively visual phenomenon. And this leads immediately to serious misconceptions as to the actual relationship between the building and its human occupants. Our very terminology reveals this misapprehension: we speak of having *seen* such and such a building, of liking or not liking its *looks*, of its *seeming* too large or too small in scale, etc., etc. These are all useful terms, of course, insofar as they convey a part of the whole truth about our relationship to our buildings. But they are also extremely misleading in suggesting that man exists in some dimension quite separate and apart from his buildings; that his only relationship with them is that of passive exposure; that this exposure occurs only along the narrow channel of vision; and that the whole experience is quite unaffected by the environment in which it occurs.

The facts are quite otherwise and our modes of thought must be revised to correspond to them. For architecture — like man himself — is totally submerged in the natural external environment. It can never be felt, perceived, experienced, in anything less than multidimensional totality. A change in one aspect or quality of this environment inevitably affects our perception of and response to all the rest. Recognition of this fact is crucial for esthetic theory, above all for architectural esthetics. Far from being narrowly based upon any single sense of perception like vision, our response to a building derives from our body's *total* response to and perception of the environmental conditions which that building affords. It is literally impossible to experience architecture in any "simpler" way. *In architecture there are no spectators: there are only protagonists, participants.* The body of critical literature which pretends otherwise is based upon photographs of buildings and not the experience of the actual buildings at all. (It seldom occurs to us to remember that even when we study the pictures of one building in a book or magazine, we always do so while sheltered by another. We could no more enjoy photographs of a beautiful building while seated in a snow-filled meadow than we could respond favorably to a concert in a storm-tossed lifeboat at sea. Most such esthetic experiences subsume as *sine qua non* the controlled environment of architecture.)

Analogies between architecture and the other forms of art are very common in esthetic literature. Obviously, architecture shares many formal characteristics with them. Like a painting or a sculpture, like a ballet or a symphony, a building may be analyzed from the point of view of proportion, balance, rhythm, color, texture and so on. But such analogies will be misleading unless we constantly bear in mind that our experiential relationship with architecture is fundamentally of a different order from that of the other arts. With architecture, we are *submerged* in the experience, whereas the relationship between us and a painting or a symphony is much more one of simple *exposure*. (Even here, however, we must be careful not to oversimplify reality. The primary significance of a painting may indeed be visual; or of a concert, aural: but perception of these art forms occurs always in a situation of experiential totality.)

Leonardo da Vinci claimed for painting a great advantage over the other forms of art — namely, that the painter had the unique power of fixing, once and for all, not only the vantage point from which his painting was to be viewed but also the internal environment (illumination, atmospheric effects, spatial organization) under which the painted action took place. Such a claim is only partly true for any art form, as we have just seen: for architecture it is preposterous. Nevertheless, architects since the Renaissance have accepted without challenge this proposition, thereby obscuring another fundamental difference between architecture and the other arts. They involve a unilinear exposure,* a one-way and irreversible sequence of events, while the experiencing of architecture, on the contrary, is poly-directional.

This Davincian error, ironically enough, has been consolidated by the development of modern photography. The photographer can capture only the visual facsimile of the building, being by definition unable to present a facsimile of its total sensuous behavior — that is, how it smells, how it feels, how it sounds. But even as a purely visual facsimile, the photograph has invisible limitations of great consequence. For the photographer, like Leonardo's painter, is limited by both choice and necessity to delineating only a few aspects (among millions of possible ones) of the building's behavior: in *time* (day or night, winter or summer, sunshine or rain); in *space* (front or back, living room or kitchen, aerial or worm's-eye view); *condition* (empty or furnished, occupied or vacant, clean or dirty).

---

* This linearity is most obvious in novel or play, ballet or symphony, where esthetic satisfaction is dependent upon the orderly unrolling of a fixed line of narrative or musical development.

All of these inherent limitations of photography make it in the highest degree unlikely that, upon such doubly limited sensory data, we could arrive at a viable estimate of the experiential reality of the building. And yet the fame of most of the monuments of modern architecture often rests upon exactly such a narrow factual base. In some cases this is inevitable, the photographic facsimile having long outlived the original (e.g., Mies van der Rohe's Barcelona Exposition building of 1929) (Fig. 1). In other cases, the photograph has become more famous than the house itself! (The view from below the falls of Wright's house at Bear Run, Pa., Fig. 2.) These photographs are not mendacious. Such aspects of these buildings do (or did), of course, exist: and what these facsimiles bring us of their vanished presence is important. But they represent at best only the merest fraction of the total, polydimensional experiential reality of the actual building. And we shall have constantly to bear this in mind if we are to comprehend the full complexity of architectural design.

BUILDING REGULATES THE BODY'S TRANSACTIONS

As continuously as the fish in water, man is submerged in his own environment, the limits of which appear to be fixed in both a temporal and a spatial sense. But, unlike the fish, man acts upon his environment as well as being acted upon by it. Conscious attempts at manipulating it are at least as old as man himself. And the cumulative results of such attempts have been — especially in recent times — to give contemporary man a much wider knowledge of his environment, and much greater control over it, than ever before. It lies within neither the scope of this study nor the competence of its author to delineate more than a small portion of the complex relationship between man and his natural environment. Nevertheless, as a result of the rapid expansion of both the earth and the life sciences, it is imperative for architects to understand the essential nature of this relationship, since building is the most important instrument used to modify it.

Our physical environment must be thought of as being of composite structure, formed of many distinct, coextensive and coexistent yet interacting elements which may actually be viewed as complete

Fig. 1. German Pavilion, Barcelona Exposition, 1929. Ludwig Mies van der Rohe, architect. The fame of this building is based largely on this photograph: yet it gives little data on actual environmental conditions it afforded at hot Spanish noon.

Fig. 2. House at Bear Run, Pa., 1935. Frank Lloyd Wright, architect. Taken from an improbable vantage point in midwinter, this photograph tells us nothing about conditions inside where cascade is invisible, perceivable as noise, humidity, chill.

subenvironments. (Indeed, for the purposes of analysis, they *must* be so regarded in order to resolve the contradictions they pose for the architect.) In this book, we shall only be concerned with those factors which act directly upon the human body and which can be immediately and directly modified by buildings. These may be listed as (1) thermal; (2) atmospheric; (3) aqueous; (4) luminous; (5) sonic; (6) world of objects; and (7) spatio-gravitational.

Evolving in this external matrix, the human body has developed an analogous specialization of function: in a sense, this can be compared to a system of channels designed to carry the two-way, highly specialized commerce between the body and the outside. These channels are likewise distinct, coexistent and interdependent. For example, the main task of the skin is to maintain the critically important "balance of trade" between the body's internal and external thermal environments. The respiratory system handles the essential exchange between the body and its atmospheric environment — importing the oxygen required for combustion, exhausting the waste product, carbon dioxide. Similarly, the digestive system handles the fuel supply — ingesting food and water, excreting body wastes. These are fundamentally metabolic functions which are locked together in a complex feedback system of controls. They exist independently of our perception of them; indeed, they precede consciousness itself and are its indispensable basis.

This is, of course, a necessary oversimplification, for, with the marvelous economy of the body, all these systems for *responding* to the environment are integrated with mechanisms for *perceiving* changes in its qualities and dimensions. Thus the skin provides the sense of touch for perceiving the texture, form, resistance and temperature of the world of objects. The respiratory system includes provisions for our sense of smell while the digestive yields the closely allied sense of taste. Even the musculature, which contains, supports and moves the body in space, provides that synoptic sense of orientation known as proprioception. And superimposed upon these are the most wonderful senses of all, those of sight and hearing. (These last, ironically, are so completely independent of the rest that life is possible without either or even both of them, as the life of Helen Keller proves.)

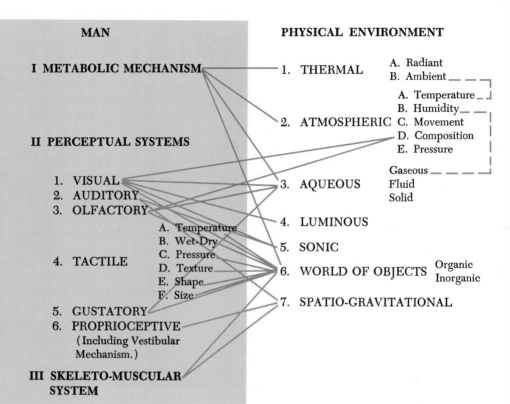

Fig. 3. Man is totally submerged in the physical environment, wholly dependent upon it. The relationship between the metabolic process and its environmental support is uterine. Since the process itself constitutes the platform of consciousness, sensory perception depends upon the satisfaction of the body's metabolic needs.

The external physical environment into which the human organism is projected at birth differs profoundly from that in which its fetal development occurred. Instead of a habitat designed specifically for its optimal development, it now finds itself in one many of whose properties are hostile to survival, and all of whose properties, friendly and hostile alike, are in continuous and often violent fluctuation across time and space. The metabolic requirements of the individual organism are constant. Its capacity for adaptation to external change, though fairly broad, is strictly limited. Thus arises the fundamental paradox of human existence.

Immersed in its physical environment, the animal body is never for a moment free of paradox, since its existence depends upon the *maintenance of an internal equilibrium which external nature does not afford*. The higher the form of life, the more complex will be the function and the more intricate the structure of the body: hence the more important its internal equilibrium. The body's dependence upon external nature is absolute — in the fullest sense of the word, *uterine*. And yet, unlike the womb, this external environment never affords optimum conditions for the development of the individual. The contradictions between internal requirements and external conditions are normally stressful. Hence, as Pavlov put it, "the animal organism as a system exists in surrounding nature only by means of a constant balancing, [between] this system and its environment." By means of this balancing, the body maintains a private, internal environment whose most extraordinary feature is its constancy. Walter B. Cannon, the great Harvard physiologist, described it thus:

So characteristic is this constancy, and so peculiar are the processes which maintain it, that it has been given a special name, *homeostasis* . . . there is the steadiness of our body temperature, a trait which we share with most other mammals and with birds. The development of a nearly thermostable state in higher vertebrates should be regarded as one of the most valuable advances in biological evolution.[1]

Thanks to the flexibility of its metabolic and perceptual mechanisms, the body is able to accommodate itself to a fairly wide range of fluctuations in the external environment. Thus the skin with its sweat glands and capillaries can greatly speed up or slow down the rate of heat transfer to the thermal environment. The heart and lungs can acclimatize themselves to fairly wide variations in oxygen content and atmospheric pressure. The range of physical intensities which the eye perceives is enormous; while for the ear, "a sound so intense as to be painful is of the order of *ten trillion* times the minimum audible intensity." But the limits of such accommodations are sharp and obdurate, and occur only within the overall limits established by the body as a whole. Beyond these limits, an ameliorating element, a "third environment," is required.

Because the external environment seldom affords the human body the precise "mix" that it requires at any given moment, man has perfected two ameliorating devices: clothing and building. Both act as interfaces between the internal micro-environment of the body and the macro-environment of external nature. Both modulate the play of raw environmental stresses on the body's surfaces and orifices; simultaneously, they create a third, meso-environment whose characteristics can be tailored to meet human requirements (Fig. 6). The principal difference between clothing and building is, of course, that the one protects the individual only while the other shelters social process as well. Traditionally, the function of clothing (aside from conventions of modesty and display) has been to manipulate the thermal environment. But as men increasingly enter new environmental circumstances (submarine, outer space), their clothing comes more and more to resemble buildings, with its life-support systems for manipulating temperature, air pressure and chemical composition, even body-waste disposal systems.

Because of the continuous fluctuation of all environmental factors across time, however, the building wall must be visualized not as a simple barrier but rather as a selective, permeable membrane with the capacity to admit, reject and/or filter any of these environmental factors (Fig. 69). All building walls have always acted in this fashion, of course, as we shall see in Chapter 8. Modern scientific knowledge and technical competence merely make possible much higher, more elegant and precise levels of performance than previously.

Before birth, the womb affords this to the fetus. But once born into the world, man enters into a much more complex relationship with his environment, for existence is now on *two* levels, not one: the metabolic and the perceptual. The two are indissolubly connected, as we have seen, the metabolic being the material basis of consciousness. Many of life's fundamental processes transpire at this level: heartbeat, respiration, digestion, hypothalmic heat-exchange controls, etc. Metabolic disturbance occurs only when external environmental conditions begin to drop below the minimal, or rise above the maximal, limits of existence. And sensual perception of the environment can come into play only *after* these limiting requirements are met. Loss of consciousness (fainting) is one of the body's characteristic responses to extreme environmental stress — e.g., loss of oxygen, extremes of pressure, acceleration, heat, cold, etc.

One might in all justice say of each of these systems, metabolic and perceptual, that each has its own "native habitat" in the external world — i.e., a general set of environmental conditions under which it operates and an inner zone in which it operates most effectively. The topologies of these habitats can be described by three values:

1. by the magnitude of support or the intensity of stimulation offered the system
2. by the spatial organization and physical dimensions of that relationship
3. by the temporal limits or duration of the experience

THE HABITATS OF METABOLISM AND THE SENSES

The habitat of our metabolic system extends across four environmental components: thermal, atmospheric, aqueous and nutritive. For the average, well-nourished adult, at rest and lightly clothed, this metabolic habitat has a well-known shape and location on the psychometric chart (Fig. 9). But any change in the metabolic rate of the body due to activity or other causes, will immediately require a change in habitat. Contrariwise, any radical changes in the external thermo-atmospheric environments will require a complementary modification in the protection offered the body by building and clothing.

The systems of sensory perception have also their respective "habitats" whose topologies can be similarly described, though such descriptions are only now being attempted in a systematic manner, as we shall see in the following chapters. Vision, hearing and olfaction are fundamentally processes for scanning the middle and far reaches of the environment: being distance receptors, they occupy habitats that are spatially three-dimensioned. The boundary of vision (Fig. 24) extends across the wave band from ultraviolet (3800 angstrom units) to infrared (7200 au); vertically, it extends from a lower threshold of perception to an upper threshold of pain; axially it extends out to infinity. The habitat of hearing (Fig. 45) has comparable boundaries of width (wave bands of energy), height (from lower threshold of audibility to upper one of blast and pain) and axial orientation (echo, reverberation). Although the mechanism of olfaction is only partially understood, its habitat is known to cover a horizontal spectrum of seven stereo-chemical categories of odor and to extend vertically from the lowest level of perceptible odor to an upper one of intolerable stench or asphyxiation. Its fantastic capacity to perceive odors in dilutions of one to one billion, or to discriminate between compounds of great chemical complexity, make it a scanning sense of the highest order though we are seldom conscious of employing it.

The senses of taste and touch are means of exploring the near environment. That of touch comes from a complex system of sensors in the skin and muscles which give us the tactile, haptic and kinesthetic capacities to perceive the temperature, humidity, pressure, shape, texture and weight of objects. Though the subject is enormously complex and very incompletely explored, it is apparent that the habitat of this sense has limits analogous to the others. The thermal sensors have upper and lower limits of tolerance to heat and cold. Those of pressure can register a range of stimuli all the way from the gentlest breeze to the stab or the blow, those of texture from that of butter to that of tree bark. And of course the entire kinesthetic-proprioceptive capacity is completely wedded to its "own" special habitat of terrestrial gravity.

But all of these perceptual habitats occur in space. To move through this space, man must overcome the inertia of gravity and the friction of motion. Thus his path or trajectory through space is actually the resolution of a system of forces — environmental, mechanical and psychological — which act upon him at any given moment. For this reason, the way in which that space is organized, architecturally and urbanistically, will be a factor in the esthetic aspects of experiencing it. All this is obvious: yet the malfunction of most of our urban constructs shows how inadequately we understand the consequences of ignoring it. Zoologists, anthropologists and psychologists have become increasingly interested in the impact of various spatial organizations upon animal communities. These investigations have important implications for the design of human communities. They suggest that there are minimal and maximal spatial dimensions for all of man's activities and relationships: there should therefore be an *optimal* scale for each of them.

The anthropologist Edward Hall[2] has approached this problem from the opposite point of view, that of trying to establish optimal physical dimensions for various types of contacts and relationships. Partly, the scale of such relationships is a quantification of our powers of perception — how well we can hear the words of the actor, how clearly we can see the face of the friend, whether or not we can touch the person we love. The spatial requirements of such relationships are real and they will only be satisfied when space is organized to facilitate them. But the problem is not simply one of acuity of perception. We want contact with the actor, the friend, the lover; but we do not want to be as close to the actor as to the friend, nor as close to the friend as to the lover.

Investigations of this sort throw new light on some of the thorniest problems of architecture and urbanism. They point to the underlying reason for the failure in real life of so many designs which seemed so attractive in drawings and photographs: that the spaces had been organized according to abstract principles of formal composition (i.e., to *look* good) rather than to facilitate specific experiential requirements. This complex aspect of design, involving ergonomics, anthropometrics and proxemics, is treated at some length in Chapter 7.

A SPECTRUM OF STRESS

Metabolic process is clearly the precondition to sensory perception, just as sensory perception constitutes the material basis for the esthetic process. But this process only begins to operate maximally — i.e., as a uniquely human faculty — when the impact upon the body of all environmental forces is held within comfortable limits (limits which are established by the body as a whole). Thus we can construct a kind of experiential spectrum of stress, extending from too much work to none at all, from sensory "overloading" to no sensory stimulation whatever. Both extremes are hostile to the animal body's survival. History affords an ample record of the disastrous consequences of too much stress — overwork, exposure, exhaustion — and current scientific investigations fully confirm it. The recent work of aerospace psychiatrists establishes this end

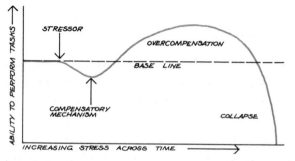

Fig. 4. The individual's capacity to accomplish assigned task drops under stress. Although, with adequate motivation, he can compensate, recovery is limited across time. Continued overload leads to decline, ending in collapse.

of the experiential spectrum (Fig. 4): sensory overloading is destructive, first of effective performance; then of balanced judgment; finally of rationality itself.[3]

Not until recently has it been possible to approach the other extreme, that of *too little* stress, even at the laboratory level. For, just as we cannot conceive of the animal body removed from its environmental matrix, we cannot imagine its being literally at rest — free of the stimulation which comes from the very processes of living. Now, investigations of the effects of sensory deprivation indicate that too little stress is as deleterious to the body as too much. Volunteer subjects for such experiments were reduced to gibbering incoherence in a matter of hours by being isolated from all visual, sonic, haptic and thermal stimulation[4] (Fig. 5). One investigator of the effects of sensory deprivation concludes:

Prolonged exposure to a monotonous environment, then, has definitely deleterious effects. The individual's thinking is impaired; he shows childish emotional responses; his visual perception becomes disturbed; he suffers from hallucination; his brain-pattern changes.[5]

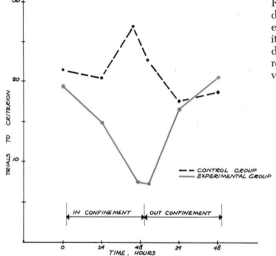

Fig. 5. The effect of sensory deprivation on the individual, expressed in terms of his capacity to learn: note rapidity and depth of decline, slowness of recovery. (Each point is mean value of 4 subjects.)

Psychic satisfaction with a given situation is thus directly related to physiologic well-being, just as dissatisfaction must be related to discomfort. A condition of neither too great nor too little sensory stimulation permits the fullest exercise of the critical faculties upon that situation or any aspect of it. But even this proposition will not be indefinitely extensible in time. As the above-quoted investigator concluded (in a paper significantly entitled "The Pathology of Boredom"):

. . . a changing sensory environment seems essential for human beings. Without it, the brain ceases to function in an adequate way, and abnormalities of behavior develop. In fact . . . "variety is not the spice of life: it is the very stuff of it."[6]

The psychosomatic equilibrium which the body always seeks is dynamic, a continual resolution of opposites. Every experience has built-in time limits. Perception itself has upper and lower thresholds. One set is purely quantitative: the ear cannot perceive sounds of very high pitch (above 18,000 cycles per second); the eye does not perceive radiation below 3800 angstrom units. But another set of thresholds are functions of time: constant exposure to a steady stimulation at some fixed level will ultimately deaden the capacity to perceive it.

Physical comfort cannot be mechanically equated with esthetic satisfaction, however. For while all human standards of beauty and ugliness stand ultimately upon a bedrock of material existence, the standards themselves vary astonishingly. All men have always had the same sensory apparatus for perceiving changes in the qualities and dimensions of their environment. All men have always had the same central nervous system for analyzing and responding to the stimuli thus perceived. Moreover, the physiological limits of this experience are absolute and intractable. Ultimately, physiology, and not culture, establishes the levels at which sensory stimuli become traumatic. With such extremes—high temperatures, blinding lights, cutting edges and heavy blows, noise at blast level, intense concentrations of odor — experience goes beyond mere perception; outrage and insult to the organism become somatic stress. Excessive loading of any one of these senses can prevent a balanced assessment of the total experiential situation. (A temperature of 120 degrees F or a sound level of 120 decibels can render the most beautiful room uninhabitable.) Only as long as these stimuli do not reach stressful levels of intensity, rational assessment and hence esthetic judgments are possible. Then — and only then — formal criteria derived from personal idiosyncrasy and socially conditioned value judgments come into play.

The value judgments that men apply to these stimuli, the evaluation they make of the total experience as being either beautiful or ugly — these will vary: measurably with the individual, enormously with his culture. This is so clearly the case in the history of art that it should not need repeating. Yet we constantly forget it. Today, anthropology, ethnology and archaeology alike show us the immense range of esthetically satisfactory standards which the race has evolved in its history: from cannibalism to vegetarianism in food; from the pyramid to the curtain wall in architecture; from polygyny and polyandry to monogamy and celibacy in sex; from hoop skirt to bikini in dress. Yet we often act, even today, as if our own esthetic criteria were absolutely valid instead of being, as is indeed the case, absolutely relative for all culture except our own.

Our esthetic judgments are substantially modified by non-sensual data derived from social experience. This again can be easily confirmed in daily life. It is ultimately our faith in antiseptic measures which makes the immaculate white nurses' uniforms and spotless sheets of the hospital so reassuring. It is our knowledge of their cost which exaggerates the visual difference between diamonds and crystal, or the gustatory difference between the flavor of pheasant and chicken. It was our knowledge of Hitler Germany which converted the swastika from the good luck sign of the American Indians to the hated symbol of Nazi terror. All sensory perception is modified by consciousness. Consciousness applies to received stimuli the criteria of digested experience, whether acquired by the individual or received by him from his culture. The esthetic process cannot be isolated from this matrix of experiential reality. It constitutes, rather, a quintessential evaluation of and judgment on it.

Simply as an animal, man might have survived without the capacity to construct a "third environment." Theoretically, at least, he might have migrated like the bird or hibernated like the bear. There are even a few favored spots on earth, like Hawaii, in which biological survival might have been possible without any architectural modification. But, on the base of sheer biological existence, man builds the vast superstructure of institutions, processes and activities which is civilization: and these could not survive exposure to the natural environment even in those climates in which, biologically, man could survive without either one (Fig. 6).

ARCHITECTURE — THE "THIRD ENVIRONMENT"

Thus man was compelled to invent architecture in order, ultimately, to become man. By means of it he surrounded himself with a new environment tailored to his specifications, interposed between himself and the world. The building, in even its simplest form, invests man, surrounds and encapsulates him at every level of his existence, metabolically and perceptually. Thus it must be regarded as a special container whose central function is to intervene in man's favor. The building — and by extension, the city — has the task of lightening the stress of life; of shielding man from the raw environment stresses; of permitting *homo fabricans* to focus his energies upon productive work. Again the uterine analogy, and not accidentally, for the building permits man to modulate the play of environmental forces upon himself and his processes, to guarantee their uninterrupted development, in very much the same way as the mother's womb protects the embryo. (See Chapter 8.)

The matter by no means ends here, however. The architect does not build for individual man, man alone and at rest. Typically, he builds for social man, man at work. And this confronts him with another set of contradictions. Work, as Hannah Arendt has reminded us, is not a "natural" activity.[7] According to this definition, only labor is "natural" — that is, those activities we share with the entire animal world where the whole body is used to meet its biological needs, to feed it, bathe it, dress it, protect it from attack. Work, on the other hand, is "unnatural" — i.e., the uniquely human use of the hand and the brain to produce the artificial, nonbiological world of human artifice (skyscrapers, textbooks, paintings, space

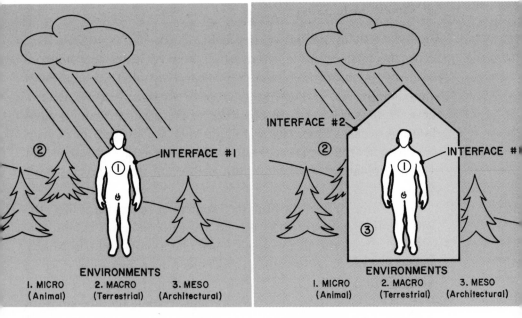

Fig. 6. Interaction between animal organism and its environment occurs across one interface — that of the epidermis. But civilization introduces two artificial membranes to modify this relationship — clothing and architecture. Clothing lifts the environmental load off the individual. Architecture, by creating a third "built" environment, takes the environmental load off both man and his institutions and processes, freeing a greater portion of human energies for socially productive activity.

ships, highways, symphonies and pharmaceuticals). Both levels of human activity are, of course, fundamental to civilization: the world of work can only exist as a superstructure on the world of labor. But insofar as we share the world of labor with the beasts, it can fairly be described as at once natural and subhuman. Only the world of work, of human thought and artifice, is uniquely human.

This distinction, by no means as fine as it might at first appear, has important consequences for architectural design. For, if the architect ever builds for the wholly "natural" man, it will be in his house, at his biological activities of resting, eating, lovemaking and play. Most other modern building types involve man at work, engaged in a wide spectrum of "unnatural" processes. Each of these involves stress. Stress, as we have seen, comes either from too much or too little stimulation, from sensory "overloading" and "underloading" alike. Biological man requires a dynamic environmental balance, a golden mean between extremes. But modern work knows no such requirements: on the contrary, for maximum output and optimum quality, it usually implies environments of absolute constancy (e.g., pharmaceuticals, printing) and often requires extreme conditions never met in nature (e.g., high-temperature metallurgy, cobalt radiation therapy, etc.). When plotted, these two sets of requirements — those of the worker and those of the work — will seldom lie along the same curve. From this it follows that architecture must meet two distinctly different sets of environmental criteria — those of man at some "unnatural" task, and those of the "unnatural" process itself.

Variety may indeed be the very stuff of man's natural life. But most of our human activities are, to a greater or lesser extent, "unnatural." From the moment we place the young child in kindergarten, we are imposing "unnatural" tasks upon him — placing his eyesight, his posture, his capacity for attention under quite abnormal stress. And this situation grows more acute throughout his education and his normal working life. As an adult, his biological existence will be linked to processes which are never completely congruent with his own. Often they involve work which is fractionalized, repetitive and hence often unintelligible to the individual; often, the processes are actually dangerous to him. Only in agriculture does he confront work whose "natural" environment, rhythms and wholeness correspond to his own; but only three out of one hundred American workers are nowadays involved in this type of work.

Each kind of work, each social process or activity in which man finds himself engaged, represents a different level of commitment or participation on his part. We have said that there are no spectators in architecture, only protagonists and participants: but the *levels* of participation will vary immensely, from being largely passive to being totally active or engaged. Participation may be largely emotional (like that of the theatergoer); primarily intellectual (like that of the child learning to read); largely manual (like the worker in the assembly line); or total (like the surgeon and his patient in the operating theater). We go to the theater for what we call "entertainment" — that is, for an experience which, however important, is not central to animal existence. In surgery, on the other hand, we are involved in a process where the issues are literally those of life and death. Yet this does not mean, as architects often seem to think, that the theater is less "real" than the surgery or that the experiential needs of the theatergoer are more simply met than those of the surgical patient.

HIERARCHY OF COMMITMENT:
THEATER, CLASSROOM, FACTORY, HOSPITAL

It is in the theater that we find man engaged in one of the most complex of all his esthetic acts. And for this reason, the performance is very sensitive to the spatial and environmental qualities of the architectural container in which it is projected.

Here the requirements of the eye and ear must indeed be well met. Optimal satisfaction with the theater must subsume optimal acuity of perception. And this is a function of the size and shape of the container, no less than its luminous, acoustical and thermal response. The notorious malfunction of many modern theaters and auditoriums is a reflection of how little we understand the subtleties of this problem. In the first place, it seems quite probable that the physical dimensions are not really susceptible to the sort of unlimited extension so common today. No matter how plausible electronic amplification of sound and light may make that extension seem, the unaided sweep of the eye and the ear together establish an optimal range of perception. Beyond this radius, there will be a progressive lowering of the esthetic impact of the experience, no matter what technological means of amplification are available. For this reason, the form and size of the classic Greek theater (Fig. 46), based upon its understanding of the habitat of eye and ear, is probably still the paradigm.

But there is unquestionably another and more subtle explanation for these modern theatral failures: our tendency to regard the process of design as primarily a matter of visual selection and organization. (See Chapter 5.) By their very appearance — the forms, colors, patterns and decorative motifs they employ — these theaters establish the fact that they are conceived *primarily to delight the eye and only incidentally to satisfy the requirements of the ear.* No ear ever "asked for" these gold-leafed hexagons, plaster pinwheels, enormous chandeliers of chrome and crystal. Such forms are not, *a priori,* hostile to good acoustics: they are merely irrelevant. The ear has a habitat which may or may not be pleasing to the eye; it cannot in any case be discovered or mapped by the eye alone. The ear will be indifferent to the color which is so important to the eye, but it will be highly sensitive to the form and texture beneath it. It will not "object" if the balcony fascia is decorated in baroque swags; it will merely require that they offer the acoustically proper profile and molecular structure. Under such circumstances, the architect errs when he tries to work backward from a visually pleasing to an acoustically satisfactory form; and the acoustical engineer errs when he accepts the task of trying to convert the architect's visual cliché into aurally satisfactory experience.

While the child's physical relation to teacher and blackboard is nominally the same as that of audience to actor, his actual involvement is much more profound. He is being asked to work, and a whole series of rewards and punishments are set up to enforce this demand. Under ideal circumstances, his physical growth and intellectual development should be steady and parallel throughout the year. In theory, his learning capacity should be as high at the end of his school day as at its beginning. In reality, of course, this is impossible. His energies will flag as the day advances and nothing but rest, food and play will restore them. The question for architects is: how can the building intervene in his favor? How shall we manipulate his external environment so that the "unnatural" task of becoming literate advances with optimum speed and with minimum stress?

It should be immediately apparent that the child's requirements are dynamic and imply a dynamic relationship with his classroom. No classroom should confront the child with a fixed set of day-long environmental norms — e.g., 72 degrees F air, 50 per cent humidity, 60 foot-lamberts of light at desk top, 30 decibels of noise, etc. Far from being held at some fixed level, the probability is that environmental conditions should be continually changing. *But this change cannot be casual or statistically indeterminate* (if change alone were all that was required, the class could be held in a nearby meadow). It must be a *designed* response to the child's changing requirements. The child may well need less heat at 2 P.M. than at

9 A.M. At day's end he may need less humidity and more oxygen; he may require more light and of a different color; he may need a chair that gives a different posture or sound levels higher or lower than in the morning. Whatever the requirements are, they could only derive from the child himself, in the experiential circumstances of study. They cannot be met by mechanistic engineers (windowless classrooms, "steady state" controls) nor by formalistic architects who design as though visual perception is the whole of experience.

For the adult at his place of work, the problem is yet more intricate. The functional task of the building is to remove the environmental load from his shoulders, permitting him to focus his energies upon the work to be performed. This proposition is most obviously valid for the factory, where the stress of manual labor is clear and conditions of work are often hazardous; but it applies with equal force to the office, the shop or the kitchen. This aspect of building design carries the architect into the very center of an extremely complex problem, involving questions of physiology and psychology upon which even specialists in these fields find it hard to agree. The level of commitment or participation required of the worker will vary immensely — from the constant alertness and discrimination required of the cook or the mechanic to the stupefying monotony of the assembly line. The connection between work and environment, on the one hand, and fatigue, on the other, is umbilical but the mechanism of fatigue itself is by no means understood.*

Fatigue is a perfectly "natural" phenomenon, part of the basic metabolic cycle of impairment and recovery in the living organism. One of the most puzzling aspects of fatigue is its duality: it is at once objective and subjective, physiological and psychological. No two men respond in exactly the same way to the same task; and the same man will respond quite differently to the same task under varying emotional or environmental circumstances.

Four factors whose values can be objectively measured are involved in fatigue: (1) the time spent at work; (2) the character of the work itself; (3) the environmental conditions under which the work is performed; and (4) the condition of the worker himself —

---

* In fact, the term covers so wide an area that some experts are opposed to its very use.

i.e., age, health, nutrition, emotional state, etc. In this complicated field, which is discussed in more detail in Chapter 7, the architect seldom controls more than one of these factors — the third. But to accomplish even this effectively, he needs to know much more about the others than, commonly, he does. Only thus can he avoid formal solutions which violate the experiential situations upon which they are imposed.

But the symbiotic relationship between the architectural container and the men and processes contained is nowhere clearer than in the modern hospital. Here we find every degree of biological stress, including those of birth and death; a wide range of highly specialized technologies, each with its own environmental requirements; and the narrowest margins for error of any building type — success and failure are literally matters of life and death. Here, if anywhere, we can observe the integral connection between metabolic function and esthetic response.

The seriously ill patient — above all, the major surgery case — will traverse the full experiential spectrum during his stay at the hospital. Stress will be greatest under surgery. His relationship with his environment can be almost wholly defined in somatic terms. Since he is under total anesthesia, there is no esthetic aspect to his experience. (It is significant, in this connection, to note that the two words anesthesia and esthetic have a common origin in the Greek word meaning "to feel" or "to perceive.")

The patient's process of convalescence — through the recovery room, intensive nursing, regular nursing and ambulatory state, on up to discharge — will take him through every level of stress. Precisely as the metabolic crisis diminishes so will his esthetic response rise to the front of consciousness. Colors, lights, noises and odors which he was too ill to notice can now become major factors of experience. And their satisfactory manipulation becomes a part of active therapy.

The surgeon and his staff, too, will meet their greatest period of stress during surgery. At this juncture, their requirements will be opposed to those of the patient. Where the latter requires warm, moist air (and anti-explosive measures demand even higher humidities), the staff — under great nervous tension — should ideally be submerged in dry, cool air. But since stress for them is of limited duration, while any added load might be disastrous for the patient, the room's thermo-atmospheric environment is usually designed in the latter's favor. The staff will sweat and recover later. On the other hand, the luminous environment of the operating room must be wholly designed in the surgeon's favor. The color of the walls, of the uniforms, even of the towels is quite as important to visual acuity of the surgeon as the lighting fixtures themselves.

Thus, every decision made in design of the operating room will be based upon functional considerations, objectively evaluated. The very nature of the intervention prohibits any abstractly "esthetic" considerations. The margin of safety is too narrow to allow the architect the luxury of any formalistic decisions based upon sub-jective preferences. In varying degrees, this situation will obtain in other specialized areas of the hospital. And it will increase as the hospital comes to be regarded not merely as a container for men and processes but as being itself an actual instrument of therapy. There are many evidences of this tendency already: the hyperbaric chamber where barometric pressure and oxygen content are manipu-lated in the treatment of both circulatory disorders and gas gan-grene; the metabolic surgery suites where body temperatures are reduced to slow the metabolic rate before difficult surgery; the use of saturated atmospheres for serious burn cases; artificially cooled dry air to lighten the thermal stress on cardiac cases; the use of elec-trostatic precipitation and ultraviolet radiation to produce com-pletely sterile atmospheres for difficult respiratory ailments or to prevent cross-infection from contagious disease. Here the building is not merely manipulating the natural environment in the patient's favor but actually creating totally new environments with no precedent in nature as specific instruments of therapy.

The exact point in hospitalization at which these environmental manipulations cease to be purely therapeutic and become merely questions of comfort or satisfaction — i.e., the point at which they cease to be functional and become esthetic problems — is not easy to isolate. Objectionable odors; disturbing noises and lights; un-comfortable beds; lack of privacy; hot, humid atmospheres — all these will work against "beauty" in the hospital room. They may also delay convalescence. We cannot hope to make modern medical procedures "pretty" and the well-adjusted patient will probably want to leave the hospital as soon as possible under any circumstances. All the more reason, then, that every external factor be analyzed as objectively as possible, with a view to expediting his recovery.

All of this suggests the possibility of establishing, much more precisely than ever before, an objective basis for esthetic decision. It cannot, in any case, be avoided. Everything the architect does, every form he adopts or material he specifies, has esthetic repercussions. His problem is thus not Hamlet's: to act or not to act. It is rather to act wisely, understanding the total consequences of his decisions. For if the architect's esthetic standards are to be placed on a firmer factual basis than the one on which they now stand, he will need the help of physiologists, psychologists and anthropologists to do it. Architecture needs a much more systematic and detailed investigation of man's actual psychosomatic relationship with his environment than has yet been attempted, at least in architecture. It is not at all accidental that we can find the broad lines of such research appearing in the field of aerospace medicine. For man can only penetrate space by encapsulating himself in a container of terrestrial environment. To accomplish this he must ask fundamental questions: what, actually, *is* this environment? What specifically is its effect upon us? What is its relation to human pleasure and delight?

In the design of the space vehicle, for example, it is no longer possible to say where problems of simple biological survival leave off and more complex questions of human satisfactions begin. Clearly, they constitute *different ends of one uninterrupted spectrum of human experience.* It is very probable that the upper end of this spectrum, involving as it does man's innermost subjective existence, can never be fully explored or understood. But it could certainly be far better understood than it is today, especially among architects.

American society today employs some 270 distinct building types to provide the specialized environments required by its multiform activities.[8] Most of them embody contradictions which must be resolved at two different levels: first between the persons and processes contained and then between their container and the natural

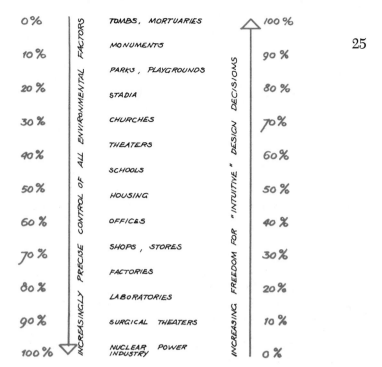

0%	INCREASINGLY PRECISE CONTROL OF ALL ENVIRONMENTAL FACTORS	TOMBS, MORTUARIES	100%	INCREASING FREEDOM FOR "INTUITIVE" DESIGN DECISIONS
10%		MONUMENTS	90%	
20%		PARKS, PLAYGROUNDS	80%	
		STADIA		
30%		CHURCHES	70%	
40%		THEATERS	60%	
		SCHOOLS		
50%		HOUSING	50%	
60%		OFFICES	40%	
70%		SHOPS, STORES	30%	
		FACTORIES		
80%		LABORATORIES	20%	
90%		SURGICAL THEATERS	10%	
100%		NUCLEAR POWER INDUSTRY	0%	

Fig. 7. The fundamental contradiction in architecture is always between the requirements of functional and formal criteria. The more complex or vital the process to be housed, the more critical this contradiction becomes. Hence the architect's freedom to create necessarily diminishes in inverse proportion to criticalness of his task.

environment. Respect for these two conditions is mandatory if the building is to be operationally successful. And yet, respect for these two conditions will often leave the architect with little room in which he can manipulate the building for purely formal — i.e., esthetic — ends. If we examine the specifications for these various building types, we will see that they can be classified according to the degree of participation they subsume on the part of the users of the building. And from such a classification, it becomes apparent that, as participation becomes more total, the architect's opportunities for subjective expression will steadily diminish (Fig. 7).

Most contemporary failures in architecture stem either from a failure to understand this situation or else from a refusal to come to terms with it. Of course, no building can grow like an organism. Architects do not work with living tissue, with its powers of cellular division and genetic memory. In this sense, buildings must always be designed by men and these men will always bring to the task preconceived ideas of what forms they ought to assume. As Ernst

Fischer, the Austrian philosopher, has said, a good honeybee will often put a bad architect to shame. "But what from the very first distinguishes the most incompetent of architects from the best of bees is that the architect has built a cell in his head before he constructs it in wax."[9] Good or bad, beautiful or ugly, the building is always the expression of somebody's creative ambitions. Today, more than ever in history, these ambitions must be contained, structured and disciplined by objectively verifiable terms of reference.

2.

THE SOCIAL CONSEQUENCES OF ARCHITECTURAL INTERVENTION

If, as we have seen, the central function of building is to lift the raw environmental load of the physical environment from our backs and to create that third meso-environment required by civilization — then we must judge building as we do any other instrument or tool: i.e., by its performance. And the central criterion for judging building performance must necessarily be amenity, well-being, ultimately *health*. Does the building regulate the relations between the individual and his environment in such a way as to guarantee his optimal well-being? And, from the standpoint of society as a whole, does the total stock of building provide that control of environmental factors which guarantees maximum productivity to all its manifold processes and activities?

Clearly, these are questions easier to ask than to answer. A bewildering variety of forces play upon the life of the individual or the activities of the group; and only a limited portion of them will be subject to manipulation by architectural means. It must also be remembered that, in human society, each level of cultural development establishes its own internal standards of health, amenity, efficiency. Its architecture can thus be measured only against its own potentials. The Eskimo igloo would offer few of the amenities required by middle-class American families. But, relative to the material resources and technological potentials of Eskimo culture, it represents an instrument of architectural intervention of simply astonishing precision and refinement.

The very word "health" may describe a real state of being but it nevertheless has ambiguous parameters. Medically, it implies a state of normal function which can vary with age, sex and genetic stock. Here, we do not confront two separate states of being — healthful and unhealthful — with a division between the two. Rather we face a spectrum of conditions which progresses, often by slow and imperceptible degrees, from health through discomfort, distress, disease and disablement, to end in death. For the individual, of course, the progression is not necessarily even or direct. For the victims of Hiroshima, it was telescoped into a split second; for the miner in the pit, an agonizing progress of silicosis may drag out for years; with the modern nutrition and medical care available to him, the average middle-class American may enjoy six or seven decades of uninterrupted health; while — lacking all this — the average citizen of India dies at 35. In one way or the other, it is the characteristic spectrum through which we all pass on the journey from the cradle to the grave. The object of medical and public health endeavor is to extend the period of health over as long a time and as broad a base as possible by systematically isolating and eliminating those factors which contribute to discomfort, disease and disablement (Fig. 8).

The whole subject is extremely complex and it would be dangerous to overestimate the role of architecture as a contributing factor; but it would be equal folly to underestimate it. For clearly health, disease and death *always* occur in real experiential situations. The environment is *always* a factor (whether large or small) in the progression and it is the task of architects and city planners to examine their responsibilities here much more clearly than they do at present.

This examination must proceed at two distinctly different levels: that of the individual buildings; and that of networks or nuclei of buildings organized into urban tissue — i.e., the city as a whole. For there will be a qualitative difference between the performance of the individual unit and that of a group of units, even when they are internally identical. It is one of the paradoxes of modern technology that it makes possible an unprecedentedly high order of performance in the individual building; and yet organizes them into cities whose environmental conditions are more dangerous, hazardous or less comfortable than ever before.

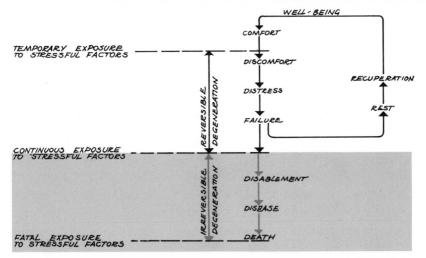

Fig. 8. The biological phenomenon of work-fatigue-rest-recovery is cyclical. Any exogenous factor which distorts or disrupts this rhythm is inimical to the well-being of the individual. All experience occurs in situations in which the environment itself is one exogenous factor: architecture intervenes to optimize its effect on the cycle.

One way in which individual buildings affect our health is well exemplified in that type with which we are most familiar: the home. In addition to being most familiar, it now appears that the home is also the most hazardous. Accidents in the home annually *kill* about 27,000 Americans — 56 per cent of all fatal nontransport accidents.[1] Home accidents are the eighth largest cause of death, being exceeded only by such diseases as cardiac attacks, malignancies, vascular lesions, etc. In addition to these deaths, the home accounts annually for 20,000,000 accidents requiring medical attention which lead, in turn, to 162,860,000 days of restricted activity. Thus, as a cause of disability and death, the home-induced accident can be ranked among the major diseases of mankind.[2]

What is the cause of these appalling statistics? How can they be reduced? Their cause lies overwhelmingly in deficiencies in the building, rather than to the building's occupants. Their cure, therefore, is primarily a problem of redesign of the dwelling. No home can be 100 per cent accident-proof, of course: the factor of human fallibility enters into the use of a house just as it does that of a motor car. Education of the occupant must parallel redesign for safety. But in a statistical sense, *the main burden of blame* lies on the house, not its user. This is clearly established by census surveys which show that home accidents do not occur at random. On the contrary, accidents of a given type happen only to persons of a given age and sex, while occupied at given tasks, at given places within the house. If the accident were the fault of the person, and not the tool, there would be no such pattern to their distribution.

Falls, for example, are the source of over two-thirds of all serious injuries occurring in the house. At first glance, this might seem a most difficult thing to pin on the building itself: in fact, it is very easy. Elderly people, for example, fall often, but they do not fall everywhere equally: a majority of their accidents occur in the bathroom, especially while climbing out of or into the tub. This suggests that the process of bathing and the equipment required — tubs, showers, grab bars, soap, etc. — have not been very carefully studied either by manufacturer or architect. The housewife who prepares, assembles and serves a meal has to make many movements around the kitchen — up to the pantry shelf, down to the oven, into the dining room, etc. There is much lifting, beating, rubbing, cutting, and stirring connected with the whole chemistry of cooking, and much of it is hazardous. Yet, unlike the industrial worker, the housewife has been the subject of few really fundamental time and motion studies. Most of her equipment — cabinets, stoves, dishes, pots and pans — is poorly designed and poorly organized with reference to her physical and psychic requirements: often it is worn out. No wonder, then, that she falls from a bad ladder while trying to reach an archaic utensil, from a cupboard shelf which should never have been there in the first place! No wonder children and old people slip on stairs whose pitch is too steep, surface too slippery, rail too high — and with none of it adequately lighted. All buildings should be designed for optimum ease, speed and safety of movement. This movement usually resolves itself into two characteristic patterns — people moving toward things or things moving toward people. In the case of the house, movement is almost exclusively of the first sort, while in the factory the opposite is the case.

Much of the same thing holds true for the burns, cuts, suffocations, poisonings and other accidental injuries which occur in the home. Thorough investigation of the causal relations of burns (929,000 serious cases in 1959) would indicate how cooking and heating units should be redesigned. Many danger points in our houses are unconsciously avoided without our being aware of the issue of safety *per se;* but many others remain for the same reasons. Accidents in the home are the result of characteristic movements and processes which require the closest scrutiny if they are to be reduced or eliminated. This does not always imply that the house is structurally bad. An interior stairway may be inherently dangerous because it is steep, slippery, badly lighted, and/or winding; but it may be none of these, and still be a source of accidents because the only telephone is at its bottom and the housewife is always in a hurry when running down to answer it. The first instance would imply redesign of the stair; the latter would indicate need for two telephones — one at the top and one at the bottom.

This problem arises in many forms throughout the building. Thus, there is the problem of collision with objects in a dark room — stumbling over furniture in the bedroom or over toys on the living-room floor. Both of these are statistically important sources of accidental injury. In the first case, either the plan of the bedroom does not make adequate provisions for the necessary furniture or the furniture is not suitably arranged in the room, or the lighting is inadequate. In the second case, the children of the household should have either a room of their own or (at the minimum) storage space for their toys. (And then, of course, be taught to put them there!)

Not all areas of the house are equally dangerous, nor are different types of accidents evenly distributed throughout the house. Outside stairs and porches are over seven times as dangerous as the bathroom. This of itself constitutes impressive proof that accidents in the home are not due merely to "human nature," but to very specific factors which can be isolated and eliminated by scientific design. Where there's an accident there's a reason; and this reason may be partly due to what safety experts call "unsafe conditions" and partly to "unsafe practices."

Reference to industrial experience sheds new light on this situation. Here scientific research has yielded many control and preventive measures which have resulted in marked reductions in accident frequency and accident severity. In such industrial safety work, three factors are investigated: the condition of the building itself; the processes carried on in the building; and the practice of the workers. The same analysis must be applied to the home if we are to understand why it is so dangerous and how it may be made safer. Take the kitchen, for instance — the most dangerous single area in the house. What characteristic processes are carried on here? To what extent can redesign of the room itself increase its safety (omission of live storage space above eye level, inclusion of electric dishwasher, and the like)? To what extent can the processes themselves be made safer (elimination of deep-fat frying or the washing of cutlery by hand)? And to what extent must the housewife herself learn safer practices (to cut bread away from the body, to keep explosive or poisonous chemicals locked out of children's reach, and so on)?

The large-scale opportunity to apply this analysis to house design has occurred in public housing. But the results indicate that an effective set of safety standards can achieve marked reductions in accident frequencies. The general home accident rate of 4.65 per thousand has been lowered in public housing projects to 1.85 per thousand — that is, by 61 per cent. Subsequent investigations have shown that further changes in design would result in a further reduction in accidents of 31 per cent, and in fires of 59 per cent.

Whether accidents result from poor building design or human frailty, it is thus amply clear that they are entirely susceptible to scientific analysis and prevention.

AMERICAN BUILDINGS: SOURCE OF ILLNESS AND DISEASE

The foregoing applies only to one type of damage to the health of the building consumer — the accident. There is yet another (and perhaps even more important) one to consider — the contribution of buildings to illness and disease. Current practice makes a sharper distinction between accident and disease in relation to building use than the facts seem to warrant. Both constitute an impairment of health, and both may be wholly or partially traced to deficiencies in the building. Obviously, the sequence of cause and effect is more apparent in the case of a sudden fall down a stair (an accident) than an obscure and imperceptibly worsening case of allergy from the dust-laden air of a felt factory (disease). But the precise difference between the two is likely to be more important to the medical statistician than to the building consumer, who is merely interested in preserving his health against both forms of attack.

However, it is a difficult and risky business to try to plot the causal relations between deficient buildings and disease. As a study by the United States Public Health Service puts it:

> The existence of excessive rates of sickness and mortality in the slums or overcrowded districts of cities is an accepted fact, but the extent to which poor housing *per se* is responsible for these differences is very difficult to ascertain because of the interaction of many economic and sociological factors.[3]

In other words, one must be careful not to attribute to deficient buildings those maladjustments, illnesses, and diseases which in fact are caused by deficiencies in the social order. Thus, the coincidence between tuberculosis and bad housing at one time led many housing specialists to conclude that slums were the *cause* of this social evil. Subsequent investigation has shown this to be incorrect: the fact is that both slums and tuberculosis are the *result* of poverty. No amount of clean, sunny interiors can cure starvation; nor can ample space in which to relax prevent the destructive tensions of unemployment, insecurity, and want. These are the products of our social environment, against which no building yet devised can offer any protection.

Nevertheless, there are many aspects of illness and disease which are demonstrably dependent upon bad building, and which can be demonstrably reduced by good building. In subsequent chapters, we shall see in more detail what these aspects are and how building can reduce or eliminate them. Here it will suffice to cite one example — the significant relationship between a group of digestive diseases (diarrhea, enteritis, colitis, typhoid and paratyphoid fevers) and the presence or absence of private indoor flush toilets. The Public Health Service found that the frequency of such digestive diseases in households without sanitary facilities was 70 per cent greater than in those with them! Any interpretation of such findings, the survey adds, must bear in mind that

> . . . in households not meeting this standard (of indoor toilets) there will probably be concomitant deficiencies (especially, lack of screening and poor facilities for refrigeration of food) which may have an effect on the illness rate from this group of digestive diseases . . . We are confronted

with an expression (or standard) which tends to measure poor housing as a whole.[4]

In other words, buildings which do not provide adequate protection against germs and insects are not likely to provide the special equipment necessary for food preservation. Deficiencies in one direction usually imply deficiencies in others; the task of exactly tracing out the relation of each to the maintenance of health only emphasizes the overall importance of good building.

The discovery of the relationship between building and health has served to expose the complete inadequacy of existing criteria for analyzing building performance. Most discussion of building has been always in primarily visual terms. Consciously or unconsciously, explicitly or implicitly, judgments based on vision have dominated architectural opinion. Actually, of course, there is quite as much justification for measuring buildings on any other sensory bases: Have you *heard* the new Jones house? What does the kitchen *smell* like? How do the stairs *feel?* Do the windows *get on your nerves?* Though we are trained to think otherwise, we experience building through all our senses equally; our entire sensory and muscular systems are involved in our use of buildings.

But the matter goes much deeper, for none of the senses is very reliable in estimating a building's performance. How woefully inadequate they are is amply testified to by the number of persons who — despite the use of their senses — are annually killed or injured in buildings. The nose is sharp enough to smell only the smoke from the actual fire, not to detect the hidden defective wire which causes it. The eye can tell you if the column is perfectly proportioned, but it can't read the internal stress organization or estimate how near it is to collapse. The ear will accurately register more noise than the nerves can stand, while the sense of touch comes into play too late to save you from breaking your neck on a slippery floor.

There is, in addition, a host of situations which arise in the day-to-day use of all sorts of buildings which cannot be sensed at all: they have to be *understood*. Under such a head fall the accidents involving electric shock, spontaneous combustion, and explosions; hookworm, typhoid, and dysentery spread by bad or nonexistent sanitary systems; silicosis, asphyxiation, and allergy due to atmospheric pollution; fatigue due to bad lighting, ventilation, or acoustics. To measure accurately such factors, more than the rule-of-thumb techniques of the past are required. In the light of modern knowledge and in the face of modern building requirements, it is no more possible to measure the performance of a building by the senses alone than it is to operate a jet plane without instruments.

The corollary is obvious: it is no more possible for an architect to design a satisfactory building by traditional methods than it would be possible for the local tinsmith to design a modern space capsule. Thus, from both the standpoint of the user and that of the designer, health-protecting and health-extending building implies the fullest application of the scientific method, the widest use of technical resources.

But urban society seems to create two new environmental problems for each one that it solves. The nineteenth century virtually completed the systems of utilities, services and amenities which make possible the modern city. Many of the epidemiological diseases which once wracked mankind were thus largely eliminated by bringing under control the vermin and filth which were the vectors of those diseases. Many of them — such as malaria, plague and smallpox — have but all disappeared from the civilized world. Effective transportation guarantees the adequate supply, and sanitary measures the quality, of the food we eat and water we drink. Sanitation systems effectively handle the removal of garbage and disposal of human waste. These urban facilities make possible the comforts and amenities of modern urban architecture, constituting the environmental support without which the individual building could not for a moment survive.

But cities, in the radical modifications of the landscape which they entail, produce their own ecologies, in which "natural" hazards to health and well-being are too often replaced with artificial, man-made ones. And there is mounting evidence that these hazards have disastrous implications. (See Chapter 9.) The typical bathroom, served by municipal water and sewerage systems, permits the average city dweller to enjoy a higher level of personal hygiene than ever before. But these same systems, on a regional scale, are polluting the environment alarmingly. (New York City in 1965 was still dumping *half a billion* gallons of raw sewage per day into the waters around it, while Miami Beach pumped all its raw sewage into the very ocean which is its only economic reason for existence!) The same mechanical systems which give us clean, conditioned air *inside* the building are simultaneously polluting the outside atmosphere with the waste ash and gases of faulty combustion (in New York City, a sootfall of 1.18 lbs. per sq. ft. per year). The automobile, paradigm of privatized luxury in transport, dumps increasing quantities of carcinogenic pollutants into the same air, as do most of the manufacturing plants of the nation. The lethal smogs of Los Angeles, St. Louis, Tokyo and London are the composite result of this atmospheric pollution.*

There can now no longer be any doubt that this generalized pollution of the environment was the root cause of new epidemiological phenomena — the startling increase in deaths from lung cancer and emphysema, for instance — even though the exact mechanism has not been explicated. (The direct results of smog are not open to controversy: following the London smog of December 13, 1952, death rates soared above normal: bronchitis 1083 per cent; influenza 720 per cent; pneumonia 486 per cent; tuberculosis 453 per cent; high blood pressure 294 per cent.) The scale and complexity of such ecological problems may outrun the comprehension, not to say the professional jurisdiction, of the average architect. And yet he is an active party of the whole process, whether or not he wills it or recognizes it. Each time he provides parking space for another auto, each time he cuts down a tree, or replaces a square yard of turf with one of blacktop, or installs a heating plant burning fossil fuels, so, each time, he modifies the microclimate in which his building stands. Sooner or later, he must face the consequences of his acts, if not as architect, then certainly as citizen.

The causal relation between building and accident, discomfort, and disease is today a generally accepted concept, however complex the line of cause and effect may be and however much of it remains to be explored in detail; and this in itself marks a great advance over the architectural theory of even a few years ago. Yet it remains

---

* Meanwhile, in the agricultural hinterland, to facilitate the production of those foodstuffs required by the city, the wide use of insecticides, fungicides and herbicides has been poisoning atmosphere, water bodies and soils alike.

merely the negative side of a much greater discovery; for these techniques of environmental control promise not merely the eradication of age-old deficiencies in building; they also yield totally new concepts of human comfort, health, and safety.

Of course, given the present structure of the building field, the architect can argue that many of the factors contributing to the low performance levels of architecture and urbanism are beyond his control. What architect is offered the opportunity to design the fixtures and furnishings of his buildings? What architect has a voice in the way his building is to be maintained after it is finished? What architect has a hand in drafting the ordinances which determine the atmospherc pollution that threatens the health of his clients or the highways which despoil the cities in which he builds? Legally, his responsibility may be limited: morally, it is very great. In fact, the future of the profession rests in large part upon the degree to which it can formulate and then apply a comprehensive and unified theory of environmental design.

3. FAIR AND WARMER: CONTROL OF THE THERMAL ENVIRONMENT

The thermal habitat of human metabolism is established by the play of solar radiation upon the surfaces which surround us and the oceans of air in which we are submerged. But this same solar radiation contains also those wave bands of energy which we call visible light, and hence establishes simultaneously our luminous environment. The temperature, movement and humidity of the atmosphere are of course operative in man's metabolic function and must consequently be reckoned as integral factors of his thermal environment. But the oxygen of the atmosphere is also a chemical prerequisite of metabolism. Hence man exists in these three co-extensive environments — thermal, atmospheric and luminous — and any manipulation of one causes repercussions in the others (Fig. 3).

This confronts the architect with a bewildering range of problems. In order to manipulate them with precision, he must analyze them as though they were separate and distinct entities. Only by this analytical method have the immense advances in heating, air conditioning and illumination been possible. In order of magnitude, control of our thermal environment is first. The question as to why we should heat buildings in winter or cool them in summer seems too obvious to require an answer; but the obvious response — to "heat" or "cool" the people in them — is actually so crude as to be almost meaningless. Our very concepts of warmth and coolness are relative and highly subjective. Ultimately, they are inaccurate, since in thermodynamics there is no such thing as "cold" above absolute zero ($-460°$ F), the point at which molecular activity theoretically ceases: above that point there are only varying degrees of heat. But buildings, in any case, neither "warm" nor "cool" us. Human metabolism, the whole life process, is one of slow combustion. Under all circumstances, it produces more heat than it needs. In its conversion of energy it is only about 20 per cent efficient. Hence it must always dissipate to its environment approximately 400 out of every 500 Btu's which it produces.

What is decisive in the body's thermal equilibrium is the *rate* at which this heat is dissipated. If the rate of heat loss is too slow, we say we feel "hot"; if it is too rapid, we say we are "cold." Of course, the *amount* of heat produced by the body varies widely with activity, age, sex and health. A man walking rapidly up a stairway produces 17 times as much heat as when he is sleeping. A ten-year-old boy will produce more heat than his grandfather at the same task (Chapter 7).

This heat must be dissipated at a rate exactly balanced with the rate of production. Otherwise, it begins to accumulate — a condition to which the body is extremely sensitive. Indeed, maintenance of this thermal balance is the fundamental condition of existence, not merely the fundamental requirement of comfort and well-being. Recent studies show that, as heat accumulates, thermal stress increases, the body passing through a characteristic spectrum of response from comfort to discomfort, distress, and failure (Fig. 8). A strong motivation may make possible the temporary extension of these limits. Continued exposure to moderate stress can lead to a certain degree of acclimatization. But the upper and lower limits of thermal existence are fixed and obdurate.*

Within these limits, however, the human body has an extraordinarily effective system for balancing heat loss against heat production to maintain a constant interior temperature close to 98.6° F. Only when this temperature rises toward 105 or falls toward the lower 80s, is the body brought into imminent collapse and death. To maintain this steady state, called *homeostasis* by the physiologists, the body employs a complex system of feedback and control. As the exterior

---

* A classic exposition of man's relationship with his thermal environment is to be found in *Temperature and Human Life*, by C. E. A. Winslow and L. P. Herrington (Princeton, N.J.: Princeton University Press, 1949).

environment grows colder, the pores of the skin contract, the rate of perspiration drops, the capillary veins contract and the heart — pumping at a slower rate — husbands the blood in the deep body cavities. (This withdrawal of blood from the body's surface explains the phrase "blue with cold.") If these measures are inadequate, shivering takes place to create muscular heat. As a last resort, the body assumes the so-called fetal position to reduce the exposed body areas to a minimum. If these measures are inadequate, collapse and death ensue.

Under opposite conditions of high external temperatures, the body reverses this procedure. Now the heart accelerates, the arteries and veins expand, and the blood is moved from inside the body to the surface for more rapid cooling. If this proves insufficient, the pores expand and the sweat glands increase their production. (Hence the expression "damp and flushed with fever.") But beyond this, the body has no further resources. Either the rate of heat loss must be externally increased by lower radiant and ambient temperatures, lower humidity or higher air movement around the body, or some combination of these; or the body will slip into irreversible coma and death.

The responsibility for maintaining a stable internal temperature rests with a complex feedback system, ultimately monitored by the hypothalamus. In periods of overheating, it is the sole mediator of the temperature control mechanisms described above. In periods of heat deficit, it teams up with the thermodetectors in the skin to accelerate all forms of muscular activity.

The body has four channels for disposing of its excess heat: by radiation to surfaces colder than itself (44 per cent); by convection from skin and mucous membrane (32 per cent); by evaporation from skin and mucous membrane (21 per cent); by conduction, ingestion of chilled foods and drink, etc. (3 per cent). Conduction — due to walking barefoot on cool floors, sitting on cold stone — is normally the least important form of heat transfer. For persons bathing or swimming in cold water, it is a rapid method of heat exchange and can have disastrous results: when persons saved from drowning in cold seas subsequently die from "exposure," they are victims of conductive heat loss carried beyond the point of no return.

All these means of heat exchange are employed by the body at all times, since nowhere in nature could conditions be otherwise. All four seem to be equally effective physiologically. The body does not "prefer" one means over another, though it does react unfavorably to uneven rates of loss from different parts of the body at any given moment (e.g., a draft on the back of the neck, chilled hands, wet feet, etc.). But the degree to which these channels of heat dissipation are individually effective depends upon the balance of external thermal factors. This will be the algebraic sum of (1) the radiant temperature of the immediate environment; (2) the ambient air temperature; (3) the moisture content of the air; and (4) the rate of air movement across the body. These establish the "thermal habitat" of man (Fig. 9). Under natural conditions, all four factors are in continual flux and very infrequently achieve that exact balance which we describe as comfortable.

Fig. 9. The thermal habitat of man is defined by four interacting environmental forces — radiant and ambient temperatures, relative humidity and air movement. "Comfort zone" in psychrometric chart (below) is for an adult male, young, healthy, lightly clothed, doing light work at sea level.

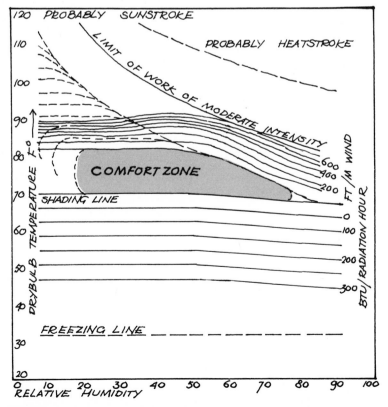

When the air temperature is below that of the skin, its movement across the skin will remove heat by convection; and the more rapid the movement, the greater the cooling effect. Even when the air is warmer than the skin, its movement can still remove body heat by evaporation of sweat. However, the evaporative process is always limited by the relative humidity of the air; the higher the humidity, the lower its cooling capacity. In any case, increased velocity is effective only up to a given temperature, beyond which the air will add more heat to the skin than it can remove by evaporation. (Thus, in desert climates cross ventilation is not always desirable.) Finally, and irrespective of atmospheric conditions, the body is always losing heat by direct radiation to surfaces cooler than itself (e.g., the cold, uncurtained window on a winter's night) or gaining heat by radiation from bodies warmer than itself (e.g., the unshaded asphalt of a parking lot). Since all objects radiate some heat above absolute zero, this radiant heat exchange balance is always algebraic.

HEAT, COLD, AND HUMAN WELL-BEING

The actual metabolic relation of the human body to its thermal environment can thus be described in largely objective terms. But human consciousness complicates this relationship for, in addition to mechanisms for *responding* to changes in the thermal environment, the body has very delicate sensory means for *perceiving* them. The thermo-sensors in the skin register the effect of heat as radiation (an open fire), as conduction (a hot bath) and as convection (a blast of hot air from the oven). And this perception undoubtedly acts to reinforce our state of thermal comfort or distress at any given moment. Finally, there are purely subjective factors, unconnected to our thermal condition, which can further complicate a given situation (e.g., anxiety about the task at hand, worry about health or finances, etc.). Clearly, architecture can only hope, at best, to alleviate the objective aspects of this complicated problem of thermal stress.

It is easy to dramatize extremes of thermal stress — heat so intense or cold so severe as to lead directly and spectacularly to disablement or death. Actually, in the normal peacetime activities of industrialized societies like our own, such cases would be statistically insignificant. For one farmer who dies of heat prostration or seaman who dies of exposure, there are millions of city dwellers who, in a long life, will never be subjected to stress approaching this intensity. Nevertheless, they will suffer from much less apparent deficiencies in their thermal environment; and the long-range consequences for them may often be quite as disabling as heat stroke or exposure. Unfortunately, even for specialists in the new field of environmental health, this sequence of cause and effect is not easy to trace out. Few cases of disablement or death can be attributed to any single environmental cause. Life is seldom that simple. A nexus of interacting factors, centered on the individual, will usually be involved, each of which may contribute to the end result. This necessarily ambiguous situation often serves to discourage any serious architectural diagnosis. Too often, instead, a sort of shell game is played in which *cause* (bad building, bad diet, bad clothing) can never be directly related to *effect* (discomfort, distress, disability, disease, death).

Nevertheless, it is perfectly obvious that most American experience today has its actual locus in real buildings and real cities; it is therefore inconceivable that architecture and urbanism do not play a vital role in their health. As the physiologist C. E. A. Winslow has put it in his study of human thermal requirements:

. . . we can predicate with certainty that extremes of heat and cold are harmful; and that even moderately hot conditions increase susceptibility to intestinal diseases, and moderately cold conditions increase susceptibility to respiratory disease. These are simple conclusions but they are of far-reaching significance both from an epidemiological and from a physical standpoint.[1]

And environmental health specialists and human ecologists recognize that thermal stress and atmospheric pollution play roles of prime importance in respiratory ailments like pneumonia, tuberculosis, influenza, grippe, and the common cold. The U.S. Public Health Service has found that debilitation and breakdown in human resistance to cold in ill-heated and ill-ventilated buildings are conducive to such ailments; and that dampness and cold are predisposing factors to rheumatism. Winslow and his colleague, L. P. Herrington conclude that minimum mortality rates from bronchial diseases occurred in the authentically temperate range of 60°–70° F and

60–70 per cent relative humidity[2] (e.g., a climate like that of San Francisco).

Excessive heat has always been a serious environmental hazard in heavy manufacturing and extractive industries. But only in recent times have we developed the rational means for evaluating the stresses imposed by hot environments, identifying contributing factors, and thus being able to predict and prevent the resulting physiologic stress. Architects involved in the design of industrial buildings now have access to skilled assistance which makes error unnecessary, indeed impermissible. As a matter of fact, however, with the rise of automation in heavy industry, the very problem of extremely hard or hazardous labor begins to recede into the background. The day may not be far off when such noisome and destructive jobs have been entirely eliminated by mechanized, automated and computerized production methods.

But if architects are seldom involved in designing for processes which demand heavy or laborious work, they are increasingly charged with creating satisfactory thermal environments for a wide range of less strenuous but more exacting tasks. Modern industrial processes have their own precise environmental requirements. Many of them will demand an absolutely constant thermal environment: computers, for example, are intolerant of even small variations of ambient temperature and humidity. Such process requirements will not always coincide with human requirements; typically, they will deviate; sometimes, they will be irreconcilable. Hence modern man at his workaday tasks will often be submerged in thermal environments not tailored to his own psychic and somatic requirements.

Even where process requirements are not stressful from thermal overload, the opposite may often be the case — i.e., *under-* rather than over-stimulation. The monotony and boredom of modern work is almost without precedent in human history. Only the galley slave of Classic antiquity would have experienced the monochromatic, atomized and repetitive experience which is characteristic of many blue-collar tasks today. This new situation raises many vital but extremely subtle problems of comfort, efficiency and productivity. If modern work, by its necessarily fragmented and repetitive character, suggests the need for variety in the environment in which it occurs, it will be the task of the architect to supply it. Each level of activity has its own metabolic rate and thus its own internally established rate of heat loss. But, as we have seen in Chapter 1, *even this is not indefinitely extensible in time.* The typist, doing the same work at 3 P.M. that she did at 9 A.M., may very well require a somewhat different thermal environment, even though the difference may be below the level of conscious perception. (The same proposition would hold true for other areas of sensory perception — light, sound, odor, posture, etc.) In any case, contemporary misgivings about the anesthetizing effects of "controlled environments" probably have a sound basis in day-to-day experience.

The typist, like the schoolchild or assembly-line worker, requires the sensory stimulation of change and variety. But this change must lie within a "golden zone" of thermal balance and — if the work is not to suffer — the changes must be structured and not indeterminate. (If change alone were all that was required, the typist could work in an open field.) In many activities, of course, questions of boredom or monotony will not arise. Buildings designed for entertainment and play — theaters, stadiums, swimming pools, ball courts — will shelter experiences which have their own built-in patterns of variety, suspense, satisfaction. Each is complete and intelligible in itself. Thus each can have a thermal environment designed for its particular level of metabolic activity.

Nowhere are the unfortunate consequences of thermal stress more clear than in the riots which appear to be becoming a permanent feature of the Negro ghettos of American cities. Although the basic causes of these disturbances are to be found in the profound social and economic injustices of which the Negroes are victims, it is not at all accidental that they occur in the hottest months of the year. The microclimates created by these masonry deserts exacerbate the already difficult summers of Boston, Newark, Cleveland and Chicago. Wretched conditions inside the slum dwellings (absence of cross ventilation, lack of fans, insulation, air conditioning) drive the people out into the streets. But the neighborhoods are as unbearable as the individual buildings which make them up. Urbanistic amenities which might compensate for lack of private comforts are missing. The shadeless pavements, paucity of parks and green spaces, scarcity of swimming pools — in short, the lack of any possibility of escape from high radiant and ambient temperatures and high humidities combine to make life literally intolerable. Explosions are inevitable. It would be nonsense to argue that reconstructing the ghettos would, by itself, suffice; the grave inequities which underlie them must also be wiped out. But it would be equal folly to imagine that American Negroes, once given their full rights, would tolerate the squalor and discomfort of the slums.

HOW BUILDINGS ARE HEATED AND COOLED

The task of architecture, then, is not merely to abolish gross thermal extremes (freezing to death, dying of heat prostration) but to provide the optimal thermal environments for the whole spectrum of modern life. The technology of heating and cooling aims not merely at introducing the proper amount of heat into, or extracting the proper amount of heat out of, the building: but to do it in such a manner as to achieve a thermal "steady state" across time and a thermal equilibrium across space. Neither of these criteria is easy to achieve, since radiant and ambient heat are very unstable forms of energy. As long as we had to depend upon simple combustion in fireplaces and stoves, the fire itself was a point source of heat, so that its effectiveness diminished rapidly with distance (Fig. 10). Moreover, the enclosing surfaces of the heated space would always be subjected to the shifting stress of sun and wind. Since the insulation properties of walling materials were very incompletely understood (see Chapter 8), a thermal environment constant across time and symmetrical across space was an impossibility in preindustrial architecture (Fig. 11).

To achieve these criteria today, architect and engineer have at their disposal two greatly refined instruments: a theoretical apparatus for accurately calculating the flow of heat; and a sophisticated range of building materials and heating/cooling equipment for producing the desired thermal regimes. In real life, one builds the thermal vessel and then installs the heating and cooling equipment. Conceptually, it is the other way around: one cannot design the enclosing vessel until one has a clear concept of the internal environments to

Fig. 10 (below). Traditional heating methods could not achieve a thermal steady state across time or space. Simple combustion of wood or coal in the fireplace was inefficient and uncomfortable. Introduction of free-standing metal stove increased control of radiant temperatures; but air temperature and movement remained uncontrollable.

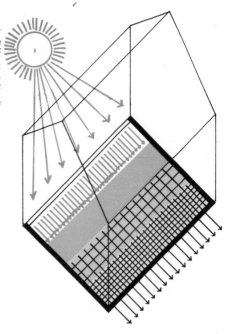

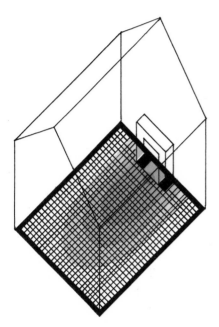

Fig. 11 (above). Traditional structural methods and building materials offered limited means of thermal insulation. The efficiency of the building as a thermal container was low; and this was exacerbated by the fundamental asymmetry, across time and space, of the natural thermal environment around it.

be created and maintained. The criteria for these environments must, in turn, be derived from the needs of the people and processes who will inhabit the building.

All thermal control systems have common functional characteristics, whatever their special features (Fig. 12). They all require a primary source of energy — coal, oil, gas or electricity.* They must convert this energy into heat or cold by the processes of combustion, compression, evaporation or electrical resistance. They require a me-

---

* Wood is too scarce and valuable a material to be used as fuel in any advanced economy. The potentials of solar energy are immense but largely unexplored and unexploited. Because of the environmental hazards of nuclear fission, energy from it will always be converted into familiar forms — electricity, steam or hot water.

ENERGY SOURCE	CONVERSION METHOD	CONVERSION UNIT	DELIVERY MEDIUM	DELIVERY MEANS	TRANSFER METHOD
gas, oil, coal	*combustion*	furnace	warm air	fans, ducts, registers	convection
		boiler	hot water	pumps, pipes, radiators	convection
				pumps, pipes, panels	radiation
			steam	pipes, radiators	convection
electricity	*compression*	compressor	warm or cool air	fans, ducts, registers	convection
			hot or cold water	pumps, pipes, panels	radiation
gas	*evaporation*	evaporative condenser	warm or cool air	fans, ducts, registers	convection
electricity	*resistance*			wires, resistance coils	radiation

Table 1. Components of modern thermal control systems. Electric motors and electronic monitors offer new levels of precision; new sources of energy, new methods of conversion and transport make possible systems which can produce a thermal steady state.

dium of distribution for this manufactured heat or cold — air, steam, water or other fluids of special properties. Finally, they must employ one of two methods of heat transfer — convection or radiation.

It is within these limits that heating and ventilating engineers have been working for over a century and a half (Table 1).* The direction of these efforts, however, has been largely conditioned by historical chance. Because wood, coal, gas and petroleum became available as fuels in approximately that order, eighteenth- and nineteenth-century heating systems were premised upon simple combustion. But the *forms* in which these fuels were available made possible increasingly sophisticated equipment, notably in automatic fueling and controls, as is obvious in the sequence fireplace–stove–furnace–stoker–oil burner.

The fireplace had many disadvantages: it was wasteful, dangerous, messy and very limited in its effect. Franklin took the first important step away from this with his lightweight, prefabricated and demountable cast iron stove (vol. I, pp. 18–20). Even the stove had the disadvantage of being a point source of heat. And this led naturally to the idea of the furnace, lost since Roman times, of heating air in a central *plenum* and carrying it by air to the various rooms. Such early furnaces relied entirely upon gravity-flow — i.e., the natural tendency of heated air to rise; and this placed obvious limitations upon the size and efficiency of such systems. Thus use of fans to push the air through the ducts awaited the perfection of the electric motor as a prime mover: this appeared in the last quarter of the nineteenth century. From this it was but a step to the modern air-conditioning system in which air is heated or cooled, moistened or dried, filtered and then forced through ducts at any rate or volume desired.

But early experience with the steam boiler set in train another set of developments in heating. Unlike the furnace, the boiler used either steam or hot water as a heat delivery medium, steam having the obvious advantage of being under pressure and therefore requiring no auxiliary pump or fan. (Gravity-flow in hot water systems was also moderately effective, in small systems.) Hence the early per-

* Thomas Tredgold's treatise, *Principles of Warming and Ventilating Public Buildings . . .* (London: J. Taylor, 1824), marks the first theoretical attempt to explore the field.

COILS IN CEILING ONLY

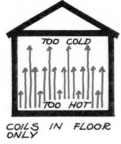
COILS IN FLOOR ONLY

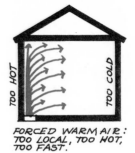
FORCED WARM AIR: TOO LOCAL, TOO HOT, TOO FAST.

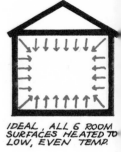
IDEAL, ALL 6 ROOM SURFACES HEATED TO LOW, EVEN TEMP.

Fig. 12. Basic types of heating installations. Even with modern equipment, heating systems often fail to meet normal criteria of comfort and health. Optimal application would be one in which transfer method was exclusively radiant (right above), with heat source distributed across all enclosing surfaces: but this is seldom practicable.

fection of central steam and hot water systems, with a central boiler supplying radiators in each room. The radiator, incidentally, is misnamed: less than one half of its heat is emitted radiantly, the balance being discharged by convection. By placing a fan behind the radiator and forcing air across the surface of its heated fins, the element was converted into an almost pure convector.

Techniques and equipment for cooling buildings are of much more recent origin. Most early developments in refrigeration occurred in the food processing industries (vol. 1, Chapter 4) and were only subsequently applied to the cooling of buildings. All the necessary components for cooling and drying air, including appropriate electronic controls, were available in the U.S. even before World War II. But, except for industrial applications and in some building types like theaters, they were not widely applied to architecture in general until the end of the war. Since that time, however, development has been so rapid that a new building without summer cooling is almost as obsolete as one without heating would have been in 1920.

Endless permutations and combinations of these various systems are in common use (Table 1). Together with parallel improvements in combustion, propulsion and refrigeration (burners, pumps, fans, compressors) and in automatic control devices (thermostats, aquastats, time and pressure controls), control of the thermal environment has become a reality. The mechanical efficiency of such equipment is now so high that it has, for all practical purposes, removed all limitations of size and location from our building activity. A small house or an entire city can be automatically conditioned by a single plant. Any kind of thermal environment can be created and maintained anywhere — at the equator, at the poles, even in outer space. This is an historic accomplishment in the evolution of architecture, permitting thermo-stable states comparable to *homeostasis* in man.

THE CONVECTIVE SYSTEMS

The majority of thermal control systems are largely convective in their method of heat transfer; those involving summer air conditioning are almost wholly so, since radiant cooling raises such serious condensation problems as to be impractical in most cases. Convective systems have certain advantages over other methods, including economy and simplicity. But they all have certain real shortcomings. The first is their general sluggishness in responding to changing external conditions. Since they depend for effect upon manipulation of the entire air mass inside the building, a time lag in completing the change is inevitable. In old-fashioned buildings with high-heat capacity walls, this lethargy was not too serious, since the building itself was slow to respond to external changes. But modern architecture, with its wide use of glass and light-weight materials, results in a thermal container of quite different properties. Its very transparency implies rapid heating up and cooling off and hence demands instantaneous response on the part of the thermal control system. This an air system cannot do, since it depends for its effect upon the temperature of the whole air mass in the vessel in question. Moreover a large part of the heat gain through glass is *radiant* and not directly modified by air temperatures. Of course, the convective system *ultimately* catches up; but it is small consolation to the occupant overheated by the radiation to know that in thirty minutes or an hour, he will be cool again. Thermal stress is metabolic and immediate, not a matter of statistical averages. For this reason, serious discomfort is all too common in many glass-walled buildings, despite their advanced air conditioning.

Convective systems have another related disadvantage. Since warm air rises and cold air falls, the tendency toward vertical temperature stratification is always operative. Most rooms will show higher temperatures at the ceiling than at the floor. From a physiological point of view this is almost the exact reverse of the desirable: ambient temperatures at the feet should be equal to or higher than those at breathing level. Modern air systems can overcome this tendency toward stratification: but to do so without drafts and noise requires a more complex duct-and-damper system and redundant capacity in the system as a whole.

THE RADIANT SYSTEMS

Well known to the Romans and the Chinese, and widely used in their more important buildings, radiant heating was all but forgotten in Europe and America until recent years. Increased experience with it since has led to important advances in both theory and technique. Mechanically, the radiant system differs in only one important respect from convective systems — the actual method of heat transfer — but it is an important difference. Using a plane surface (ceiling, walls and/or floor) as the actual heating element, the radiant panels offer an almost ideal method of manipulating the thermal environment. If installed in all six surfaces of the room, as the Romans often managed to do, they surround the body of the occupant with a balanced thermal perimeter. That is to say, the rate of heat exchange between the body and its surrounding surfaces will be equal in all directions (excepting, of course, the soles of the feet, where the heat exchange is conductive) and constant in time. This exchange is independent of the temperature, humidity and movement of the surrounding air. For example, a convective system would surround a normally clothed man at rest with 71° F air in order to maintain comfort. But with radiant surfaces at 85° F, the air temperature could drop to 59° F and the same man would be comfortable. Contrariwise, air temperatures could rise to 90° F and, with walls held at 60° F, the man would be quite at ease. It is this relative freedom from having to manipulate ambient temperatures that makes radiant heating so attractive.

From an experiential point of view, radiant systems have the obvious advantage of acting directly and immediately upon the occupants of the building and only indirectly and secondarily upon the air mass.* In any case, if they use hot water or electricity as a

---

* Obviously, in any closed and unventilated room, the atmosphere would ultimately reach the same temperature as the enclosing surfaces. In actuality, this would seldom, if ever, occur.

medium, they eliminate space-consuming fans, *plenums* and duct-work. For the same reason, they are simpler to install and operate. The elements themselves are invisible and, because of the low temperatures at which they operate, permit any type of decoration.

In practice, however, there are limitations to radiant systems, too. The optimal installation, from a physiological point of view, would use all six room surfaces as radiant sources. But construction methods and budgetary limitations often make this ideal distribution imprac-tical. Then the coils will be concentrated in one or two planes only — e.g., floor and/or ceiling. But because of such restricted areas, sur-face temperatures may have to be raised beyond the comfort level: hot feet or headaches can be the result. Also, if heating coils are confined to one plane — such as the ceiling — desk and table tops will block the rays, producing cold spots under them. Another haz-ard in systems using water as a delivery medium is the danger of leaks developing in coils embedded in plaster ceilings or concrete slabs. Thus, the electric resistance coil is the safest installation.

The Roman system employed heated air, circulating it through continuous ducts in floors, walls and ceilings. It was wood-fueled and gravity-flow, a simple and comfortable method of heating. Its limitation was that it presupposed heavy-load-bearing masonry struc-tures of the sort one would rarely find practical today. A combina-tion of such labyrinths in a masonry floor with conventional con-vective air systems, however, makes a highly satisfactory set-up for single-story buildings.

Though the high cost of electricity in many parts of the country limits the use of the electric resistance coil in radiant heating, it is the most attractive of all methods. It requires almost no space, has no moving elements, is relatively simple to install and all but fool-proof in operation. The coils themselves are usually embedded in plaster walls and ceilings, somewhat less frequently in masonry floors; but a wide variety of supplementary applications suggest themselves. For example, the electric elements used in bed sheets or blankets have been incorporated into curtains for large glass areas. They could also be built into folding or sliding screens and shutters. In cold climates, where the low surface temperatures of even insulating glass raise serious comfort problems, such applications would make significant contributions to the overall thermal balance of the room. In such applications, the coils would be employed to slow down radiant heat loss from the room's occupants to chilled glass surfaces, not to raise the air temperatures of the room as a whole.

The above considerations apply to the use of radiant panel systems for heating. But air and water systems also offer interesting potentials for summer cooling. In hot weather, as we have seen, comfort can be maintained quite as well by losing heat to cool surfaces as to cool air. Thus, by circulating chilled water or cool air through the coils, we would have "radiant cooling" independent of the temperature, humidity or movement of the surrounding air. The drawback here is condensation: except in the American southwest, summertime humidities are high and chilled surfaces would produce heavy sweating. Thus "radiant cooling" could only be used in conjunction with dehumidification equipment which could hold room air at low humidities. But from a physiological standpoint, radiant "cooling," like radiant heating, offers an exhilarating thermal environment.

Because it operates independently of air temperatures, radiant panel heating can be productively employed in a wide range of outdoor installations — e.g., in theater and hotel marquees, in sidewalk cafés, and for removal of ice and snow on sidewalks, streets and plazas. Moreover, since infrared radiation can be focused, like the visible wave band, all sorts of special problems can be solved by means of radiant heating and cooling which could not readily be met with convective systems. Thus, for example, a surgical team in an operating theater might be cooled by radiant cooling panels focused on them from the walls while the patient was submerged in the warm, moist air supplied by the central air conditioning system.

ANIMAL ANALOGUES FOR THERMAL CONTROL SYSTEMS

The objective of all these heating and cooling systems would be, of course, to produce a stable, balanced and symmetrical thermal environment — i.e., to achieve in architecture that homeostatic state which Cannon called the highest stage of evolutionary development in animals. The analogy is apt, for the building confronts the same paradox as the animal body. It seeks to establish and maintain this internal thermal state while being submerged in a continually fluctuating set of external forces. The analogue would be that the building, as a thermal vessel, requires a skin or enclosing membrane which, like the animal epidermis, is capable of variable response to shifting environmental stresses. This is why the wall cannot be thought of as a simple barrier but must rather be visualized as a permeable filter, capable of admitting, modifying or rejecting the various forces which play upon it (Fig. 69).

Hence, in thermal control, the design of the building wall is quite as important a matter as design of the systems. The malfunction of much modern architecture can be traced to neglect of this principle, where stereotyped curtain walls are used in highly formalistic designs which seldom pay serious attention to climate, latitude, and orientation. The entire task of maintaining required internal conditions is thrown upon the heating and cooling systems, with inevitable waste, inefficiency and malfunction. The advantages of standardization of industrially produced parts and components are obvious. But a comparable standardization of entire buildings which will have to meet the wide climatic variations discussed in Chapter 9 makes no such sense at all. A building in Bangor and a building in Tucson may well use identical materials — metals, insulation materials, glass and plastics: but the *way* in which they are assembled into a wall must be quite dissimilar to function equally well.

It is possible to visualize in broad terms the characteristic features of several different types of building skins to meet these requirements:

1. The most direct analogue of the animal epidermis would be a solid opaque membrane (with few windows of limited size) with an overall capillary system of coils embedded near the outer surface (Fig. 13). The coils would circulate either chilled or heated water as called for by individual thermostats for each exposure and roof. In cold weather, such a capillary system would circulate heated water in those walls which were chilled by wind or shade, transferring heated water from sunny exposures and supplementing it as required. In summer, when heat gain would be excessive on all walls, the capillaries would circulate chilled water on all outer surfaces, transferring heat thus accumulated into a storage system.

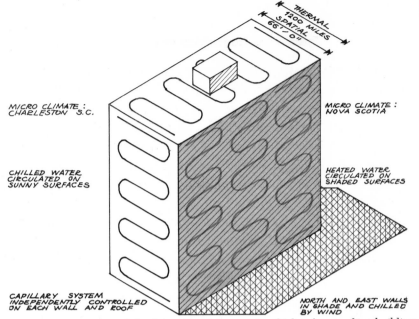

MICRO CLIMATE :
CHARLESTON S.C.

CHILLED WATER
CIRCULATED ON
SUNNY SURFACES

CAPILLARY SYSTEM
INDEPENDENTLY CONTROLLED
ON EACH WALL AND ROOF

THERMAL
1200 MILES
SPATIAL
66' - 0"

MICRO CLIMATE :
NOVA SCOTIA

HEATED WATER
CIRCULATED ON
SHADED SURFACES

NORTH AND EAST WALLS
IN SHADE AND CHILLED
BY WIND

Fig. 13. The asymmetry of the thermal environment in which a freestanding building is submerged is very marked; during daylight hours, it becomes acute. Then the spread between thermal environments along sunlit and shaded walls will be the equivalent of hundreds of miles rather than tens of feet. A capillary system in the building's epidermis, operating independently of internal heating and air-conditioning system, would facilitate the maintenance of an internal thermal steady state. It would also reduce redundant capacity and yield economies in energy consumption.

Such a capillary system would be supplementary to conventional conditioning of enclosed volumes, serving largely to hold the perimeters in a thermally symmetrical state. It would be most valuable in building types where very precise environmental controls are required. It would have the obvious disadvantage of opacity for any building type which required natural light or view.

2. There are other dynamic solutions to the problem of equalizing the unequal and continually shifting thermal stresses upon the building. One type of response would be to design the building so that two adjacent walls were opaque to thermal transmission and the opposite pair transparent. The building could then be rotated so as to keep the opaque walls normal to the sun in periods of overheating; in cold weather, the cycling would be reversed — i.e., the transparent walls would be held normal to the sun (Fig. 14).

A less complicated version of the same principle would be to rotate a free-standing screen, large enough to shield the building, around it, cycling it to correspond to periods of over- or underheating as above (Fig. 15). Such methods would be especially adapted to dry climates of extreme insolation (e.g., Yuma, Phoenix, Las Vegas) or to regions with high winter winds (Duluth, Buffalo). Since either building or screen could be floated on tracked pontoons, the mechanical energy for such rotation would be moderate — probably less, in fact, than the redundant cooling capacity saved.

3. The most familiar architectural response is that of shading the wall by manipulating the forms and materials of the wall itself. This response takes two forms: (a) planar extensions of the wall itself, in the form of vertical and horizontal *brise-soleils,* louvers, screens, etc., and (b) use of materials with special photo-thermal properties — heat- and/or light-rejecting glasses, plastics, etc.; or some combination of the two. Because of the constantly shifting path of the sun, the geometry of the first method is complex. Consequently many "sun-shading" devices are often more photogenic than functional (Fig. 17). Automatically powered louvers can overcome this hazard but are not practical in many climates because of icing, corrosion, and mechanical failure (Fig. 18).

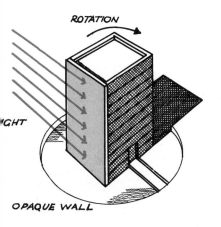

Fig. 14 (left). Another form of architectural response to changing solar loads would be rotation in phase with moving sun. Rate of admission or exclusion of solar energy could be held constant by holding transparent or opaque walls normal to sun's position. Even fairly large buildings, floating on tracked pontoons, might be rotated. Control of internal thermal and luminous environments would be improved; capital costs of redundant equipment and excessive energy consumption might be reduced. For prototype installation, see Fig. 29.

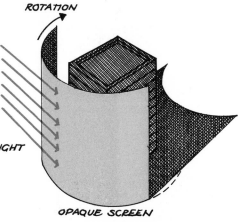

Fig. 15 (right). A variant of the rotating building might be a screen, opaque to solar energy, which rotated on tracks around building. In climates where a deficiency of solar energy or high winds are an environmental problem, such a tracked screen might be used as a windbreak to reduce excessive chilling of walls to windward.

Fig. 16. Law Building, Columbia University, New York, N.Y. Harrison and Abramowitz, architects. Fixed vertical fins, identical on all four façades, offer unpredictable, hence inadequate protection against insolation to continuous glass walls behind. Truly effective sun-shading devices would necessarily show different pattern on each side.

The most sophisticated solution to this particular problem is the type of wall analysis and design suggested by the work of Ralph Knowles (Fig. 17). Here a cellular geometry has been developed by computerizing the many thousand variables involved in rejecting solar radiation for every minute of every day. In addition to being highly effective, the resulting patterns are extremely handsome and suggest once again that the origin of rich and satisfying esthetics is always found in functional effectiveness.

Fig. 17. Hypothetical study for an office building at 30°N. Ralph Knowles, architect. The shape of the building, its orientation and the geometry of its surfaces derive from geometry of sun control. Result is a kind of bearing wall in which structural material is organized normal to wall plane. This assures complete diurnal and seasonal control of sunlight, maximum transparency from inside and wide spans.

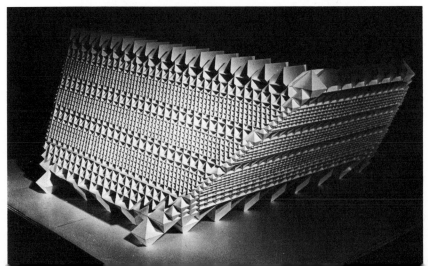

Fig. 18a. South-facing solar collector wall is tilted at a 30° angle from vertical for maximum heat absorption. It consists of sealed, glass-faced boxes containing coils.

Fig. 18. Solar-powered office building, Albuquerque, N.M. Stanley and Wright, architects; Bridgers and Paxton, air-conditioning engineers. Instead of rejecting high heat input of American Southwest, this building is designed to absorb it, employing it as prime energy source for heating and cooling around the year. System consists of a flat-plate solar collector of 830 sq. ft. (above), using water as transport medium; 7.5-ton heat pump for winter heating and summer cooling; an evaporative water cooler (for summer only). There is a 6000-gal. underground water tank for heat storage and the necessary circulating pumps for radiant heating and cooling panels, ventilation system, etc. Extraordinary efficiency of heat pump (1.2 Btu delivered for every 1 Btu put into it from collector) is reason for system's success: additional advantage of installation lies in reduction of seasonal redundant capacity in equipment.

Fig. 18b. For 90 per cent of heating season, system uses stored solar heat exclusively.

Fig. 18d. As cooling loads peak, evaporator acts as cooling tower for refrigeration.

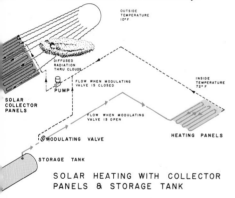

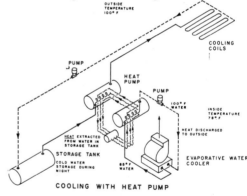

Fig. 18c. During long cold spells, when stored water cools, pump "concentrates" heat.

Fig. 18e. This cycle is used in spring and autumn to cool building while storing heat.

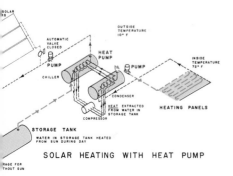

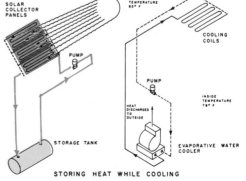

4. PURE AS THE AIR YOU BREATHE: CONTROL OF THE ATMOSPHERIC ENVIRONMENT

In popular opinion, the ideas persist that somewhere — in Atlantic City, in the Smoky Mountains, at Yellowstone — there is such a thing as "pure air," that such atmospheres are "good for you," and that they constitute the ideal habitat for all of man's activities. The first opinion is wrong and the latter two are only relatively right. There is no such thing in nature as "pure" — i.e., completely clean and sterile — air and there never has been. The nearest approach to such an unnatural state would be found either at the poles or in the upper levels of the atmosphere. But scientists have found dusts and pollens deep in the ancient ice of Antarctica; and some terrestrial impurities are carried to the outer limits of the earth's atmospheric envelope. The great air currents of the globe are Nature's most important transportation network, and she uses them to the maximum. Natural atmospheres are by definition impure, freighted with a vast cargo of bacteria, molds, viruses, pollens, spores and dusts — not to mention flying insects (which are the vectors of some of mankind's worst diseases) and birds.

What we usually mean when we speak of "pure air" is air which is free of *man-made* pollution: and here, of course, conventional wisdom is correct. There are few man-made pollutants which are not actively inimical to us; and the amount of them now being discharged into the atmosphere is verging on the catastrophic. In the undisturbed natural atmospheres of the Siberian *taiga* or the Canadian far north, however, only people with allergies or asthma would find any cause for alarm. The botanist Fritz Wendt has pointed out that Longfellow's "whispering pines and hemlocks" are among the world's greatest sources of pollution, discharging molecular substances known as terpenes; and that some plant species have such noxious discharges that other plants cannot grow near them![1] But in common experience, such discharges are the source of some of our most pleasant olfactory sensations — e.g., the scent of the lily, the rose or the pineapple.

We are completely submerged in this ocean of air and we are as completely dependent upon it as any fish is upon the sea. Our relationship with it is very complex: as we have seen in the preceding chapter, the thermal balance of the human body is largely dependent upon the temperature, humidity and movement of the air around it. They become, in fact, functions of the thermal environment (and this is confirmed by thermal engineering practice, where the handling of air masses within the building is regarded as an integral part of heating and cooling). But this relationship can only partially be described in thermal terms, for the air is also the habitat of the respiratory system, including the sense of olfaction, for which the free oxygen of the atmosphere is a prerequisite. Animal life is fundamentally a process of slow combustion: thus the air plays a critical *internal* role in the metabolic process, this time on the heat-producing side of the metabolic cycle. Of the body's three requirements for combustion — air, water, and food — air is most urgently needed. The average man will consume five pounds of air for every one of food or water, and a few seconds of lack exhausts his reserves: collapse, coma and death follow within moments of a cutoff in his supply.

Thus, while the respiratory system is only indirectly involved with the temperature, humidity or motion of the air, it is vitally linked to its pressure and composition. It is to this latter relationship that we must now turn, since it plays an increasingly important role in design at both the architectural and the urbanistic level.

THE HABITAT OF THE RESPIRATORY SYSTEM

The natural habitat of the human respiratory and olfactory systems has a topology which can be described in terms of *pressure, gaseous composition* and *non-gaseous aerosols.* The normal pressure — i.e., the level to which our lungs, heart and blood circulation are adjusted — is that of sea level, about 14 lbs. psf. In undisturbed conditions, the air is a gaseous mix of nitrogen, oxygen, carbon dioxide and water vapor with minute traces of argon, helium, krypton, neon and xenon, together with varying small amounts of ammonia, nitrous and nitric acids. Until comparatively recent times, this mix would have supported a physical burden of aerosols of natural origin: bacteria, viruses, pollens, etc.; water particles; dusts from storms, and smokes and ashes from forest fires and volcanic explosions.

Normal preindustrial man going about his daily tasks would never have experienced violent shifts in the pressure or composition of the atmosphere comparable to those diurnal and seasonal fluctuations which are characteristic of the thermal and luminous environments. He would encounter stressful changes in pressure only in such activities as diving or mountain climbing. The chemical composition of the air would only rarely be disturbed by natural phenomena (marsh gas, volcanic eruptions); and, aside from allergens, the only noxious particles would be dusts or insects. The design of his respiratory system reflects these relatively stable conditions. His lungs had the built-in capacity for accommodation to the low pressure and thin oxygen of high mountains; or even the capacity to acclimatize him to life on the *alto planos* of Tibet and Peru. But against poisonous gases he had only the warning system provided by his sense of smell.

IMPURITIES IN SUSPENSION

All atmospheres carry a suspended burden of foreign matter — spores, pollens, dusts and particulates of all sorts. But if nature produces all these pollutants, she has also evolved a series of mechanisms for holding them in check. Washing them out with rain is, of course, the most general; but a natural landscape of forest or meadowland acts as a vast impingement filter, trapping many of these aerosols out of the air as it moves across it. This natural filtration effect will produce atmospheres at the center of the forest which may be 25 per cent cleaner than that at its fringes, while a mown lawn is also an extremely effective filter of larger airborne particles. (See

Chapter 9.) It is only within the last few decades that we have been able to define — much less to construct — a perfectly pure and sterile atmosphere. Yet men have for centuries understood that apparently clean air could, on occasion, carry a lethal burden. Thus, in medieval plagues, the people wore masks against contagious diseases, some of which are in fact airborne. (Others were carried by water, food or personal contact, of course.) A fear of "night airs" was widespread in the Western world. And not without reason: in ante-bellum New Orleans there was a great fear of the "miasma" which rose at night from the swamps, carrying the danger of malaria (literally: "bad air") to all who inhaled it. Buildings were supposed to offer some protection against this menace, though in both Rome and New Orleans a flight to the hills was considered advisable in hot weather. Even so great a scientist as Darwin, lacking the assistance of bacteriology, was forced to fall back upon the miasma to explain the propagation of certain tropical diseases. It remained for Walter Reed, the great American doctor and epidemiologist, to convict the swamp mosquito (and not the swamp air) as the vector of malaria and yellow fever. Without this discovery, the Panama Canal would have been impossible.

The natural atmospheric environment has always been immensely important to Nature as an avenue of propagation, and she has loaded it with spores and pollens. Not all of these are "good" for the human respiratory system and it is probably erroneous to think that allergic contemporaries of John and Priscilla Alden were any more comfortable, submerged in them, than are we today. There is no reason to suppose that asthma, hay fever and allergies are modern inventions — though there is every reason to suspect that man-made pollutants have enormously complicated the picture in recent times. As with most of the diseases which afflict mankind, we are constantly learning more about them. Our diagnoses grow more accurate all the time, so that last year's statistics are not comparable with those of fifty or even ten years ago. Even today, we have no accurate information on how many persons suffer from pollen- and spore-induced disturbances. But at least, for the first time in history, we understand something of the pathology of allergy; and we have perfected equipment which can filter out a large proportion of the allergens.

The ocean of air also supports another complicated hierarchy of microorganisms — bacteria and viruses. Many of these are beneficial to man: some of them (the antibiotics, yeasts and bacilli like those which sour milk or fix nitrogen in the soil) are indispensable. But collectively these organisms are the cause of most of the contagious diseases of mankind. Some of them are free agents, riding around on drops of moisture from human throats or nostrils; many of them hitch rides on insect hosts. For many others the exact method of transmission is not fully understood. The viruses — those strange substances that bridge the gap between the living and the nonliving and thus obscure what was once considered to be a sharply defined line between living cell and chemical molecule — these viruses can apparently move on the tsetse fly to cause encephalitis; on the house fly to spread infantile paralysis; on droplets from the nostrils to scatter influenza and the common cold.

There is now no doubt that airborne pollens cause hay fever, that airborne dusts lead to silicosis and that smokes cause lung cancer and emphysema: together, these constitute a large and growing percentage of American disabilities and deaths. But oddly enough the whole theory of infection by airborne microbes is still the subject of cautious speculation, though there is growing evidence to support it. The layman who thinks he "catches" cold or influenza from exposure in a crowded bus or elevator has common sense on his side but not yet completely proven fact. For scientific investigators, the problem is complicated by the fact that viruses appear to be the cause of such ailments; and their behavior is not completely understood.

But if architects must, with the experts, withhold final judgment on the airborne transmission of disease, they might at least observe that the air inside any building supports billions of organisms of all sorts; that the population of such organisms per cubic foot rises in direct proportion to human occupancy; and that many of these organisms closely resemble those known to cause respiratory disturbances. To this can be added the notorious coincidence between overcrowding and contagious disease; and the moral responsibilities of architect and urbanist in this area become clear.

Finally, the atmosphere is the habitat for many insects, most of which are a nuisance to man. A few, of course, are essential: aside from his no longer significant task of producing honey, the honeybee carries on the immensely more important task of pollenization. But relative to most of modern man's activities — especially those which occur in cities and buildings — insects are uniformly *personae non gratae*. For the average middle-class American city dweller, municipal sanitary measures have largely eliminated the problem of airborne insects. (The problem of eradicating land-based vermin — roaches, bedbugs, fleas and termites — is altogether another matter, as most slum dwellers can readily testify. But the elimination of these vermin is a matter of social responsibility, not technical competence.) Nevertheless, in rural areas and especially in tropical and semitropical climates, insect control is a prime architectural problem, from not only a sanitary but also an esthetic point of view. The necessity for insect-screening works directly against the open plan, with its integration of indoor and outdoor space which a tropical climate makes desirable. The recent tendency here, especially in residential buildings, is to place the entire house and garden in a screened cage, thus placing this environmental filter at the outer perimeter of family life.

Insect control at an urban or even regional level has been immensely advanced by the use of chemical pesticides sprayed from the air. Thus whole sections of the Florida Everglades have been ridded of the mosquito, the Mississippi Delta of the boll weevil, Adirondack resort areas of the deer fly — if only on a local and/or temporary basis. But, unexpectedly, such aerial use of pesticides has had disastrous ecological side effects, not only in the insect world itself (e.g., the destruction of the Florida honeybees upon which fertilization of the orange groves depends) but also upon bird life and aquatic life. The intricate and far-reaching consequences of this kind of chemical warfare are already leading to legal limitations. It seems entirely possible that much of it will ultimately be outlawed altogether, as called for by the late Rachel Carson in her epochal book, *Silent Spring*.

Modern life confronts man with other new atmospheric situations, as when it takes him deep under the sea or far out into space. Here he is exposed to such barometric pressures as would either collapse or explode his respiratory system were he not encapsulated in a submarine or spacecraft. These remarkable vehicles have required the development of a para-military technology which, while very advanced, has little application to terrestrial activities. Research needs its vacuum chambers, aviation its wind tunnels; and there are specialized medical procedures in which atmospheric pressure is manipulated for therapeutic purposes — e.g., hyperbaric chambers for the treatment of caisson disease, gas gangrene or severe cardiac cases. However, the architect will seldom be called upon to design buildings for anything other than normal ambient pressures. The one important exception to this generalization would be in the new and promising field of inflated structures, in which internal air pressures are slightly higher than outside in order to support the nonrigid envelope. The differentials are too small to be physiologically significant and the structural possibilities appear to be spectacular. (See Chapter 8.)

THE POISONED AIR

It is above all the chemical composition of the atmosphere which is being radically altered by modern industrial society. Every human activity has always had waste products and much of this waste has always been dumped into the open air. But in preindustrial times, neither the nature nor the concentration of these wastes was ever a matter of much consequence. It is urban life and modern technology which have brought about a qualitative change in this "atmospheric sewage," as it has been quite aptly called. There is incomparably more of it; and it is composed of thousands of new substances, gaseous and particulate, whose actions upon one another and upon human life are scarcely guessed at. It is true that there are many activities which require atmospheres whose composition, purity or cleanliness are without precedent in the natural world (e.g., pharmaceuticals, surgery, baking, brewing and food processing, etc.). But it is simultaneously true that these same industries, along with all our activities (heavy industry, transportation, space heating) are annually dumping some 133 *billion* tons of pollutants into the American atmospheric environment. We are destroying the "old-fashioned" natural atmospheres on which all biological existence is premised.

Things have already reached critical proportions. In fact, there are those ecologists who are seriously beginning to fear that this pollution — result of over two hundred years of fossil fuel combustion — may have already irreversibly altered the structure of the upper atmosphere and hence the future climates of the whole earth![2]

In the light of current research in environmental health, it seems incredible that the smoke and fumes of industry could have once been considered beautiful — at least by those upper-class people who were not compelled to toil in the factories and mills. The smoke and flame of the iron foundry were even raised to the level of architectural ornament in Ledoux's design for the royal French munitions monopoly (Fig. 19). It is now apparent that, from the very beginning, these industrial wastes of gases, smokes and ashes had profoundly serious implications for the health of the working people. The striking thing is how long it took to establish the causal links between air pollution and disease. Even when the first movements against it appeared, in the early part of this century, they took the form of "smoke abatement" or "smoke prevention" campaigns.

Fig. 19. *Forge à Canons*, project for a metallurgical plant for the French military establishment, 1804. Charles Nicholas Ledoux, architect. In this early scheme for a model factory town, the utopian designer celebrates the smoke, flame and noise of a coal-powered industrialism. It was too early to visualize the disastrous consequences for the atmospheric environment of inefficient combustion of fossil fuels.

Although they recognized the health hazards of pollution, there was little concrete medical data to support them. Hence these campaigns used arguments of a largely visual nature — i.e., smoke should be eliminated because of the way it cut out sunlight, damaged plants, soiled buildings and clothes, etc.[3] Obviously, these are perfectly valid arguments against atmospheric pollution: they merely turn out to be, in the light of current knowledge, much less serious than those involving health and well-being.

Atmospheric pollution had to reach the level of major natural disasters in order to attract adequate scientific attention to the pathological consequences of even low concentrations of pollutants. The last few decades have, unfortunately, provided a lengthening list of such disasters. All these incidents have occurred within a fixed environmental reference frame. The underlying cause (discharge of large amounts of industrial waste into the air) had to be triggered by a meteorological phenomenon. This occurs when, because of both topographical and meteorological reasons, a metropolitan region finds itself submerged in a cold, moist air mass which is trapped under an overlying mass of still, warm air. Since the condition is the reverse of normal it is called an *inversion*. Typically, these cause fogs: and since the inversion prevents dispersion of pollution to the upper atmosphere, the concentration of pollutants increases and we have a poisonous mixture now called a *smog*.

Smogs occur most frequently in winter, when the heating season is at a peak and effluents from thousands of stoves and furnaces are dumped, so to say, on top of the normal industrial wastes. Wintertime smogs are more significant physiologically because cold weather always produces the peak of respiratory diseases — bronchitis, influenza, common colds. Even in clean air, the greatest number of persons would be having respiratory problems. Thus, all factors combine to make the smog most severe just when the population is most vulnerable to such an added environmental stress.

One of the first serious smogs to be recognized and studied[4] as such was that which occurred in the heavily industrialized Meuse Valley in Belgium. Submerged in a heavy fog for four days in December, 1930, with the atmosphere more poisoned hour by hour, the population witnessed 63 deaths and 6000 illnesses serious enough to require medical attention. This represented a death rate 10.5 times the normal; and most of the victims, in what has since come to be recognized as a normal pattern, turned out to have had previous histories of respiratory or cardiac disturbances. The effects of the smog can thus be seen as being most severe on those with serious ailments. Now there is growing evidence that many of these ailments are themselves the pathological results of longtime exposure to lower concentrations of exactly the same pollutants which finally killed them!

Almost identical environmental circumstances produced the first well-documented American disaster at Donora, Pennsylvania.[5] A manufacturing town of 13,000, Donora extends along the banks of the Monongahela River, which forms a crescent-shaped valley sunk between 400-foot-high hills. In the town at the time of the disaster were three big plants fabricating steel and zinc products on a 24-hour day. In such a classic topography for inversions, this one began with a fog on Tuesday, October 26, 1948, and did not lift until the following Sunday. The deadly concentration of pollutants from trains, tugboats and factories* rose steadily — and with it, the roster of dead and disabled. At week's end, there were twenty dead (as against a usual rate of one or two) and almost 6000 cases of respiratory distress of varying degrees of severity (many of whom were saved by oxygen inhalators belonging to the fire department). Scientists of the U.S. Public Health Service found that "pre-existing diseases of the cardio-respiratory system appeared to be a single common factor among the fatally ill." They also found that of Donora citizens who were 65 or over, more than 60 per cent had reported some discomfort from the smog, almost one-half of them having been severely affected. In trying to isolate the exact mechanism of the attack, the investigators were forced to the conclusion that it was "probably a combination of [such] substances, rather than one, which was responsible for the trouble."

* The U.S. Public Health Service reported that, even after eliminating those substances "which were either known or suspected to be irritants of the respiratory tract," the following gases remained to be studied: fluoride, chloride, oxides of nitrogen, hydrogen sulfide, cadmium oxide, sulfur dioxide and excessive amounts of carbon dioxide which, being a stimulant of the respiratory tract, makes one breathe more deeply and often!

London has been famous for her fogs since long before Dickens; but she only began seriously to analyze them from an epidemiological point of view after the disastrous smogs of December, 1952, and January–February, 1953. Here again a very durable inversion was responsible, accompanied by unseasonably cold weather. Deaths during the first smog ran to 4000 above average for the period, while those during the second soared to 8000 above normal. Here again the hardest hit by these two atmospheric disasters were persons with previous case histories of cardiac and respiratory diseases.[6] Analyses of recent New York City smogs have revealed comparable situations. In one which ran from January 29 to February 12, 1963, mortalities ran 647 above normal for the period. Even allowing for the fact that it was the coldest such fortnight in ten years, and for the fact that there was concurrently an epidemic of influenza, investigators figured that at least 400 deaths could be directly attributed to the smog.[7]

Another Public Health Service study, this time of deaths due to respiratory ailments for a twelve-year period ending in 1960 in Nashville, Tennessee, revealed a significant correlation between income, place of residence, and death rates from respiratory ailments. The study showed that the lowest-income groups in the city (black, in this instance), living in those wards where air-sampling stations showed air pollution to be highest, had a mortality rate almost two and a half times as high as that of higher-income groups living in the much cleaner suburbs.[8]

The smogs of Los Angeles are perhaps the most notorious of all, though because of two special conditions (semitropical climate and the world's highest population of automobiles), they take an unusual form. Because of the climate, there is comparatively little need for winter heating; and because the winters are mild and dry, there has been (until recent years, at least) a low incidence of bronchitis, influenza and colds. But this same preponderance of clear, sunny days exerts an exaggerated photochemical effect upon the effluents of four million automobiles, many oil refineries and thousands of trash burners, to produce many complex gases in the atmosphere. The most widely publicized result of such smogs was their "tear gas" effect on the eyes: but since several of the pollutants are known to be carcinogenic, the long-range impact upon the health of Los Angeles residents is certain to be more serious.

By dint of heroic control measures adopted in the past decade, Los Angeles has succeeded in greatly reducing air pollution from stationary sources — i.e., oil refineries, power and heating plants, trash burners and incinerators.[9] It is estimated that gaseous wastes from such sources have been reduced from 6375 tons per day to 1375. But the discharge from automobiles remains largely untouched. No one knows what reductions will be effected by the new fume-control equipment now required on new cars; and of course millions of old cars without such equipment will continue to circulate. The amount of atmospheric sewage produced in the city is incredible. Dr. Jack McKee of California Institute of Technology has calculated that it amounts to 9580 metric tons per day, equivalent to

1470 grams (about three pounds) per person per day on a dry weight basis — twice as much as solid refuse disposal (i.e., garbage and trash), and six times as much as the contaminants in waste water.[10]

It must be assumed that the air pollution in any urbanized area will differ little from that of London, Donora or Nashville. The situation is reflected in a rapidly expanding corpus of national and local legislation aimed at correcting it; the creation of new agencies to enforce it; and a literature too vast and complex to be more than indicated in a volume such as this.[11]

For architects, the situation is full of paradox. From a social point of view, they are parties to the act of pollution, since most of the wastes involved are generated in buildings designed by members of their profession. Yet the architect *qua* architect is usually powerless to intervene at any scale larger than the individual project. His client will have neither the power nor the inclination to control more than the air in his own building; nor the inclination to meet more than the minimum legal standards imposed on the disposal of his own building wastes (e.g., venting of noxious fumes, smoke abatement, incinerators, etc.). From a purely technical point of view, the architect's dilemma is also full of paradox. He is called upon to correct atmospheric conditions which are largely or wholly of his own collective making. Unlike the thermal or luminous environments, which the architect must manipulate to correct all sorts of natural deficiencies by means of heating/cooling, illumination and the like, the natural atmospheric environment has little "wrong" with it, as we have seen. Theoretically, the architect need only let it fill his building as water fills a bowl. Instead, however, he is compelled to spend more and more of the building dollar on elaborate equipment designed merely to return the air to its normal state. The result is another of those misapplications of technical virtuosity with which America is filled. In the last analysis, no isolated architectural solution to the problem is possible — there can only be an urbanistic or regional one.

USES OF FILTRATION

All the foregoing is very recent history. It is only within the past few decades that we have begun to realize the degree to which the atmosphere is loaded with impurities, gaseous and particulate, natural and man-made. It is even more recently that filtration equipment has been developed to combat the situation. Characteristically, the first steps were taken by industry, and more to promote efficiency than employee health *per se*. It was in those industries where pollution interfered with the process itself that the first effective measures were taken and the most efficient filters evolved. Industrial dusts in the paint shops of Detroit's auto plants and the film laboratories of Hollywood picture-makers made first-rate paint jobs and films impossible. In mining or quarrying, on the other hand, dust did not affect the process itself, though it had most destructive effects on the lungs of the miners and quarrymen. In the first instance, we find industry eagerly fostering the development of advanced filtration equipment; in the latter case, we find Congress itself reluctant to pass legislation protecting the most elementary health demands of the workers.

Several methods of ridding the air of its unwelcome burden of particulates have been developed. (None have been developed for filtering out gaseous substances.) Air can be *washed* by passing it through a fine water spray: this will remove most of the larger particles — ashes, dusts, pollens. However, smaller particles are not caught, and the air comes out of the spray much wetter than it went in, which will often be undesirable. A second method is that of *mechanical filtration.* Here the stream of air can be forced through a many-layered filter of fine metal filings or glass threads; sometimes these filters are covered with oil to hold particles by impingement. This method traps only larger airborne particles and has the further disadvantage of offering high resistance to air passing through it. A third method, that of *electric precipitation,* passes the air through a charged grid or ionizer which bombards the particles and thus gives them an electrical charge. The air then passes through another grid whose plates are alternately positive and negative. Here the charged particles are caught and held, from whence they can be periodically removed by slipping out the grids and washing them.

Of the three methods, precipitation is the most efficient, since it removes dusts, pollens and bacteria whose diameters are too small for the other filters to catch. Its applications are many and interesting. A large film manufacturing company uses it for reclamation of airborne silver nitrate previously lost in the ventilation system. It is used in most laboratories, telephone exchanges or computer banks where extremely delicate electronic equipment demands dust-free atmospheres. It is useful in libraries and archives, where books and documents must be kept dust-, insect- and mildew-free. It offers hospitals and clinics the first completely clean air for the treatment of serious cases of asthma and related allergic disturbances of the respiratory system.

Despite their very high efficiency, however, the electric precipitators are not wholly effective against bacteria, bacilli and virus. They can remove up to 85 per cent of all particulate matter: but the smallest of these organic substances slip through in the remaining 15 per cent. Besides, the only safe germ is a dead one: it is not enough to catch it, it must also be killed. For this purpose, the germicidal lamp can be used to irradiate the air after filtration. Emitting radiation in the invisible portion of the spectrum, the ultraviolet lamp has been found to be highly effective against both microbic and viral populations. It can be employed in several ways besides being tied into the filter. It can be used to irradiate the air in any room or portion of a room, including its surfaces, since it has been proved to be effective against bacterial colonies on any surface on which the rays fall — e.g., furniture, clothes, floors, etc. Finally, the germicidal lamp can be used to form an invisible "germ lock" between different areas of the same building.

Obviously, this type of irradiation could be applied to many building types. The atmosphere of an entire hospital can be kept completely sterile; or certain areas like surgical suites and baby wards can be sterilized; or contagious diseases can be effectively isolated to prevent cross-infection — a particular hazard with central air-conditioning systems. In controlled experiments in three Pennsylvania schools, ultraviolet irradiation of primary-grade classrooms reversed the trend of a measles epidemic: only a third as many cases were reported there as in the upper classes, whose rooms were not irradiated. (There are usually three times as many such cases in lower grades than in the upper ones.) The U.S. Navy has found that similar equipment, installed in selected barracks, reduced cases of common colds, German measles and scarlet fever by 25 per cent: samples of air from these barracks showed only half as many micro-organisms as that from non-irradiated buildings.[12] Application of this type of bacteriocidal light has also proved valuable in theaters and in public transport.

There are some specialized processes, on the other hand, in which the presence of certain micro-organisms is essential: thus, in brewing and baking, a particular strain of cultivated yeast is introduced into the atmosphere. Thereafter, any contamination by wild airborne yeasts and other fermentative agents must be avoided by sterilizing all incoming air. Cheese-making requires both bacteria and molds, but certain cheeses require special cultures and close control of atmospheric and thermal conditions. Until recently, such cheeses could only be produced in some special cavern in Greece or Italy. Now it is possible to re-create and maintain these exact atmospheres — complete with their special microbic population — in any building anywhere. Other fields in which absolutely sterile air is essential are the manufacture of pharmaceuticals and cosmetics and food processing generally.

Advanced equipment of this sort should, in theory, be employed to create such new and special environments required by modern life, for which there are no precedents in nature. Yet all too often it is employed merely to re-establish conditions which under "ordinary" circumstances would be free for the asking. Thus many a modern building employing electronic filtration and irradiation internally is simultaneously dumping the wastes from its own heating and power plant into the outside air around it! The insanity of this proposition does not make it any the less common. On the contrary, it is a characteristic contradiction of architecture and urbanism today. Yet it becomes ever clearer that either the whole environment must be cherished and maintained intact or ultimately even the finest building will be doomed to fail.

THE AERODYNAMIC BEHAVIOR OF BUILDINGS

The need for structural stability long ago compelled architects and engineers to come to terms with the force of moving air. Relatively wind-resistant structures were designed empirically — i.e., on the basis of trial and error — for millennia before the development of mathematical means for calculating wind loads and converting them into stress formulas which would yield structural members of appropriate size and shape. Such computations are today routine; and now, with the computer, mathematical models of any conceivable aerodynamic condition can be easily simulated.

Of course, the impact of moving air on buildings has consequences other than purely mechanical ones. Air currents moving through and around the building have important impacts upon the thermal state of that building as a whole. The factor of wind chill is especially critical in cold climates, since it greatly exacerbates the thermal stress of submersion in cold air. This phenomenon has long been understood by heating engineers and is a standard component of heat loss calculations.

But there is still another side to this question: for, if the problem of what moving air "does to" buildings has been rather thoroughly explored, the obverse — i.e., what the building "does to" this moving air — has been almost completely ignored by architects and landscape architects alike. True, the consequence of this aerodynamic interaction is micro-environmental in scale, but this is precisely the scale at which human experience takes place. It is obvious that any building, no matter how small, will modify pre-existent wind patterns by its sheer presence in the air stream. It is equally apparent that when the exterior surfaces of this building are heated, whether externally by the sun or internally by the heating plant, convective air currents will be set up. These will interact with local winds, still further complicating the aerodynamic situation in the immediate environs of the building.

Such factors have always been fairly well understood by pre-industrial societies and compensated for in their architectural and town planning. But the small scale and low height of preindustrial buildings held them within manageable (or at least tolerable) limits. The great height of modern buildings and their unprecedented density in modern cities has raised this problem to new levels of acuteness. Any modern complex, with its masonry masses and paved streets and parking lots, absorbs and then reradiates immense amounts of solar energy. This effect alone is enough to set up strong convective currents; but superimposed upon this is the effect of large vertical surfaces which create powerful rising and falling currents. If these surfaces are in close juxtaposition, as they usually are in downtown districts, these currents are often accelerated into gale-force winds.

As a result of these accumulated factors, the micro-environment of most urban areas is radically altered from its natural state. And, because this is never taken into account in either the design of the individual building or the complex of which it is a part, the alteration is usually for the worse. There is an unanticipated drop in the levels of amenity, comfort and safety which the designs were supposed to have raised and reinforced. The wind-chill factor reduces the time span in which plazas in the north are actually pleasant to be in or possible to use. Blowing dust and trash is an offense to eye and nostril alike. Snow is drifted into unsafe and unpretty patterns. Entrance doors become difficult to operate and lobbies drafty. Falling icicles and window glass sucked out of curtain walls by pressure differentials become a serious hazard to pedestrians. Such aerodynamic dysfunction is familiar to all city dwellers — excepting, ironically, the building designers themselves!

It is, of course, impossible to *prevent* the generation of local wind systems in built-up areas. (In hot climates it might even be desirable!) The real point at issue here is their *control*. Though such control involves many variables, aerospace technology has raised to very high levels the possibility of analyzing the interaction between the form and the moving air around it. The principal research tool is the wind tunnel: these are widely distributed across the country and could readily be used to test scale models of individual buildings, building complexes, and indeed entire towns. Such analyses should become an integral part of all architectural and landscape designs.

THE HABITAT OF OLFACTION

To *be* in the atmospheric environment is the basic fact of animal existence. To be able to *perceive* some of its qualities is an altogether different aspect of the same experience. A room could simultaneously be filled with attar of roses and carbon monoxide: the olfactory sense would register pleasure with the one without detecting the mortal danger of the other. Contrariwise, the atmospheric environment might meet all objective criteria for health and still be rendered esthetically unsatisfactory by harmless concentrations of a noisome odor (rotten eggs, putrefaction). It is an odd fact that the critical literature of architecture pays so little attention to its olfactory behavior, since odor plays an important experimental role in all buildings. Anyone who has entered the old churches of Italy and Greece will realize that the experience is conditioned, in about equal parts, by four factors: illumination, acoustical response, ambient temperatures, and *odors* in those great masonry vessels. Stepping into them, one is immediately submerged in co-existent pools of light, sound, temperature and odor which differ sharply from the work-a-day world outside. The sensuous impact is very powerful, even on the nonbeliever; and the scent of candles, flowers and especially incense is a very important constituent of the total experience. As a matter of fact, the extensive use of incense in Orthodox and Catholic churches has important *visual* consequences as well, since without the smoke in the cool, still air, the rays of sunlight coming in through the windows would be invisible. This "finger of God" effect is especially important in Baroque churches, where the size, shape and location of windows is often calculated to focus such rays on a given spot at a given time of day.

All buildings generate their own olfactory environment, whether or not the architect has anticipated the fact in his considerations. Too often, in the modern world, he has not. Here, as in other aspects of the design process, purely visual criteria will often tend to dominate design decisions, to the detriment of other avenues of sensory perception. For example, the "open plan" of upper-class suburban houses often yields visual sequences more dramatic than would be possible with conventional rooms. But the plan through which space flows without interruption will be one in which odors (and sounds) behave the same way. This condition will not show up in the photograph and is not apt to be mentioned in the caption; but for such reasons many open plans are, in experiential reality, disastrous.

Every act of the architect has olfactory consequences: at the very least he should be able to anticipate them. This becomes especially important in buildings like schools or hospitals, where centralized air-conditioning systems introduce the hazard of accidentally distributing obnoxious odors across the whole building. (This would be the olfactory dimension of the danger of cross-pollution discussed earlier in this chapter, though it might not involve identical gases or aerosols.) Such considerations raise basic questions: what is odor? how is it perceived? how can odors be manipulated architecturally?

For any substance to be olfactorily perceptible, it must have two physical properties. It must be at least partially volatile (otherwise the atmosphere would not support it); and it must be soluble in water (otherwise it could not penetrate the watery film that covers the mucous membrane of the nose). Beyond this, surprisingly little is known about odors; and this is expressed in the fact that there is not yet an objective, quantitative unit of measurement for odor, as there is for light or sound. We do not yet have even a means of describing or identifying various odors except by analogy.

Nor do we fully understand the process of olfaction. It is a chemical sense and, to the chemist, its sensitivity is astounding:

The mechanism through which a tiny area within the nasal fossae is able to receive an unlimited number of dissimilar odor stimuli, sometimes from a remote distance and sometimes in dilutions as weak as one part in billions of air, constitutes a prime biologic mystery. In the case of the eye and the ear, the perceptive apparatus is confronted with a limited and precise range of vibration. Exactness attends the two sensations. [Even] for taste, only four primary stimuli are involved. Not so for odors. The varieties of odor stimuli requiring appraisal and identification are to be reckoned in tens of thousands.[13]

Moreover, the capacity of even the human nose (let alone that of the wild animal) to sort out and characterize various substances is almost beyond belief:

. . . it deals with complex compounds that might take a chemist months to analyze in the laboratory. The nose identifies them instantly, even in an amount so small (as little as a ten-millionth of a gram) that the most sensitive modern laboratory instruments often cannot detect the substance, let alone analyze and label it.[14]

Thus we cannot yet accurately measure the habitat of olfaction nor describe in precise terms the mechanism whereby we perceive it. Nevertheless, this habitat must be conceived of being as concrete as those of the other senses of vision and hearing.

Like vision and hearing, olfaction is a scanning sense, permitting us to analyze the middle reaches of our environment. (The sense of taste, with which it is closely allied physiologically, depends of course upon actual contiguity.) The horizontal dimension of its habitat would be a spectrum of thousands of mixes of the seven primary odors, though these odors cannot be arranged in an orderly progression, like those of light or sound, because different substances can have the same smell. Along this scale would lie all those pleasant olfactory experiences which we associate with roses, incense or *bœuf Bourguinon;* or unattractive or repellent ones connected with sweat, feces or putrefaction. The vertical dimension of this olfactory habitat would be one of intensity, ranging from a lower threshold of perception to an upper one of concentrations so intense as to be stressful, nauseous or asphyxiating. The third dimension of the habitat would be that of time. Continued exposure to a steady concentration of a given substance will lead to a steadily declining capacity to perceive its odor. As with the other senses, steady stimulation tends to anesthetize perception itself. This is the experience of all heavy smokers and explains why the "smoke-filled rooms" of political conventions soon cease to be objectionable, even to nonsmokers, after a short while.

Not only are odors hard to quantify; they are even more difficult to arrange according to any valid esthetic scale. The qualitative judgments we pass on any given set of olfactory conditions are highly subjective, deriving in about equal parts from personal experience (e.g., the scent of lilies at the funeral of a parent) and culturally derived criteria (e.g., the Elizabethan attitude toward body odors). Sometimes even the same odor provokes different value judgments, depending upon our knowledge of its origin (e.g., the scent of putrefaction in meat as against certain cheeses). This cultural component of what "smells nice" and what "smells bad" varies widely from one society to another, as both Hall[15] and Bedichek[16] have demonstrated.

Olfaction clearly plays a larger role in the life of animals than it does in the life of contemporary man. Part of this loss of acuity may indeed be evolutionary, but it is probably more due to a kind of acclimatization to the conditions of modern life, which do not compel us to exercise our ability in the same ways or to the same ends as earlier cultures did. This becomes very apparent with blind people, who are compelled to develop their other perceptual senses to compensate for the loss of vision.[17]

It may also well be that the polluted urban atmospheres we have discussed earlier in this chapter are not only deleterious to the respiratory tract as a whole, but also that they exercise an anesthetic effect on the olfactory mechanism. In any case, olfactory monotony would only be another sensual expression of the monotony of the urban landscape as a whole. Part of it is due to personal and munic-ipal hygiene, whereby body cleanliness is extended to the social aspects of eliminating wastes of all kinds, including the noisome odors which would have been an integral part of any pre-twentieth-century city.

The other side of the same coin — the disposal of obnoxious odors (your own or your neighbor's) — is not a pressing problem on an American farm today: before the Civil War it would not have been too serious even in the American city. Densities were low enough to permit one to "open up the windows and air the place out." By the same token, few operations were large enough to pollute very large areas around them. Some of the earliest sources of industrial stench on a neighborhood scale were the tanneries, meat-packing houses and soap and tallow factories of Cincinnati and Chicago. Today, on the other hand, noisome industrial wastes have become regional in scale (e.g., along the middle Northeast Corridor from Baltimore to Staten Island). Even a single large plant can pollute an entire city, as the citizens of Charleston, Savannah and Mobile who live downwind of big paper mills can attest.

ARCHITECTURAL CONTROL OF ODORS

Under circumstances such as these, it is literally true that the only effective way to control obnoxious odors is to prevent them — often a complex and expensive process. Inside a given building, odor control usually falls to the air-conditioning engineer, who has three stock responses — dilution, masking, or removal.

1. *Dilution* is the commonest method of odor control when the odor is of internal origin. This involves simply recirculating less of the used air and adding more outside air to the mix. (But this is merely a technical way of saying that more of your odors are being dumped on your neighbor; very tall chimneys serve at least to distribute them more widely, as in the case of the paper mills.) This method involves the moving and conditioning of greater volumes of air per cycle, with corresponding increases in fan, duct and conditioner capacities.

2. *Masking:* Some objectionable odors can be masked by superimposing a stronger concentration of a putatively more pleasant scent "on top" of them. This is the technique commonly applied in public washrooms in lieu of more adequate ventilation. As long

as the original stench is not toxic, this technique is permissible, although it is not apt to be very successful esthetically.*

3. *Removal:* Some of the techniques already described for cleansing the air of particulates may also have the side effect of reducing odors associated with those offending substances. The most direct method of odor removal, however, is by chemical adsorption. Here the air to be de-odorized is passed through a thin filter of activated charcoal which adsorbs (i.e., physically catches and holds) the offending gas molecules. This method requires that the filters be periodically removed for cleaning and reactivation. But adsorption (or some of the more complex methods like vapor neutralization or catalyctic combustion) should be mandatory for any industrial process yielding noisome or noxious airborne wastes.[18]

The control of the olfactory habitat is not an easy task for the architect, involving, as we have seen, a number of incompletely explored areas of experience. But that should constitute no reason for his abdicating responsibility for it, as he all too often does. Olfaction constitutes an important dimension of his client's sensory perception of architecture and hence of his total esthetic experience of it.

---

* It is paradoxical, to put it mildly, that this masking technique is widely used in insect sprays for household use when the toxicity of the basic chemical is prominently announced on the container itself. One might expect the printed warning to be reinforced with an *unpleasant* odor rather than a pleasant one!

5. "OH, SAY, CAN YOU SEE . . .":
CONTROL OF THE LUMINOUS
ENVIRONMENT

A sunset is a pretty thing to look at and a leaping deer a lovely thing to see. But it is scarcely in such terms that the evolution of human vision, or its uses today, can be productively analyzed. Vision is indeed the material basis for much of our richest esthetic experiences; but we did not, as Hans Blumenfeld once succinctly put it,

. . . develop the ability to see just for the fun of it but in order to grab and avoid being grabbed. The good, the true, the beautiful light is the light which enables us to perceive real bodies. We want to perceive their exact size, shape and distance; and to perceive them safely, easily and quickly.[1]

Of all the sensory means of perceiving the qualities and dimensions of the real world, the visual is by far the most comprehensive. Psychologists estimate that, for adults, as much as 90 per cent of all information about the external world comes in the form of visually perceived data. Since, as Edward Hall says, "the optic nerve contains roughly eighteen times as many neurons as the cochlear nerve, we may assume that it transmits at least that much more information . . . the eyes may be as much as a thousand times as effective as the ears in sweeping up information."[2] For the literate person, the relative weight given to visually received information is enormous and unbalanced, outrunning by far the importance we attach to data perceived by other sensory means — hearing, touch, olfaction and taste.

The implications of this visual bias are serious and by no means fully comprehended. It would be as difficult for us to imagine a blind architect as to conceive of an illiterate nuclear physicist. Visually acquired data is the bedrock of all specialized education. But by this same token of ubiquity, we consistently overlook the dangers implicit in this visual bias, which leads us to act as though the entire esthetic process were an exclusive matter of vision. Common sense should tell us that much of the data we think of as visually acquired has actually been perceived by other sensory means and only subsequently abstracted and synthesized into visual constructs. Thus vision-based estimates of the shape, size and relation of objects would be impossible without previous tactile and kinesthetic explorations of them. When we say, "It looks far away," or "It looks like velvet," or "It looks like a pineapple," we are actually recasting in visual terms a whole body of information which we originally acquired, in whole or in part, by other sensory means — i.e., by walking, reaching, feeling, smelling, tasting. The architect conventionally expresses his concepts of spatial phenomena in visual terms. We "see" distances and dimensions; but our original understanding of distance, and of the friction and gravity to be overcome in exploring it, comes originally from kinesthetic experience. Architects talk of balance, rhythm, symmetry as though they were purely visual qualities, but our perception of them rests on complex factors of heartbeat, vestibular apparatus and sensors in skin and muscle.* Finally, of course, there is the fact that many important aspects of human experience cannot be visually perceived at all — e.g., electric shock, the smell of roses or the taste of wine, symphonic music or the sexual orgasm.

Nevertheless, the visual experience of architecture remains the dominant one, above all for the architect himself. The tendency to base important design decisions on narrowly visual criteria seems to have steadily increased with literacy. The more books and magazines he reads, the more TV and cinema he scans, the more apt is the architect to rely largely or wholly upon visually acquired data, divorced from its matrix of multidimensional sensual reality. This failure to recognize the enormous significance of the nonvisual impact of architecture leads to the impoverishment of all perceptual

---

* See Chapter 7 for a more extensive treatment of the role of touch in architectural experience.

experience — including even, ironically, that of vision itself! For if the satisfaction of our complex sensory requirements is to be vulgarly simplified in such a fashion, then whole areas of environmental manipulation, with all their important visual consequences, will be excluded from the design process. Having thus abandoned the one real source of originality, the architect is reduced to the mere *invention* of novel forms; and these, as in modern painting and sculpture, tend to become increasingly idiosyncratic, subjective, frivolous.

Actually, as the whole history and prehistory of architecture demonstrates, visual richness is the almost automatic by-product of the correct solution of most environmental problems. Their very complexity assures this. As both primitive practice and the most advanced research demonstrate, the proper control of sunlight, with its inordinate number of luminous and thermal variables, will yield far more photogenic surfaces than any amount of formalistic invention (Fig. 17). And precisely because the forms will have been derived in response to environmental necessity, they are bound to be more durable stylistically.

Fig. 20. Mud-walled huts, Kordofan, Republic of Sudan. For primitive societies living in hot climates, most work takes place out of doors. Hence control of luminous environment indoors is less critical than protection against thermal extremes. Mud masonry is topped by thatched parasol roofs as protection against short wet season.

Fig. 21. Millowners' Association Building, Ahmedabad, India. Le Corbusier, architect. The great French pioneer was among the first of modern architects to recognize the sheer esthetic possibilities of the geometry of sun control. He employed it in many forms in many buildings. In some of his buildings, however, he made inadequate distinctions between the luminous and the thermal characteristics of sunlight. While reinforced concrete, his favorite material, might be formed to manipulate the visible component satisfactorily, its thermal behavior is less satisfactory.

The paradox is that, despite the contemporary architect's obsession with the visible aspects of his work, he often displays serious misunderstandings of even basic optical phenomena. This is expressed in many ways. For all the new means at his disposal, his use of color — either as pigment or as light — is both more timid and less expert than in many previous periods. For all his extravagant use of glass, he seldom recognizes the basic optical fact that it is only transparent under certain objective conditions. For all his wide use of artificial illumination, few buildings are actually well lighted, while well-designed lighting fixtures are all but nonexistent. And notwithstanding new knowledge of insolation and orientation, many new buildings display serious malfunction, expressed in glare, overheating and faulty integration of natural and artificial light sources. In short, the architect pays at once too much and too little attention to the visual world — too much to its formal superstructures, far too little to its experiential foundations.

HISTORIC CHANGES IN THE VISUAL TASK

The natural luminous environment shares with the thermal and the atmospheric the quality of discontinuity. There is not only the regular alternation between night and day, but the constant fluctuation in both intensity and color composition of daylight itself. Unlike variations in the other environments, however, such fluctuations were not of themselves either stressful or the cause of much inconvenience to preindustrial man. Nightfall, naturally, had always brought terror as well as rest to primitive peoples, but it did not seriously interfere with their activities. Or rather, their activities were geared to the diurnal luminous rhythm. There was ample daylight for hunting and fishing, agriculture and shepherding; and long, unilluminated nights provided for the necessary recovery of energy from the day's activities. This remained true for even so relatively advanced a society as that of pre-Revolutionary America. There might have been an occasional cobbler or engraver who felt that "God had made the night too long": certainly, the means of artificial illumination at their disposal were primitive and expensive. But by and large, the day was long enough and bright enough; all society remained geared to a dawn-to-dusk rhythm.

It remained for the industrial revolution first to raise the question of, and then to produce the means for, continuous illumination around the clock. George Washington's America had relatively little need of artificial lighting. In his day, nineteen out of every twenty workers had to spend their days producing food for themselves and the twentieth person. In Lincoln's day, eight people out of ten had to work the soil to feed the whole ten. Today only two people are needed to feed ten. It is thus apparent that 95 per cent of early Americans had relatively little need for artificial illumination, since agriculture then (as now) was a daytime operation. Our forefathers rose with the dawn, worked by the light of the sun, and stopped at dark. They went to bed early both from choice (manual labor made them sleepy) and from necessity (they had few sources of artificial light to read by; few books; and most of them would have been illiterate anyway).

But today, this situation is almost precisely reversed. Perhaps as many as four-fifths of all Americans work in a largely synthetic luminous environment because neither the quality nor quantity of daylight is adequate for the tasks at hand. Upward of 90 per cent are literate; newspapers, magazines and books are published in the billions; artificial light sources are cheap and plentiful.

A parallel changeover must be observed: the great majority of pre-Revolutionary Americans used their eyes naturally. Their seeing tasks nearly all lay in the fields of middle- and far-vision — stalking game or fighting Indians, guiding a plow or sailing a ship. Only the craftsmen (bookkeepers, printers, jewelers and the like) and the housewives (with their sewing, knitting and weaving) had tasks which lay primarily in the field of near-vision. As we have seen, books were few, literacy low. Few children went regularly to school so that most of them used their eyes in a completely natural mix of near-, middle- and far-vision during their formative years.

Today, this situation is likewise reversed. The vast majority of us move in the world of near-vision, of prolonged and critical seeing tasks, of concentration on a visual field rarely farther from the eye than the arm's reach. With universal education, American children are pushed into the world of near-vision in nursery school and can easily remain there for twelve, fourteen or twenty years.

It is hard, even today, to visualize the consequences of this shift from a largely natural to a largely synthetic luminous environment; the conceptual lag is apparent in the scanty and uneven research on the subject. Certainly, the consequences were not anticipated at the beginning. Nineteenth-century enthusiasm for artificial illumination found its initial outlets in such applications as street lighting — understandably, for natural laws seemed to have been repealed. With the appearance of illuminated streets and plazas, the temporal limits of social intercourse were measurably extended across areas which night had closed to all but the hardy or the suspect. This is the potential that Edward Bellamy celebrated in his utopian Boston in *Looking Backward,* and that the outdoor electric illumination of the Columbian Exposition demonstrated to a dazzled public in 1893.

These were spiritual as well as physical proofs to the Victorians of their conquest of darkness.

However, it was scarcely to make streets safe or fairs beautiful that American society spent so much on the development of artificial light sources. These were by-products of the central understanding that *industrial technology could not develop in the natural luminous environment.* The need of industrialism for a luminous environment which could be extended in time and space, and manipulated in any desired direction, sprang from two distinct but closely related facts. The first was the discovery that a machine (unlike a slave or a horse) is most economically operated when it runs all the time. The second was that, even in its primitive stages, a machine is a precision instrument — i.e., works to close tolerances and hence demands visual acuity on the part of its operators. Both of these factors imply artificial illumination: the first, *more* light in time and space, the second, *better* light than nature gives us.

Thus the economy and culture of industrialism has changed not only the luminous environment of our work places but also the physical setting of our entire lives. It has even changed the way we use our eyes, in ways that are both historically and physiologically unprecedented. In general terms, we have developed artificial light sources to the point where, in many building types, they have long ago supplanted natural illumination. There is no question that our vaunted technological accomplishments would have been impossible without this mastery of the luminous environment.

Yet it is a debated point as to whether the average American eye is any better off in this new habitat than was its Colonial predecessor. (Comparable studies on hearing acuity suggest strongly that environmental attrition is much lower among aboriginal peoples than in civilized urban societies: see Chapter 6.) Certain it is that for one American building which offers its inhabitants optimal luminous conditions, there must be ten where conditions range from inadequate down to dangerous. Historically, illuminating engineering was developed primarily to expedite process, and only indirectly eye health or well-being: today it bears the characteristic imprint of this history. Its development has been uneven, with enormous qualitative discrepancies between its highest and lowest examples, with instances of gross deficiency side by side with extravagant waste. This paradox is very clear in our mechanical separation of problems of artificial illumination and daylighting when, in most building types, they could be thoroughly integrated to the benefit of both.

THE HUMAN EYE AND ITS HABITAT

Human vision is today the subject of close study on the part of a wide range of specialists in the fields of psychology, opthamology, optics and engineering. An enormously complex psychophysical process, it defies any "simple" description. Yet, just because vision plays so large a role in the experiencing of architecture, a holistic approach to the subject is of great value to architects and designers.

Current psychophysical theories as to how the visual system works suggest that

. . . it scans across space, over time, so that first one and then another point in space is "interrogated" by a neural mechanism in the brain. This scan is repeated perhaps as many times as ten times per second. Thus, during a fixational pause, the entire field may be scanned at least twice, with items of information being assimilated from various points in visual space during each neural scan.[3]

Fig. 22. The process of vision is enormously complex, involving physical, physiological and psychological phenomena. It is our most important source of information on the shape, size, location and physical characteristics of the world of objects.

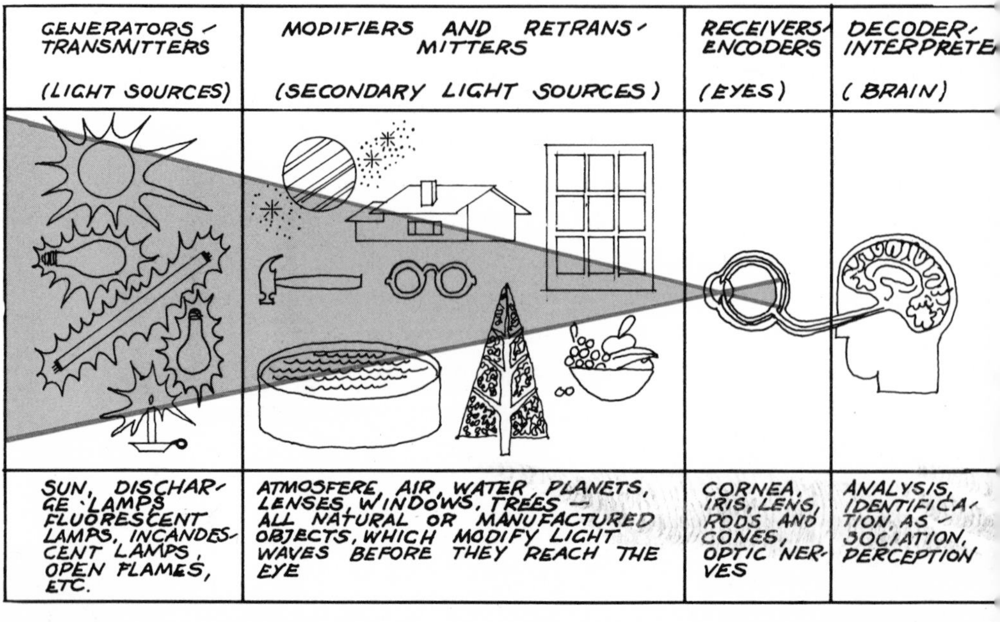

GENERATORS - TRANSMITTERS (LIGHT SOURCES)	MODIFIERS AND RETRANS- MITTERS (SECONDARY LIGHT SOURCES)	RECEIVERS- ENCODERS (EYES)	DECODER- INTERPRETE (BRAIN)
SUN, DISCHAR-GE LAMPS FLUORESCENT LAMPS, INCANDES-CENT LAMPS, OPEN FLAMES, ETC.	ATMOSFERE, AIR, WATER, PLANETS, LENSES, WINDOWS, TREES — ALL NATURAL OR MANUFACTURED OBJECTS, WHICH MODIFY LIGHT WAVES BEFORE THEY REACH THE EYE	CORNEA, IRIS, LENS, RODS AND CONES, OPTIC NER-VES	ANALYSIS, IDENTIFICA-TION, AS - SOCIATION, PERCEPTION

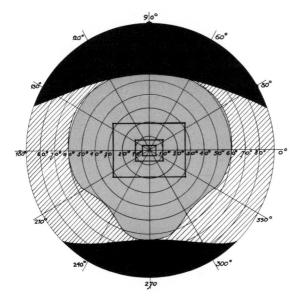

Fig. 23. The spatial parameters of binocular vision are partially represented in this diagram of the visual field. Shaded portions (right and left) are seen only by the right and left eyes respectively. The rectangles represent the sizes of various typical visual tasks.

The visual system may thus be compared to an iconoscope, though an incomparably superior one. Its capacity to perceive the limits and qualities of its environmental habitat may be defined in both spatial and luminous terms. Spatially, it is capable of scanning a wide range of distances with marvelous precision and flexibility. Basically, however, it is an instrument of far- and middle-vision.* The angular limits of the binocular visual field extend horizontally across more than 180 degrees and vertically for almost 130 degrees (Fig. 23). However, the central cone of the visual field which provides our most accurate vision is smaller.

The eye resembles the ear in that it perceives only a small portion of the sea of electromagnetic energy in which it is submerged — i.e., the visible portion of the spectrum (Fig. 24). Within these

* The normal eye focuses from a point approximately 15 ft. in front of the cornea on out to infinity. However, 3 per cent of first-grade school children will be myopic (nearsighted) and this percentage will rise to 9 per cent in the sixth grade; about 19 per cent of the first grade will be hyperopic (farsighted) and this will decline to 9 per cent in the sixth. The U.S. Naval Academy finds a consistent 25 per cent rate of attrition in visual acuity in each four-year class; and this rate appears to be independent of any environmental or vocational factors.

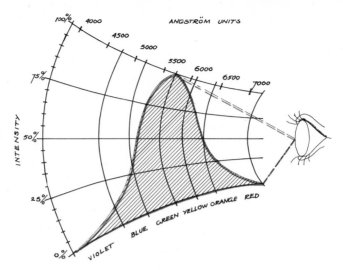

Fig. 24. The human eye perceives only a small portion of the ocean of electromagnetic energy in which it is submerged — the visible spectrum. Perception is highest in yellow-green bands, lowest in violet and red. It can adjust to large variations in intensity.

wavelengths, neural stimulation is highest in the yellow-green (around 5700 angstrom units), while down below the violet band (3800 au) or above the red (7200 au), stimulus and hence perception fall away rapidly to zero. Like the ear again, the range of energies to which the naked eye responds is enormous — from that of a lighted candle 14 miles away to a landscape flooded by 8000 foot-candles (fc) of sunshine. To accommodate itself to such a range of stimuli, the eye has a series of modulating devices: the pupil, which by expanding and contracting, controls the amount of light admitted; and the eyelid, eyelash and eyebrow, which shade it from stressful intensities.

The quantitative boundaries of the visual habitat are thus established by physics and physiology. But how well the visual system performs within this habitat is a function of several variable factors — the condition of the eye itself; the nature of the seeing task assigned to it; and the specific luminous environment under which the act of seeing takes place. Like all physical activity, the performance of any visual task involves stress, whether "at work" (typing, sewing, chauffering) or "at play" (tennis, skiing, card playing). The visual component of any task requires definite inputs of energy and will ultimately become "tiring," no matter under what subjective motivation or objective conditions it transpires. Here, as elsewhere in the world of sensuous experience, an optimal environment, one designed to facilitate the specific task in question, will lighten the load and delay the onset of fatigue. A deficient or hostile set of luminous conditions, on the other hand, will tend to exaggerate stress and accelerate fatigue.

But the need to define the mechanism of fatigue is not made any easier by the inability of the experts to trace out its causal relationships or agree upon meaningful ways of measuring it. According to John L. Brown, the concept of fatigue implies a reduction in the ability of the sensory receptors to respond to visual stimuli and a resulting depressed neural activity for a given level of stimulation.[4] But many investigators find no evidence of sensory fatigue *per se.* To resolve this apparent paradox, H. C. Weston distinguishes between visual and retinal fatigue, because vision involves motor functions as well as sensory process. Though he finds little evidence to support the idea of fatigue of the neural sensors, he finds a great deal of evidence to suggest that visual fatigue is principally due to movements of muscles within the eye, such as those which control convergence and accommodation.[5]

In any case, the eye — like any other organ of the animal body — can only accomplish its tasks by the expenditure of energy. This cannot occur without cost to the body as a whole, however complex or obscure the cost-accounting of the process may be. Some observers, therefore, take a holistic view of the process:

Vision, though primarily a function of a specific visual pathway, involves the participation of the whole organism. Since vision depends upon so many diverse components, visual fatigue is so complex a phenomenon as to be variously understood and diversely defined.[6]

The causal relation between the eye and its task can be expressed in either of two ways, each of which will be an obverse of the other: (1) how well the visual system performs its task in terms of speed and accuracy of work accomplished, and (2) at what cost it does so in terms of tension, blink rate, etc. The luminous conditions under which the task transpires — i.e., the visual "fit" — will be an important factor in either case. Generally speaking, performance improves and fatigue rates drop in direct proportion to increasing levels of illumination in the visual field (Fig. 25), though this is modified by other factors such as distribution, direction and color of light.

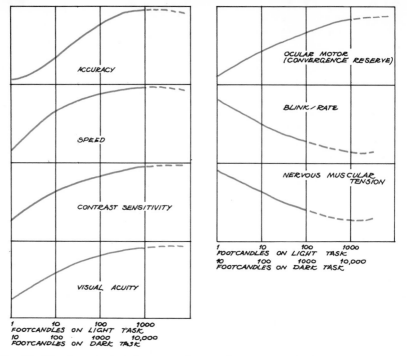

Fig. 25. Visual strain is a function of many factors, one of which is the luminous environment in which the seeing task occurs. Experimental data show that raised illumination levels lead to increased visual efficiency (left); physiologically, this lowered stress is expressed in lower blink rate and lower muscular tension (right).

A satisfactory adaptation of the eye to its task clearly implies a dynamic balance between three factors — the eye, the task, and the environment. It hardly needs saying that, in experiential reality, such a balance is rarely automatic. Some adjustments are usually called for and they can be made at any or all of several junctures. (1) By being fitted with eyeglasses, the eye can be modified optically so that its seeing task can be performed with less strain. (2) Or that particular task can be assigned to another person whose eyes are better suited to it (hyperopic for distant view, myopic for close work). (3) Or the entire task can be automatized, with the load of visual discrimination transferred to electronic devices — which can often do it better, anyway. (4) In almost all cases, the luminous environment in which the visual task takes place will be restructured in favor of the task itself. Only this last accommodation lies within the province of the architect's responsibility.

MAN-MADE LUMINOUS ENVIRONMENTS

The provision of the proper luminous environment for a given visual task or activity is clearly a prosthetic measure, not merely for the eye but for the body as a whole: it extends the body's capacity to accomplish its task by making vision easier, more precise, less stressful. And it must be reckoned as a therapeutic measure as well, for in lessening strain, it reduces the "cost" of seeing. This relationship is enormously complex and has been inadequately investigated in holistic terms; but if vision plays as decisive a role in total sensory perception as psychologists and neurologists claim for it, then it is of fundamental importance to behavior. Posture, gesture, movement are all conditioned by the luminous environment. Such effects can be observed and quantified. However, it is much more difficult to determine the long-range, cumulative effects of good or bad illumination upon our health and well-being. Here, as in other areas of organism-environment interaction, we can only assume that the connection is real and important.

Generally speaking, the eye is most comfortable in a habitat which confronts it with no great contrasts in the field of vision. But this does not imply that the eye "wants" evenly distributed, directionless illumination. On the contrary, objects seen under diffused light exclusively are very difficult to appraise correctly. Here we meet the same paradox that is to be observed in regard to other areas of sensory stimulation: optimal conditions would seem to imply variations in stimuli strong enough to be perceived but not strong enough to be stressful; and for these variations to occur in time as well as space.

The amount of light in the visual field is called *brightness*. (Light falling *on* a surface is measured in foot-candles; light flowing *from* a surface is measured in foot-lamberts.) As we have seen, the visual system has the capacity to adjust to a very wide range of brightness levels; and in recent decades there has been a steady escalation of minimum standards for various types of visual activity. For tasks involving critical seeing (proofreading, sewing, watch-repairing) two qualities are important: the illumination of the task itself should be high (100–150 fc) and the brightness levels of surrounding surfaces should not be less than one-third this value (35–45 fc). No surface anywhere in the field of vision should be much brighter than those of the materials and tools of the task itself. Of course, many tasks in the modern world require far higher levels of illumination: a machine toolmaker at his bench or a surgeon at the operating table may need 100 fc on his task. (All such brightnesses are relatively low for the animal eye, which developed in a natural environment in which levels of 8000 or 9000 fc are not unusual and would be stressful only in desert or snow-covered landscapes.)

When we illuminate the interior volumes of a building by either natural or artificial means, we are actually creating a new luminous meso-environment, designed and maintained for some specific set of visual needs. The luminous criteria will be derived from the task itself (sewing, card-playing, typing, study, etc.); ordinarily, they will be symmetrical in space (e.g., every child in a classroom will enjoy identical brightness levels) and constant in time, at least for the duration of the task itself.* But our attempt to establish such stable meso-environments occurs in the larger context of the natural world, where the light of the macro-environment is constantly shifting in amount, direction, color and distribution. To resolve this paradox of establishing a stable state in a condition of flux, the architect has at his disposal the structural devices of architecture (walls, roofs, windows, overhangs, etc.) and artificial lighting systems (lamps, fixtures, controls, etc.).

By its very presence, any building modulates the sunlight which falls directly on it and the daylight and darkness in which it is diurnally submerged. And if it is properly shaped, sited and oriented, with its fenestration properly designed for the visual tasks inside, the building will have extracted the maximum "assist" from the natural luminous environment. But, except for very simple building types located in the open country (with unobstructed access to all quadrants of the sky), satisfactory illumination by daylight alone is not probable. It must be supplemented by artificial sources: and for a vast range of contemporary social and technical processes, each with its own specialized luminous requirements, reliance upon natural

---

* It is typical of the current state of our knowledge that we do not know if — to maintain a given level of visual acuity throughout a working day — the prescribed light level should remain objectively constant (e.g., 200 fc for color grading) or whether it might be raised as the day progresses and the worker becomes more tired and consequently less speedy and less precise. Yet such parameters of work and fatigue should be established if the building is to perform at optimal levels of therapeutic intervention.

light is out of the question. Artificial lighting systems of great and increasing complexity will be required.

The integration of natural and artificial illumination is thus an extremely complex problem. From the point of view of the architect and illuminating engineer, it would be simplified if all visual tasks took place in opaque, sealed containers from which all natural illumination was excluded. With the perfection of a wide range of electrical light sources over the past half century, this has become entirely possible. The "windowless" building has become a commonplace. For many processes requiring absolute and unvarying control of luminous conditions, such sealed containers are obviously appropriate. However, it would be all too easy to extend such special cases into a general rule. As we have seen before and shall see again, the preponderance of experiential circumstances, even for modern urban man, has no such fixed or unilinear characteristics. Many activities and processes have no inherent requirement for opaque enclosure and many more actually require transparency for easy visual access (e.g., lobbies, stores and banks; airport control towers; "view windows," etc.). Moreover, there are many situations in which the eye is, so to say, at liberty, not engaged in any specific visual task. When we wait for a friend, walk in the park or listen to a symphony, the visual system is stimulated by a wide range of optical conditions. This "idle" scanning of the visual field is not only pleasant: the chances are very high that it is a psychophysiological necessity.

Instead of the deep views of nature, urban man moves in the shallow frame of man-made perspectives. Aside from the fact that most modern work lies in the field of near-vision, there is the added problem that most of our leisure time is spent in the same kind of unnatural habitat. Our horizon is usually limited by the surfaces of a room (bedroom, classroom, workshop, office) or a very limited perisphere (out the window, down the block, through the windshield of a moving car). This raises problems for building design which are only obscurely understood and very little investigated. Ever since the twin developments of year-round air conditioning and artificial illumination made possible the windowless building, observers have been conscious of hidden factors which were not being fully accounted for. In many windowless workplaces there has been accumulating evidence of employee dissatisfaction, not to say actual discomfort. Workers complain of "feeling all cooped up," of "not being able to tell what the weather's like outside." Windows are thus openings to the outside world in more ways than one. When the desk worker or the student looks out the window instead of down at his work, he is not "wasting time": he is seeking psychic as well as optical relief from a highly structured and unnaturally monochromatic experience. From this broader point of view, many of the arguments for the windowless building may turn out to be illusory, if not worse.

In designing the required visual habitat inside his building, the architect exercises control at two phases in the overall design process:

1. by manipulation of natural light across the interface between the macro-environment and building's synthetic meso-environment;

2. by manipulation of artificial light sources and surface response within this meso-environment.

The two aspects are, of course, inextricably linked. The architect will have to analyze them separately for purposes of precision; but to guarantee their successful re-integration in the final design, he must make sure that solutions to each are developed simultaneously — in tandem, so to say. To do this in buildings of any complexity, the architect will ordinarily require the assistance of the illuminating engineer. And, because of this complexity, there is a natural tendency on the part of the architect to delegate the entire illumination problem to the engineer.

There are two hazards here. The typical illumination specialist has a background in electrical engineering: he is thus all too prone to rely upon artificial light sources exclusively, paying little or no attention to daylighting. The other hazard is more subtle. Many building types will have optical characteristics that are not solved by lighting alone. For example, design decisions on questions of outlook or view, or of visual privacy versus visual access, are fundamentally architectural. Their correct solution depends upon many design decisions, often made before the illuminating engineer appears upon the scene. The luminous dysfunction of much contemporary architecture — especially that involving a wide use of glass — is traceable to confusion over this critically important phase of the design process.

ORIENTATIONAL AND STRUCTURAL FACTORS IN DAYLIGHTING

The manipulation of light falling on the building's surfaces will be a function of the orientation, the geometry and the physical characteristics of the enclosing membranes — i.e., roof, walls, windows, etc. These factors may be summarized as offering various options of control (Table 2).

It is obvious that any building above grade will be exposed to daylight: but how the building exploits this natural resource will depend upon a number of variables, many of them not directly related to control of the luminous environment. Endogenous factors (function, budget, etc.) will establish the parameters of size, shape and volume. Exogenous factors (shape, size and topography of the site; means of access; zoning ordinances, etc.) will act to mold these parameters to the exigencies of the site. Each of these will affect the manner in which incident daylight falls upon the various surfaces of the structure. But, except in those special building types in which good daylighting is an explicit requirement of the program, all of the above factors are too often decided before it has been determined what proportion of this incident daylight should be permitted to penetrate into the building (Fig. 26).

Some building types (warehouses, department stores, laboratories) will have little or no need for daylight; in others (office buildings, factories) daylighting may be desirable though not mandatory; in still others (dwellings, schools) good daylighting will be critically important — if only because that wall which *admits* light also *permits* outlook and view. The question of whether to admit or exclude daylight is, as we have seen, a modern paradox: it could not have arisen until reliable artificial light sources were available. But, now that the alternative does exist, the problem of integrating the two sources of light into a single effective system of luminous control has become extremely complex. Failure is unfortunately more common than success.

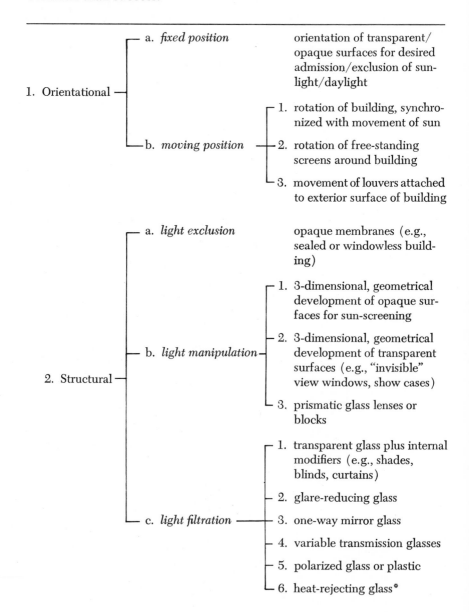

1. Orientational
   a. *fixed position* — orientation of transparent/opaque surfaces for desired admission/exclusion of sunlight/daylight
   b. *moving position*
      1. rotation of building, synchronized with movement of sun
      2. rotation of free-standing screens around building
      3. movement of louvers attached to exterior surface of building

2. Structural
   a. *light exclusion* — opaque membranes (e.g., sealed or windowless building)
   b. *light manipulation*
      1. 3-dimensional, geometrical development of opaque surfaces for sun-screening
      2. 3-dimensional, geometrical development of transparent surfaces (e.g., "invisible" view windows, show cases)
      3. prismatic glass lenses or blocks
   c. *light filtration*
      1. transparent glass plus internal modifiers (e.g., shades, blinds, curtains)
      2. glare-reducing glass
      3. one-way mirror glass
      4. variable transmission glasses
      5. polarized glass or plastic
      6. heat-rejecting glass*

* Although used for thermal reasons (i.e., to reduce transmission of infrared radiation) such glasses also affect optical behavior of the wall.

Table 2. Energy input-output relationship between building and its luminous environment is a function of: (1) location and shape of building with reference to path of sun; (2) area, geometry and exposure of external surfaces of building; (3) physical characteristics of these surfaces — opaque, transparent or selective filtration.

Because daylight fluctuates continuously across time in intensity, color and direction, its precise control in even simple buildings involves the balancing of many variables — computations which, though simple in themselves, are often so numerous that electronic computers are required for any really definitive examination of alternative solutions. Perhaps because of this, American architects tend to handle the problem summarily, shifting between two extremes: either to make the building windowless because daylighting "is more trouble than it's worth"; or to sheathe the entire building in glass and "leave it up to the air-conditioning engineer and interior designer" to solve the problem of thermal and luminous overloads with their compressors, curtains and blinds.

Since the architectural manipulation of daylight always has two components, thermal and luminous, the thermal controls discussed

Fig. 26. Residence, Stony Point, N.Y. James Marston Fitch, architect. This house is oriented to take advantage of a panoramic east-to-south view. It is partially submerged in hillside along west-to-north perimeter, to minimize impact of summer-afternoon sun and prevailing southwest-to-northwest winter winds. 88 per cent of all glass faces southeast, south or southwest. Remainder of perimeter walls are designed to minimize transmission of light and heat — opaque and insulated.

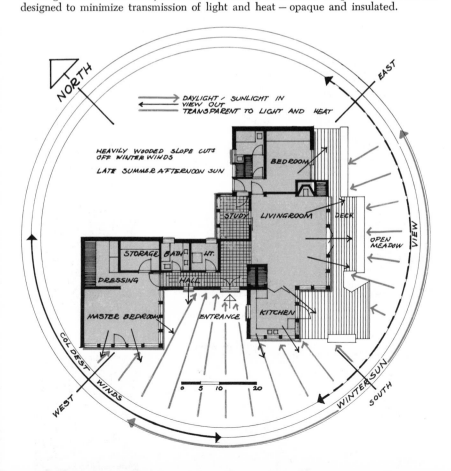

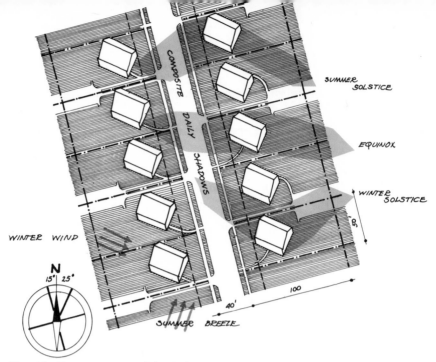

Fig. 27. Even conventional land-platting of freestanding houses on small lots can be easily manipulated so that all units get maximum exposure to sun around the year. Hypothetical study by Henry Wright for project at latitude of New York, N.Y.

Fig. 28. In high latitudes, where there is an absolute deficiency of solar heat and light, megastructures for neighborhoods or entire cities are the logical metabolic response to problems of energy conservation. Even here, height and density can be manipulated to give each unit its full share of winter sun. Ralph Knowles, architect.

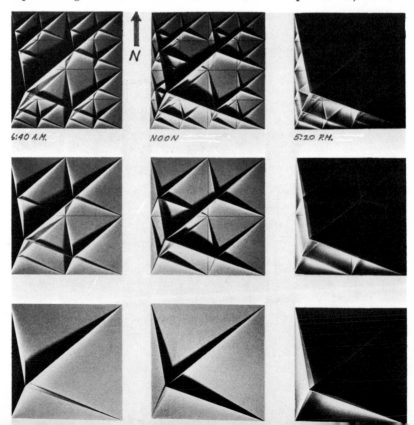

in Chapter 3 have a certain relevance here. As in the case of thermal control, so in that of the luminous: many problems can be resolved if daylighting becomes an integral part of the design process at the early stages of site selection and development. Thus the sheer deployment of buildings on the landscape can become a tool for giving each building access to its share of sunshine as well as freeing it from the shadows of its neighbors (Fig. 27). Similarly, at this early formative stage of the design, it is easier to decide which areas require daylight or direct sunlight and orient them accordingly (Fig. 28).

The building which is properly oriented to exploit the warmth of winter sunshine will also be brightly illuminated. But visual comfort is not thereby automatically guaranteed. Problems of glare, both within the room and in the landscape beyond the glass, can, under certain circumstances, become quite serious. In midwinter, one would be looking through south-facing glass *into* a low sun — an optical situation which would be further exacerbated by snow cover. (The most comfortable view is one lighted from behind the spectator). Thus proposals to maximize solar heat gain would also have to be analyzed for their optical behavior. This would undoubtedly require a further refinement of the wall membranes — i.e., more sophisticated glasses, movable blinds or curtains, etc. — and result in a more complex interface. However, in climates where the comfort problem is one of protection against excessive insolation (Yuma, California; Key West; Cairo), the parameters for thermal and visual comfort would coincide. There a building which constantly "kept its back" to the moving sun would have windows which looked out upon a view lighted from behind the viewer. At the same time, a building which presented a thermally opaque wall toward the sun would, in tropical climates, yield important economies in both capital and operating costs of cooling.

Since the sun angle changes constantly with hour and season, however, such measures can be only partially successful.* If the

* There is an adequate literature on the general subject of architectural orientation, including many mathematical and graphic systems for computing sun angles for time, season, latitude, etc. The most comprehensive exploration of the subject is to be found in *Solar Control and Shading Devices* by Aladar and Victor Olgyay (Princeton, 1957) and *Design with Climate* by Victor Olgyay (Princeton, 1963).

Fig. 29a. Steel-framed structure is cantilevered from a central concrete pedestal.

Fig. 29. House at Wilton, Conn. Richard Foster, architect. Aimed at maximizing the choice of view rather than manipulation of sunlight per se, this house has push-button controlled rotation. Its exterior walls are entirely of insulating glass shaded by continuous 6-ft. overhangs. With a diameter of 72 ft. it revolves on a ratchet track atop the pedestal, in either direction, for a full 360°. Although rotation could be continuous (at a maximum rate of 40 revolutions per 24 hrs.), its design rate is too slow to be noticeable and can be stopped or started at will. Powered by a 1½-hp motor, the structure rides on bearings. The pedestal also incorporates circular stair leading up from arrival platform. Garage and parking court are on raised platform.

Fig. 29b. Details of trackage and motive power, as well as connections for electric power, telephone, water supply, waste disposal borrow from transport technology.

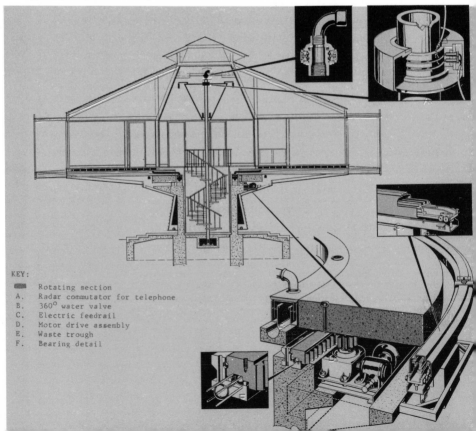

KEY:
▬ Rotating section
A. Radar commutator for telephone
B. 360° water valve
C. Electric feedrail
D. Motor drive assembly
E. Waste trough
F. Bearing detail

Fig. 29c. Like all rooms in house, living room has outer wall of insulating glass.

Fig. 29d. Plot plan (below) shows relation of house to arrival court and garage.

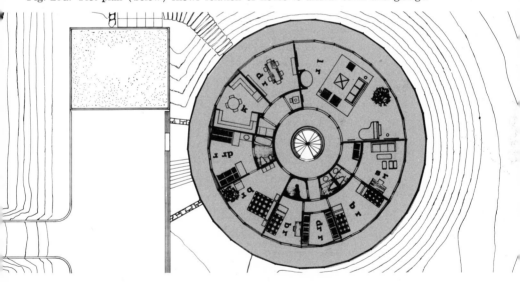

Fig. 29e. Time exposure of house at night (below) showing exterior illumination.

building were placed on a turntable and its rotation synchronized with that of the sun, luminous control would be much more precise, since both azimuthal and elevational angles of incidence could be held constant (Fig. 29). Though such means have seldom been employed, there are many situations in which they might prove effective. In regions of intense insolation (e.g., the American southwest) or of very deficient daylight (e.g., the Canadian Arctic), synchronized rotation might be both experientially desirable and economically feasible, especially if solar heat gain through glass areas was an integral part of heating and cooling design. Though synchronous rotation might be practicable only for buildings which are regular in shape and relatively small in size, such devices as tracked pontoons or efficient roller bearings would reduce the motive power required to rotate the structure. In climates like Baja California or the Persian Gulf, a built-in capacity always to hold an opaque wall toward the sun would yield important economies in both capital and operating costs of air conditioning.

A simpler variant of this same principle, and one presumably applicable to much larger buildings, would be a tracked solar screen which rotated around the building at a rate synchronized with the sun. In climates of great seasonal or diurnal variation (e.g., New Mexico or southern Tunisia) such solar screens might well be set to act as windbreaks during cold nights or cold seasons (Fig. 15).

The most familiar form of sun-shield is the *brise-soleil*, either fixed or rotating around a vertical or horizontal axis. Employing the same principle as the venetian blind, but located outside the building wall and using larger and more stable vanes, such sunscreens can be either manually or electronically controlled (Fig. 30). They afford a very precise means of luminous control. However, since they are exposed to the weather, they present problems of corrosion and freeze-up which tend to restrict their practicality to warm and/or dry climates; but these are the climates in which they would be most useful, luminously and thermally, in any case.

As we have seen, an absolutely light-opaque membrane would be the "simplest" method of handling the problems of daylighting. In certain highly specialized situations, where an absolute control of all environmental factors within very narrow tolerances is mandatory,

Fig. 30. Los Angeles Hall of Records, Los Angeles, Calif. Neutra and Alexander, architects. Vertical aluminum vanes cover entire wall area. Mechanically rotated on vertical axes, they are adjusted once a month to afford maximum shading of glass, while admitting reflected light and permitting outlook from offices. System is not practical for climates where rain or ice is common.

Fig. 31. Deere and Company Headquarters, Moline, Ill. Eero Saarinen and Associates, architects. Here a continuous membrane of heat-rejecting, glare-reducing glass is also shaded by a system of cantilevered horizontal louvers. To minimize maintenance, louvers are made of steel that develops a self-protective coat of rust.

such a solution may well be required. The world's largest building, the moon-vehicle assembly tower at Cape Kennedy, is the most dramatic example of this "sealed container" approach. Here, the very macro-environmental factors which make for good rocketry (year-round warmth, preponderantly sunny skies) also make for difficulties in rocket assembly (intense insolation, high humidities, hurricane danger). The problem is further complicated by internal require-ments for a meso-environment of extraordinary refinement, permit-ting precise manipulation of luminous, thermal, atmospheric and biological factors. Under such circumstances, environmental dis-continuities across the interface are necessarily severe and a her-metically sealed vessel is the best response.

By any conventional standard, such a design program is highly uneconomical. (For example, the complete exclusion of daylight from any workspace requiring high levels of illumination means its replacement by expensive lighting systems. Since all lamps are highly inefficient in converting electrical energy into visible light, the lighting fixtures alone can come to account for as much as 60 to 70 per cent of the total cooling load of the workspace.) Cape Kennedy is therefore a highly atypical situation.

Much more usual is the situation in which free access to daylight and view are desirable but protection against direct sunlight is required (i.e., a building wall which yields optimal transparency from inside outward, but limited or controlled transparency from outside in). This kind of shading can be accomplished by planar extensions of the wall surface itself — extensions whose geometry is calculated to prevent direct sunlight from impinging upon trans-parent wall surfaces. Modern architecture abounds in examples of this type of surface response to insolation (Figs. 30, 31). However, since most of them are designed on an "intuitive" basis — if for no other reason than that the variable conditions created by the moving sun outrun ordinary calculations — they are often more photogenic than practical.

A pioneer attempt to establish rational parameters for this problem of surface response to environmental forces has been the research of Ralph Knowles.[7] Using computerized techniques of analysis, Knowles has demonstrated conclusively that "the mathematical derivation of appropriate surface response to selected environmental forces" is entirely practical (Fig. 17). In fact, Knowles has moved on to a significant extension of this same concept — namely, that the building *form* as well as the building *surface* could be allowed to "derive as a response to the combined dictates of all environmental forces — light, heat, gravity, air and sound." And — since the individual building has little or no control over these factors beyond its lot lines — he has shown the need for extending the same criteria to the design of larger spatial increments — neighborhoods, districts, even whole cities.[8]

There are, of course, many ways in which light can be controlled with *transparent* (as opposed to Knowles' opaque) walling materials. Many types of glass and plastics can be employed to refract, focus, filter and polarize light by modifying either the molecular structure or the physical shape of the substance. There are many special cases in architecture where such materials will prove extremely useful. Perhaps the most broadly applicable form of optical manipulation of daylight is the so-called prismatic glass block. Manufactured in a range of prismatic types, these blocks can be used to refract incident daylight and deliver it to any desired area of the room. Such applications would be helpful in situations in which daylight is important to the visual task but outlook and direct sunlight either unnecessary or undesirable (e.g., color-matching). Prismatic blocks are also useful in galleries and museums, for controlled illumination of works of art (Fig. 32); or in churches, where

Fig. 32. Light-directional glass blocks. Where admission of daylight is desirable and outlook-inlook not required, these blocks offer possibility of fairly precise manipulation of daylight. One type (left, below) diffuses all incident daylight; another type has prismatic structure which can be used to redirect daylight: when used in vertical plane (center, below), onto ceiling; when used in horizontal plane, onto adjacent walls. Other variations have different light-diffusing and thermal insulation capacities, which make them adaptable to walls of different orientations (right, below).

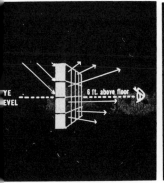
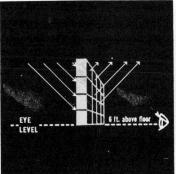
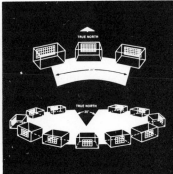

the architect might wish to focus a beam of sunlight on a spot which might not otherwise get it — the so-called "finger of God" effect of which Baroque architects were the masters.

Ordinary sheet or plate glass can be shaped or molded to achieve certain optical effects. In situations where it is desirable to preserve a panoramic view at night, like the famous Top of the Mark in San Francisco, the glass can be angled in the vertical plane so as to minimize disturbing reflections of the room itself. A variant of this is the so-called "invisible" shop window: here, where the problem is that of preserving transparency from the outdoors inward, the glass is curved so as to pick up no reflections from the much higher illumination levels of the streetscape. All such installations assume a single, relatively fixed observation point — that of a seated diner or a standing window-shopper.

As against a purely optical manipulation of daylight, however, quite another technique of light control has been opened up by the appearance of the new window glasses: that of filtration. In the case of buildings glazed with these glasses, the surface response is photophysical, a function of the molecular structure of the material rather than its geometric configuration. They have a wide range of photophysical properties which yield, singly or in combination, almost any degree of transparency for both the visible and thermal portions of the solar wave band. They afford the architect the means of filtering the daylight entering his buildings to a degree which would have been impossible even a few decades ago. As we have seen, such glasses have already become extremely important in very cold climates, making possible visual transparency *and* thermal opacity in the same membrane. They have a comparable significance in purely visual terms, since some of them can be used to filter the visible wave band alone, reducing the amount of visible light that enters the building as desired. (Since none of these latter glasses are water clear, they modify the color as well as the intensity of transmitted light.) (Fig. 33)

There is another new glass that acts as a one-way mirror — i.e., is completely opaque when seen from the outside yet is transparent and colorless when viewed from the inside. This paradoxical effect, true only for the daytime, responds to those cases in which privacy *and*

Fig. 33. Light-filtering glasses. Filtration of natural daylight, by admission or exclusion of ultraviolet, visible, and/or infrared wave bands, is now feasible with the new glasses. Shown here are four types of glass specially designed for filtration of visible band. Top left is normal plate, almost water clear and almost 90 per cent transparent. Bronze-tinted glass (upper right) transmits 51 per cent of visible wave band, gray (lower left) admits 42 per cent, and blue-green (lower right) 75 per cent. The optical differences of the four membranes are somewhat exaggerated by black and white photography.

Fig. 34. Bell Telephone Laboratories, Holmdel, N.J. Eero Saarinen and Associates, architects. A continuous glass-curtain wall acts as a selective filter: the glass, coated on one surface with a thin metallic film, rejects 80 per cent of infrared radiation while admitting up to 65 per cent of visible spectrum. During the day, the wall appears opaque from outside; night view (below) indicates its optical transparency.

outlook are simultaneously desirable. It is achieved by a vacuum deposit of a very thin, evenly distributed metallic coating on the inside face of the glass. (In this connection, it must be observed that most glass curtain walls act as mirrors under normal daytime conditions, since outdoor illumination levels are normally much higher than interior ones. Thus many such buildings which aspire to easy visual access are, in reality, as opaque as though they were sheathed in polished granite!) The one-way mirror glass eliminates need for daytime use of curtains or shades: the manufacturers claim that it is highly efficient in reflecting radiant heat as well (Fig. 34).

Two of the most sophisticated groups of light-filtering materials are the new photochromic glasses and the plastic multilayer polarizers. Both are just emerging from developmental stages;[9] they are consequently not yet generally available and still expensive. Nevertheless, they offer a whole new level of control for the designed luminous environment. The photochromic glasses, as the name implies, have the paradoxical ability to react reversibly to the ultraviolet in sunlight. Because of their complex molecular behavior, they change physical properties, becoming darker the more ultraviolet light falls upon them. They are fatigue-resistant, which means their reversibility does not diminish with time; and both the intensity of response and time-lag of recovery can be controlled within narrow limits. These glasses should prove valuable for such spaces as classrooms, libraries and museums, where a stable "mix" of artificial and natural light is desirable but where the bother of either manually or electronically operated shades and blinds makes such a stable mix impossible to maintain (Fig. 36).

The complex structure and optical behavior of the new multilayer polarizers have been described by H. R. Blackwell.[10] The visual benefits of polarized light lie in two related areas — increased ease of seeing and economy of light required. In the natural world, surfaces are concealed behind a "light veil" of reflected light — a veil which tends to blur the true colors and textures of the surface. Vertically plane-polarized light, on the other hand, is absorbed by the surface and then re-emitted. It is this phenomenon which permits us to see "behind" the light veil and perceive the true qualities of the surface with greater ease and more accuracy. This is, of

Fig. 35. A demonstration of the "self-shading" behavior of photochromic glass in response to exposure to daylight. A pane of the glass, its center unmasked, is exposed to sunlight (top left). Immediately the silver halide crystals in glass react to ultraviolet band and absorb up to 75 per cent of visible band (top right). When sunlight is cut off, darkened area begins to lighten (bottom left). In half-hour after initial exposure, darkened area has disappeared and pane is transparent again.

course, the principle of polarized sunglasses: but these materials were not applicable to architectural illumination for several reasons: they would not be equally effective from all points of the room, they absorb over 50 per cent of the light, and they are unpleasantly tinted. Moreover, they are transparent and thus could not conceal the bare light bulbs behind them. The new polarizers overcome all of these objections. Since they are not weatherproof, they could only be used internally and would ordinarily be used in conjunction with ceiling fixtures. But they would be very useful in the daylighting of galleries and museums, where they might be used as a second, inner membrane of window-walls and skylights. According to Blackwell,

. . . vertically plane-polarized light produces a fundamental improvement in the ease of seeing, comfort and pleasantness of the visual environment, with appreciable loss in luminous efficiency . . . No other lighting material produces a comparable increase in [visual] task detail, apparent saturation and textural richness for all materials, surfaces and viewing angles.[11]

LAMPS AND THEIR APPLICATIONS

An understanding of the above theories, techniques and materials is essential to the correct exploitation of the natural luminous environment; and the scientific exploitation of daylight is an integral part of the illumination of most building types. But no matter how comprehensively daylighting is handled, it alone would not meet modern requirements, either optically or temporally. The development of a satisfactory synthetic meso-environment will be impossible without exploiting artificial light sources as well. The task of the architect is to establish a "mix" of the two sources, designed for the specific visual tasks, with a criterion of stability in quality, space and time.

The perfection of the dynamo in 1877 made possible the large-scale production and distribution of electricity: since then, the electric lamp has supplanted all other types. The architectural consequences of this switch from the combustion of organic materials (rush, wood, candle, oil, gas) to electrical resistance and gaseous excitation are literally incalculable. Perhaps the most obvious expression of this shift has been, paradoxically, the diminishing importance of the light source itself. In historic architecture, artificial illumination had always been very expensive. This fact was celebrated by making the brazier, lamp, torchère, candelabra and chandelier more important, esthetically, than the flame itself. Today, the light source is apt to be either invisible (e.g., recessed reflectors, cove lighting) or else to become an entire surface (e.g., the "luminous ceiling"). At the same time, the isolated lamp or fixture has all but disappeared from non-residential building types.

The range and flexibility of these new sources of light make possible a whole new order of luminous control in architecture. The components can be categorized thus:

1. *type of lamp:* arcs, filaments, luminous vapors, fluorescents, luminescents
2. *type of lighting fixture:* bulbs, tubes; spots, floods, panels; luminaires, luminous ceilings, planar sheets
3. *type of optical accessories:* lenses, color filters; reflectors; louvers, baffles, egg-crates; polarizers
4. *type of light source:* point, linear, planar
5. *type of light distribution:* direct, indirect, focused, diffused

Dozens of manufacturers of lamps, fixtures and controls now produce thousands of variants and combinations for commercial, industrial and specialized scientific installations. In ordinary architectural applications, however, a comparatively limited number of lamps are used, in several basic types of installations. Since these lamps vary rather widely in their spectra, efficiencies and performance characteristics, they merit a brief description here.

Arcs: In these, the earliest of all electric lamps, the actual light source is the luminous bridge formed when an electric current jumps across the gap between two electrodes. A brilliant but very hot and inflexible light source, it is seldom used in interior illumination. Its principal current applications are in movie and television studios; in exterior illumination of parking lots, playing fields; and in searchlights, for military or maritime applications. Emitted light is on blue side of spectrum. It is a "point" source highly suitable for focusing by reflectors and lenses (e.g., multimillion-candle-power searchlights).

Filaments: Second oldest of the lamps, these are still the most widely used. Here the light source is passed through a coiled tungsten filament in a sealed glass bulb. The filament's resistance to the current raises it to a white heat. Its efficiency has been increased by upward of 1000 per cent in recent decades. Its advantages scarcely need listing; its principal shortcomings lie in the low percentage of visible light produced (10 per cent) and its spectral deficiencies. To modify its characteristic yellow-white color, either colored bulbs or colored filters are required: these absorb a large proportion of emitted light — 60 per cent for a saturated yellow, up to 98 per cent for a deep blue. The filament yields a point light source easily focused; but because of its high infrared output, such applications must be ventilated.

Luminous vapors: This complex and growing family is of increasing significance to architectural illumination. Each type is based on the fact that passing an electrical current through certain gases "excites" them into emitting radiant energy whose spectrum will be a function of the gas employed. This radiation can either be used as the light source itself, or be chromatically modified by lining the interior of the bulb with color-correcting phosphors.

Sodium vapor lamps are efficient, producing from forty-five to eighty lumens per watt; but they operate at very high temperatures and the sodium might be dangerous under certain conditions. Though very useful in some critical seeing tasks which do not involve color, their monochromatic deep yellow light renders them unsuitable to most indoor illumination problems: externally, they are commonly used on highways, bridges and parking lots.

Neon vapor lamps operate on the same principle: variations in the gases and in color of glass tubing yield a fairly wide range of colors. They are unsuited to general illumination, however, because of low efficiency, low intensities and dangerously high voltages. Their architectural use is thus largely confined to outdoor signs and decorative lighting.

Mercury-vapor lamps are extremely efficient — certain types yield over 100 lumens per watt — but emit a light which is almost totally deficient in red. However, when the bulb is internally coated with color-correcting phosphors, the characteristic blue-green light can be modified into a range of fairly satisfactory whites comparable to the conventional fluorescents. A small point source of high intensity, the mercury lamp can be used with reflectors for improved optical control. Because it yields near-ultraviolet in addition to visible light, it is also modified to serve as a sun lamp and a so-called "black light."

Fluorescent lamps: For architecture, the most significant application of the low-pressure mercury-vapor principle has been in the standard fluorescent tube. Here the tube is of ordinary glass, the inside of which is coated with a fluorescent material which converts the ultraviolet into visible light. Since the mercury-vapor spectrum is itself deficient in red and the light of fluorescing materials the coolest known, the result is a lamp with a low heat output. (The ordinary filament lamp is from four to five times as hot as the fluorescent tube.) Other advantages include its wide color range, including a close approximation of daylight, and its efficiency — from 25 to 75 lumens per watt depending upon the color. In unmodified form, it is of course a linear light source but, with appropriate reflectors and diffusing materials, it can be made to approach a truly planar form.

Together with fixtures, accessories and electronic controls, these lamps offer the means for an unprecedented manipulation of the luminous environment. How this remarkable equipment is employed in a given situation will depend upon what sort of environment is required and how precisely it can be described or specified. Here the architect is projected into the field of psychophysics, where a bewildering range of factors, objective and subjective, physical and emotional, confront him. If he regards the designed meso-environment as a prosthetic device and translates the eye's requirements into environmental specifications, some generalizations are possible. The first is that, within broad limits, the more light on the visual task, the easier vision becomes. And the easier vision becomes, the less will be the stress on the organism as a whole. Higher levels of illumination are a function of increased foot-candles in the source and increased reflectance values in all the surfaces of the room.

The second "law" of illumination is that the brightnesses of all areas in the room should be in balance, with no great contrasts between adjacent surfaces. For specific visual tasks, the brightness ratio between the task and its surrounding visual field should be low — not under 3:1 and not above 1:10. The third principle is to avoid direct and reflected glare (Blackwell's "light veil" on illuminated surfaces).

The recommended levels of illumination for different visual tasks have risen steadily over the past half century and may well rise even higher. Tasks which in preindustrial times might have been carried on at 10–15 fc are now specified at 100–200 fc. Some tasks requiring a high degree of visual acuity (e.g., autopsies, micro-surgery) may require as much as 2500 fc. Although the relative efficiency of all light sources has been greatly increased in recent years, the ratio of visible light to infrared is low in the best of them (about 10 per cent for the filament, 15 per cent for the fluorescent). As a result, waste heat is a byproduct of all artificial illumination. If high illumination levels are required, this heat becomes an important factor from the standpoint of both comfort and economy. Thus for a space with 100 fc illumination, the waste heat can account for about 37 per cent of the summer cooling load: if the illumination level is raised to 400 fc, this factor will rise to 70 per cent. When waste heat reaches such proportions, it becomes a major factor in summer cooling; by the same token, it can be employed in winter heating — sometimes to the extent of becoming the entire source of heat. In such installations, current practice is to siphon off this heat before it enters the conditioned space, either exhausting it in summer or feeding it back to the heating system in winter. Since such installations usually involve fluorescent tubing used in luminous ceilings, there is less waste heat, and less of it is radiant, as much as 76 per cent can be siphoned off directly into the return air system.*

The illumination requirements of many discrete visual tasks (precision machine work, surgery, drafting) can be defined with some degree of precision; and the effectiveness of the system can be measured in terms of safety, productivity and workmanship (Fig. 36). But life — and hence, architecture — is full of many other visual tasks which are subject to no such precise delineation. The illumination of retail stores and showrooms, for example, involves such subtleties as dramatizing the textures and colors of the merchandise. (Jewelry and automobiles need point sources for shine and glitter; furs and velvets show up best under floods at acute angles.) Restaurants, bars and cafés have special luminous criteria†; art galleries and museums have entirely different ones.   Theaters and

---

* For a survey of such problems see W. S. Fisher and J. E. Flynn, "Integrated Light Air-Conditioning Systems," *Illuminating Engineering*, vol. LIV (Oct. 1959), pp. 615–623.

† For some reason it is currently assumed that the proper "mood lighting" for such establishments dictates that the light level be very low and the color pink. The first

churches share very special luminous requirements. The illumination of exposition buildings and pleasure gardens poses another set of problems, including the manipulation of both luminous and pigmental color. This by no means exhausts the list of architectural situations in which sheer visual pleasure may well be the end in view. In such cases, simple "functional" criteria may be very difficult to delineate. This is probably the reason why some of our most distinguished illuminating engineers and color specialists find it so difficult to describe or objectify the principles they follow in achieving some of their most striking effects. It may well be that, beyond some limit of rational analysis, "intuition" necessarily takes over in the creation of these effects, just as it does in the great painter's use of pigments. But this should not become — as too often it *does* become — the excuse for abandoning all orderly research in this important aspect of architecture. For no matter how subtle the problems or complex the solutions, the architect must understand how such effects are achieved — if only in order to know how to replicate (or avoid) them in subsequent work.

Just as a blind architect would be a contradiction in terms, so too

---

makes it difficult to see one's companions and the second has unfortunate effects on the appearance of most foods, whatever its putative effect on complexions. If to these we add the high noise levels common to such places, the result is often opposite to the declared aim — that of facilitating interpersonal relationships.

Fig. 36. The behavioral consequences of an improved luminous environment for many industrial processes are now accepted. In a series of experiments carried on in one textile mill over a period of seven years, lighting levels were progressively raised from 16 to 70 fc on working surface; all other environmental conditions remained unchanged. Production was increased by over 10 per cent: more importantly, from the standpoint of management, the rate of rejection of faulty goods fell by 40 per cent.

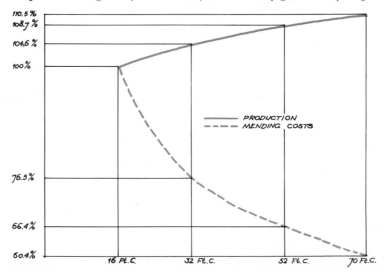

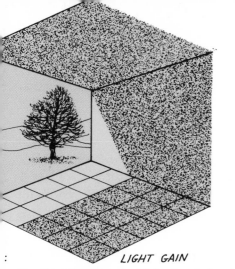
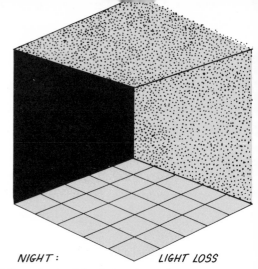

DAY: LIGHT GAIN   NIGHT: LIGHT LOSS

Fig. 37. That the optical behavior of glass is not fully understood is obvious in much current architecture. Interiors are conceived of in daylight conditions — i.e., with the glass as a source of light. But unless covered with a reflective membrane, such glass after dark becomes a light drain, destroying luminous balance of room.

would be a completely lightless room (tombs and photo darkrooms would be among the few exceptions). All designed spaces are conceived of in visual terms. Many of the architect's decisions as to interior proportions, colors and textures actually deal with matters of surface response to light. They are all made with "an eye to how it all will look." Such a conceptual approach subsumes a stable luminous state as desirable — i.e., that the room will "read" the same way, day and night, winter and summer.

In any windowless enclosure this is a simple matter; but in any room in which glass plays an important role the situation is entirely altered. Such transparent membranes are conceived of as (1) being a source of light, and (2) affording visual access to an illuminated out-of-doors. But, with nightfall, both of these conditions change (Fig. 37). Surfaces which were a source of light become open sluiceways for its escape; and the darkened out-of-doors is replaced by a dimly mirrored image of the room.* Historic architecture had no real difficulty with this paradox. Although daylighting was very important, the high cost of glass and of heating tended to keep windows relatively small and/or few. And since they were always

* The reflected image of a lighted room often seems so bright to the eye that it leads many designers to act as though the luminous equilibrium is not disturbed. Actually, the image is produced by about 7 per cent of the incident light being reflected back into the room: the remaining 93 per cent escapes to the out-of-doors. As a result, the room no longer behaves luminously in the way the architect conceived it.

covered at night with curtains or blinds whose reflectance value approached that of the walls, they did not seriously affect the luminous response of the walls.

But in modern architecture, with its wide use of glass walls and wide misconceptions of their optical behavior, the problem of nocturnal disequilibrium reaches serious dimensions. And not only visually: when people complain of uncurtained glass as "feeling cold," they are accurately describing a combination of thermal and optical stress (Fig. 39). In such cases, the interiors can only be restored to their daytime shape by one of two measures: by covering the glass with a reflective membrane — shade, shutter, blind (Fig. 38); or by raising the illumination level outside the glass to that of the room itself (Fig. 40). Both measures are technically quite feasible, though for obvious reasons the first is apt to be the simplest and least costly.

Fig. 38. House at Stony Point, N.Y. James Marston Fitch, architect. Two views of living room, photographed under identical conditions of illumination. (All light sources are normal for room, no auxiliary lights being used for photography.) Note (left, below) the deadening effect of uncurtained glass. The camera reveals that reflections which might seem important to the eye contribute little or nothing to maintenance of daytime balance. When shades are lowered (right, below), glass wall becomes again a source of light, even if reflected, and the room is returned to its daytime "shape." Painted landscape on shades is an abstract version of actual view.

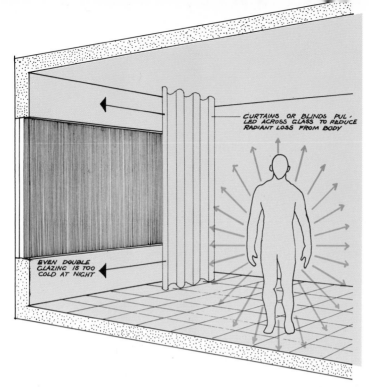

In the figure: "CURTAINS OR BLINDS PULLED ACROSS GLASS TO REDUCE RADIANT LOSS FROM BODY" and "EVEN DOUBLE GLAZING IS TOO COLD AT NIGHT"

Fig. 39. The subjective verdict that uncurtained glass walls make a room "cold" after dark may derive from purely optical sensory input: but it often has a thermal component, since the body loses heat by radiation to all surfaces colder than itself.

Fig. 40. House at Grand Rapids, Mich. Kenneth C. Welch, architect. A carefully engineered effort to keep the optical performance of a glass wall constant around the clock, this design has three elements: (1) nighttime illumination of grounds near house; (2) a glass wall slanting out from ceiling; (3) interior light sources located and shielded to minimize reflections. Actual light-meter readings show that, while nighttime values do not approach daytime ones, luminous balance is maintained. Summer condition is more effective, since trees in leaf offer more reflective surface to outdoor lighting. This "view window" thus has year-round view.

ARCHITECTURAL POLYCHROMY:
PIGMENTAL AND LUMINOUS

Color is another aspect of the contemporary architect's confrontation with psychophysics: he finds it, if anything, even more confusing than light *qua* light. Part of his diffidence has historical origins. The stylistic revolution which, in the first third of this century, overthrew the dominant psuedo-historical styles, discarded their coloration as well. Purity of form was to be matched by purity of color; banishment of ornament was to be paralleled by banishment of pattern. As a consequence, modern architecture is almost without precedent in its monochromism: and even when color has been employed, it tends to be either timid or inexpert. This situation is paradoxical, for modern technology affords the designer absolutely unparalleled resources in both colored light sources and colored surfacing materials. Such developments as polarized light, "black light," and fluorescent and luminescent paints and dyes offer him a palette of saturated colors whose range and intensity was undreamed of until modern times. Surfacing materials of every imaginable hue, texture and pattern are available to him. But so far he has ventured to employ them extensively only in some of the big international expositions, where current standards of good taste tend to be relaxed.

But the architect's hesitation to employ color widely also stems from a justified uncertainty as to the experiential consequences of its use. Here the dilemma is partly cultural, partly psychophysiological. The physical phenomena in both pigmental and luminous color may be well understood and the conundrum of the eye's capacity to perceive them now explored. The general laws that might cover the individual's response to color are much more difficult to formulate. That different colors have different appeals to different people is axiomatic. The fact that one can generalize at all about group preferences — as consumer goods interests often do quite successfully — indicates the cultural factors involved. There is a large and growing literature on the subjective aspects of color. We are told that red is "exciting," purple is "stately" or "mournful," yellow is "joyful," green is "calming," etc. But these are all affective value judgments whose direct applicability to architecture seems oddly inconclusive and nonspecific.

Experimental psychologists, by observing behavioral response to luminous stimuli, are exploring such fields as the therapeutic use of color in the treatment of the mentally ill. And Robert M. Gerard, working with normal adults, has found that submersion in red light produced more activity and in blue light less, than normal. He found that red led to an increase in blood pressure, respiration and frequency of eye-blink; blue had the reverse effect. On the basis of his experiments, he proposes two laws of color dynamics: within the visible range, psychophysiological activation tends to (a) increase with wavelength and (b) increase with stimulus intensity. Gerard advances the following general propositions:

1. the response to color is differential — i.e., different colors arouse different feelings and emotions and activate the organism to a different degree;

2. the differential response to color is a response of the whole organism, involving correlated changes in autonomic functions, muscular tension, brain activity and affective-ideational responses;

3. the differential response to color is lawful and predictable:

a. it is related to specific characteristics of the stimulus, both physical (wave-length, intensity, number of quanta and energy per quantum) and psychological (hue, saturation and brightness);

b. it transcends individual differences — i.e., it is shared to a significant extent by members of the same culture;

c. individual differences in psychophysiological reactivity to specific colors can be accounted for on the basis of (i) previous learning experience, as reflected in color preferences and color associations; and (ii) characteristics of the organism, including personality variables such as manifest anxiety level.[12]

All of which suggests that problems of architectural color, complex though they be, are susceptible of a far more systematic exploration than architects or illuminating engineers have themselves so far attempted. Our most brilliant colorists operate largely on the basis of a highly developed personal taste. This tends to limit their effectiveness both as paradigm and as teacher, and narrows their influence. As in so many other areas of architecture, color needs to be carefully researched in holistic terms.

EXTERIOR ARTIFICIAL ILLUMINATION

Modern technology has made possible another unprecedented amenity — the nighttime illumination of streets, squares and gardens. This has become such a basic part of contemporary life that it is no longer possible for us to imagine the crippling effect of nightfall upon preindustrial life. It brought almost to a complete halt the free movement and varied activities which characterized the daytime city. The appearance of electric lighting had two great urbanistic consequences: it doubled the time when the urban out-of-doors could function as a theater of action; and esthetically it made possible a delightful experience which hitherto only potentates like Nero or the Sun King could have afforded (and only they for a night or two) — the purely decorative illumination of the landscape.

This process of external illumination has been carried further in the U.S. than elsewhere — if not the best lit, American cities are the *most* lit on earth. They are very beautiful when seen from the air, on a clear night, their structures diagrammed by millions of lamps and signs. But, on the normal plane of pedestrian movement, both beauty and clarity disappear. Street and park lighting is strictly utilitarian, designed for economy and weather- and vandal-proofness. And the harsh yellow and acid blue-green of sodium and mercury vapor lamps, which looked so lovely from the air, turns out to be unflattering to the passersby and annoying to the permanent residents. Electric signs confront us with something of the same dilemma. Seen from afar, they are often a beautiful celebration of the city's focal points. Yet, here again, the picture changes at close-up — and usually for the worse. Jostling each other in space and competing in size, color and movement, the illuminated signs cancel out each other's information-giving function. They become confusing to the passerby, annoying to the resident and actually hazardous to the motorist.

Yet it is possible to illuminate individual buildings, whole neighborhoods, or even the entire city, in ways which better meet the requirements of spectacle and utility, tourist and inhabitant, passerby and tenant. Indeed, we can already glimpse such possibilities in London and Paris, where the monumental districts around

Fig. 41. Lincoln Center, New York, N.Y. The use of glass walls assures exterior nighttime illumination, whether intentional or not. Such a condition is much more satisfactory when experienced from outside looking in than from inside looking out.

Fig. 42. Château de Chambord, France. When externally illuminated for such spectacles as *son et lumière*, uninhabited historic buildings afford an unforgettable experience. Such illuminations are designed to be viewed only from fixed vantage points, however. Exterior illumination of inhabited buildings is more complex.

Fig. 43. Chapel, Château d'Amboise, France. Artificial illumination of historic buildings permits the lighting engineer to illuminate them from directions never anticipated by original designers. Shadows are reversed, color and modeling strikingly altered.

Westminster and the Louvre are skillfully lit all summer; or in Washington and Athens, where the Capitol and the Acropolis are most dramatically illuminated. An extension of this technique for purposes of spectacle is the *son-et-lumière* technique employed in French chateaux and gardens with such touristic success.

It must be observed, however, that these examples are all buildings or districts which are either uninhabited or at least not inhabited at night. Theatrical lighting can thus be freely used for maximum impact on the spectators who view from established vantage points. The inhabited building confronts the illuminating engineer with a more ticklish problem. Even if the tenant might have no objection to having the exterior of his building illuminated, his own rights to visual privacy and to outlook are jeopardized. On the other hand, if the landscape is to be illuminated for his benefit, then the spectator will be in visual distress. Of course, in ordinary residential design, only the garden areas adjacent to the building are lighted; and these would normally be screened by walls or plantings anyway. But many urban situations would demand skill and imagination on the part of the designer if everyone were to be satisfied.

From the foregoing, it is apparent that the illumination of architecture is a very complex field of action. The architect has not adequately analyzed the luminous requirements of contemporary life; nor has he mastered the technical means of meeting them. Here — as in so many other areas of the profession — the inadequacy of traditional design methods is apparent, with their heavy reliance upon taste, hunch and intuition. A whole new theory of the experiential relationship between man and his luminous environment is in order.

Fig. 44. Farnsworth House, Fox River, Ill. Ludwig Mies van der Rohe, architect. An optical paradox: the hovering planes of cantilevered terrace and roof made for beautiful photographs. But the heat of Illinois summers made outdoor living desirable while insects made it impossible without insect screening. In solving this paradox, owner increased habitability of the house while radically altering its esthetic impact.

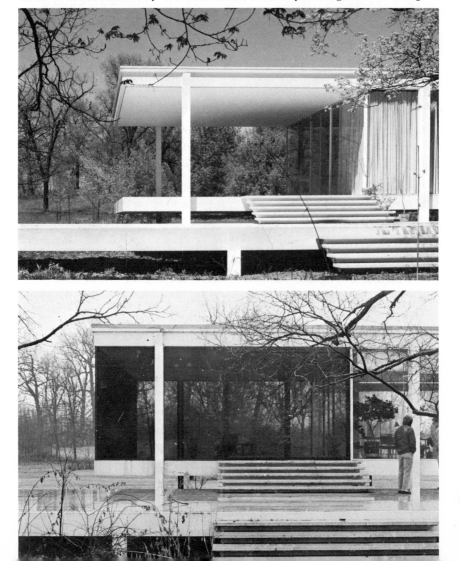

6. SILENCE — MEN AT WORK: CONTROL OF THE SONIC ENVIRONMENT

Like the other sensory perceptual systems of the human body, that of hearing occupies its own special habitat in the external world. Like the eye and the nose, the ear scans that habitat across time and space, bringing in important information on events in that world. And submerged, like the eye, in a sea of electromagnetic energy, it perceives only a relatively small portion of the total spectrum of terrestrial sounds (Fig. 45). This aural habitat can be quantified and topologically described as having four dimensions: a spectral or "horizontal" one of wavelength frequencies; an energy-input or "vertical" one of pressures per square centimeter (decibels); a depth or "longitudinal" one as expressed in reverberation period; and a fourth dimension across time. Because of the fact that many sounds can coexist in the same space at the same time, the sonic environment is very rich in aural stimulation. And as we shall see, the ear has developed a corresponding capacity to perceive much of this complexity.

But the sonic environment differs in one fundamental respect from all the others so far discussed in this book: in its natural unpolluted state, it is seldom if ever stressful to the organ of perception. The other environments may fluctuate wildly, between widely separated extremes of hot and cold, light and dark, windy and still, wet and dry. Unmodulated, these extremes carry the threat of discomfort, disaster, death. Not so with the natural sonic environment: here the upper threshold of human hearing is seldom if ever crossed (e.g., a nearby thunderclap or volcanic explosion) whereas the lower

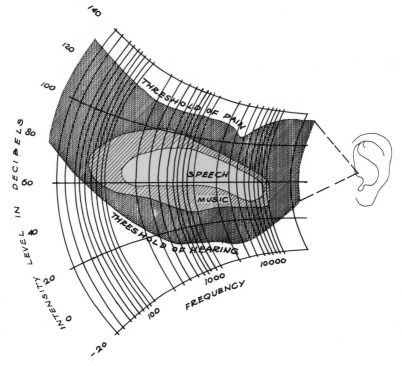

Fig. 45. The human ear, like the human eye, perceives only a small portion of the energy in which it is submerged. It scans this field, whose limits are defined in terms of decibels and frequencies, to pick up important information on environmental events.

threshold (e.g., no perceptible sound at all) is commonly reckoned as "restful."

Until comparatively recently, a simple, unpolluted sonic environment was the natural state of the American. Our Colonial ancestor would have heard few sounds, none of them physiologically stressful: conversation of neighbors or sound of churchbells; song of a bird or sigh of wind in the trees; call of the ploughman or blows of the blacksmith at his anvil. Many sounds might have been threatening by reason of the information they contained — rattlesnake whirring, panther crying, Indian warwhoop or rattle of musketry — but none of them was in itself dangerous to health.

All the more ironic, then, that man-made pollution of the sonic environment now constitutes a real and rising threat to contemporary Americans.[1] It has been left for modern industrial society to create new sound to a point where sound levels in many industrial plants and offices are at the threshold of pain; where most urban areas have an average loudness level which makes protection against it necessary; where jetports and multilane highways have already exceeded tolerable noise limits and where the new supersonic jets, with their sonic booms, threaten the physical integrity of buildings, let alone the human ear.

Almost any individual human action, and all social process, has some sonic consequences. New sound is produced deliberately (as when we speak to a friend, conduct a symphony or televise a play) and incidentally (as when we accelerate a car, stamp out a metal auto body or rivet the hull of a ship). In the first case, the new sound is the end-product of the process: this might be called productive sound. In the second instance, the new sound is a by-product of the process: this — which might be called contraproductive sound — is usually called noise.

However, even productive sound is socially useful only so long as it is confined to the immediate environment for which it has been produced. Thus the symphony, performed in a hall designed for the purpose before an audience which has paid to hear it, has maximum cultural value. Thanks to modern electronic technology, this audience can now be enormously expanded by means of radio, television and recordings. For this new audience, seated before millions of scattered sets, the symphony is still productive sound. But it is now produced in spaces designed neither to receive nor to contain it; the sound escapes, impinging on countless nearby ears which *do not* choose to hear it but which cannot escape. For all such persons, the symphony at that time and in those circumstances is apt to be contraproductive, a nuisance: plain noise.

Noise will therefore be seen as a social, not a physical, unit of measurement, developed to describe our pollution of the natural sonic environment. This pollution corresponds closely to that of the atmospheric environment in both cause and effect. Both are an index of social waste, since both represent an incomplete or incorrect conversion of energy on the one hand, and a direct threat to the health and efficiency of society, on the other. This correlation has not always been so clear: all through the nineteenth century, industrially generated noise was considered a symbol of progress ("the roar of the steel mills," "the busy hum of the city") instead of being a certain index of waste of both human and mechanical energy. Today silence has become the very symbol of efficiency in technology. But no such criteria are as yet applied to the urban environment. Because of this paradoxical situation, in which by sheer amplification, productive sound becomes destructive noise, architects and urbanists must master two distinct scales of sonic control — the traditional one of architectural acoustics (the artful manipulation of sound within buildings) and the newer one of control of environmental noise. The point of departure of both efforts must be an understanding of the requirements of the human ear.

WHAT WE HEAR AND HOW

In conventional terms, the ear is the organ of hearing. But the ear is in fact only a part of a complex auditory system which transmits vibrations (i.e., sound waves) from the atmosphere and converts them into nerve impulses. The ultimate function of this system is not merely to permit hearing but to make possible *listening* — a critical examination of the information picked up from the external environment.* For such an examination, we need two types of information: the nature of the event and the direction in which it is occurring. The binaural auditory system is nicely designed to accomplish this task. Our response to this examination of incoming auditory information is one of constant re-orientation, both intellectual and physical — the more so, since the auditory system also includes our balancing mechanism for spatial orientation, the vestibular apparatus. Through the brain, this system is linked to visual perception in a feedback process of marvelous sensitivity. Together they furnish the basic spatial orientation of life.

The normal ear perceives only a portion of the total sonic environment, its habitat being that described in Fig. 45. But within that habitat, its powers of perception and discrimination are immense. Paul E. Sabine, a pioneer in architectural acoustics, has said:

* See James J. Gibson, *The Senses Considered as Perceptual Systems* (Boston: Houghton Mifflin, 1966), especially for his clear and cogent description of the process of listening.

The range of physical intensities to which the ear responds is enormous . . . A sound so intense as to be painful is of the order of *ten trillion* times the minimum audible intensity. The intensity of speech is of the order of one to ten *million* times the minimum audible intensity, so that conversational speech falls about the middle range which the human ear will accommodate.[2]

Its powers of discrimination are, however, more limited. In theory, the human ear can discriminate among some 400,000 sounds in the sense of telling that there is a difference between any two when the two are presented in rapid succession. But in actuality, some experiments indicate that ordinary untrained people

. . . seem unable to classify sounds beyond about seven degrees of loudness and seven degrees of pitch . . . or forty-nine tones of different pitch and loudness, hearing them one at a time. It is interesting to note that this is not far from the number of phonemes we distinguish in a language.[3]

The problem is enormously complex and not fully understood, even among the specialists. But, in any case, the range of sonic stimuli perceived by the ear and analyzed by the brain is immense.

Unlike the eye, with its complex modulating devices of contractile iris, moveable eyelid and eyebrow, the ear has no comparable protection against environmental stress. This is probably an evolutionary reflection of the fact, already noted, that all sound in the natural sonic environment — hurricane, thunderbolt, volcanic explosion — fell well within the ear's limits of accommodation. However, the auditory system does have a subtle capacity for *selective* listening. In situations where a number of diverse sounds or sonic events are being picked up by the ear, the brain has the capacity to "tune out" the unwanted stimuli — the familiar phenomenon of the cocktail party. Exactly how this process of filtering is accomplished, or at what cost in terms of energy, is not understood. Obviously, in the cocktail situation, we supplement inadequate auditory information with visual data picked up from the facial expressions and lip movements of our conversational partners. But there are other situations in which such visual assistance is not available: at such times we describe our action as one of "concentrating" on hearing what we want to hear. Actually a process of filtration, it must depend upon some kind of neural action, the reflex effect of which is the contraction of blood vessels in the ear. This effect seems to take place with equal intensity during sleep and wakefulness and — since it involves energy output — cannot be accomplished without some cost to the individual. How much, and with what consequences, is currently being investigated by many people.[4]

The fourth dimension of the aural habitat is, of course, time. As in the case of the other systems of sensory perception, the aural stimulation of a steady sound diminishes with time — provided that the sound is not actually painful in either frequency or intensity. In such case, it can gradually drop below the level of conscious perception, like the "white noise" of a fan or window air conditioner. But this of course is a purely quantitative measure of stress. Whether we cease to "hear" the sound, whether or not we find it "endurable," depends also upon the informational content of that sound. This is one of the more mysterious aspects of listening. We can and do endure sounds of stressful magnitude if their message is important to us. As one acoustical engineer puts it:

Reasons for the difference between *comfort* levels and *tolerance* levels may be found in the information content of the various sounds. [Thus sounds which connote] "the fan is making it cool" or "the vacuum is making it clean" are usually tolerable at much higher levels than those recommended as good design practice . . . Moreover, when a noise source is under the direct control of the listener and is beneficial to him, the allowable noise level is considerably higher than if the device were fully controlled by others.[5]

Here again, however, we must remember that such exposure must of necessity be fatiguing, no matter how overwhelming the motivation, or concealed the cost.

Because aural perception is so closely linked to vision, our eyes play a larger role in "hearing" than we commonly realize. Developing together over evolutionary time, the two senses have comparable scanning radii of spatial reach. The degree to which we can hear the luncheon companion or the actor on the stage is also a measure of how well we can see him, though the two types of sensory input are normally so blended that we are unaware of it. "I can't hear a word he says" may well be translated "I can't read a word of his lips."

This symbiotic function has great significance for architectural acoustics, as we shall shortly see.

HOW SOUND BEHAVES

The behavior of sound in the atmosphere is strikingly like that sort of motion which occurs when a stone is dropped into a quiet pool. In both cases, the energy is dispersed from its point of origin in successive concentric waves. The difference between water and sound waves is, of course, that the former move outward in an expanding circle on a single plane, while sound waves move out in an expanding sphere. In open air, this process of dispersion continues until all the energy is finally dissipated in friction with the air.

Although a sound wave displaces each air particle as it passes, setting up a characteristic vibration, the particle itself does not move forward with the wave but rotates vertically. The time required for a given particle to complete this vibration is known as the sound's *period;* the number of completed vibrations per second is the sound's *frequency;* the distance between two wave crests is called its *wavelength;* and the maximum distance between the crest and valley of the wave is its *amplitude.* The speed of sound is much slower than that of light, and varies somewhat with air temperature — at 40° F, sound travels at a speed of 1100 feet per second; at 60° F, 1120 f.p.s. Like light, sound may be focused, reflected and absorbed. Unlike light waves, sound waves can coexist without blending.

The behavior of sound inside buildings is quite different from that in the open air. Investigation of this behavior is the basis for a whole branch of physics known as acoustics — or, when the subjective aspects are also being analyzed, psycho-acoustics. The acoustical behavior of a given vessel (church, theater, living room) at any given moment depends upon a bewildering array of factors, most of them variable. The type of sonic event; its location in the vessel; the size, shape and surfaces of the vessel itself; the number of people present (even the clothes they are wearing) — all these play a role in the total acoustical behavior of the volume in question. But in the response of any kind of vessel to any kind of sound, these physical phenomena are always to be observed: *reflection, refraction, reverberation* and *resonance*. These serve as objective criteria by which to measure acoustical performance. Thanks to modern physics, they can now be mathematically expressed.*

The reflection of sound is just what the term implies: when the sound wave meets a solid obstacle, it is bounced back. Refraction occurs when a sound wave breaks around a freestanding obstacle, such as a column. Here the action is similar to what happens when an ocean wave breaks around a pile. No surface, however, will reflect all of the sound which strikes it: a portion will also be absorbed by the surface itself. The amount reflected and the amount absorbed will depend upon the physical characteristics of the surface itself. Dense, smooth-surfaced materials like glass or marble reflect much of the sound energy while rough-textured, porous materials such as fiberboard or glass wool absorb more sound. Two other acoustical properties of closed spaces describe the response of the vessel as a whole. Reverberation time describes the time required, after a sound stops, for the intensity of the reverberation to fall to one-millionth of its first intensity. If the time gap is more than 70 milliseconds it is the echo of our childhood. The other phenomenon associated with the behavior of sound in closed vessels is resonance. This describes the special response of a room to sounds of a certain pitch or frequency. The reaction here is identical to that which occurs when one tuning fork is set into vibration by striking another of the same pitch. When we describe a room as "brilliant" or "dull," we are describing its resonance.

The foregoing describes the behavior of sound generated within the vessel. But only a portion of the sound impinging upon the vessel walls is reflected; a portion of the remaining energy is absorbed by the wall itself, the residue being transmitted to adjacent parts of the structure and to the air beyond. The proportions vary greatly, depending upon the molecular nature of the material and the construction of the wall.† Generally speaking, sheer massiveness

---

* A standard text on the subject is *Acoustical Designing in Architecture* by V. O. Knudsen and Cyril M. Harris (New York: John Wiley, 1950).

† A detailed analysis of the acoustical behavior of building materials will be found in *Bulletin*, no. 31, 1971, published by the Acoustical and Insulating Materials Association, Park Ridge, Illinois.

is the most effective barrier to sound transmission through the wall. A solid masonry wall or heavy concrete floor absorbs more airborne sound than a light one. But since massive walls and floors run counter to current trends toward lightness in structural design, light-weight, absorptive insulating materials are commonly substituted, with isolation of the various wall elements as a secondary device. Thus the vessel must be visualized, not as a merely inert and static container, but as the active interface between two sonic environments — the internal, acoustically predetermined meso-environment and the macro-environment, all too often intolerably polluted by noise.

THE COMMUNICATION ROLE OF BUILDINGS

Since all buildings are designed to facilitate some aspect of human intercourse, communication occurs in all of them. But many building types are specifically designed for communication — churches, schools, theaters, legal and legislative chambers — and they constitute, as they always have, one of the architect's most important areas of activity. This communication role has two levels, concrete and metaphysical, but we are here concerned with the first: the transmission of information, by aural and visual means, between minister and congregation, teacher and class, actor and audience, judge and jury. Before the development of the electronic ear (microphone) and the electronic voice box (amplifier), all aural communication was conditioned by the reach of human energy, vocal and muscular — i.e., the power of the speaker's voice box, the strength of the harpist's fingers. And before the invention of optical glasses and electric illumination, almost identical restraints were placed upon the visual component of communication — i.e., what the naked eye of the spectator could perceive. The spatial parameters of all pre-industrial communication were established by scanning power of the eye and ear, organs of sonic and luminous perception, working in tandem.

These parameters, in turn, governed the development of both communication structure — i.e., the formal characteristics of sermon, lecture, concert, play — and the architectural vessel in which it was

Fig. 46. Theater, Epidaurus, Greece, fifth century B.C. The Greek theater was a roofless vessel of astonishing visual and acoustical effectiveness. Its shape and size were nicely adapted to scanning range of unaided ear and eye. Since it developed symbiotically with Greek dramatic forms, it was shaped to give environmental support.

Fig. 47. Margrave's Opera House, Bayreuth, Germany, 1748. Giuseppe Galli Bibiena, architect. The Baroque theaters of northern Europe, necessarily enclosed because of climate, were designed for small audiences. Wood and plaster vessels of great acoustical brilliance, they afforded lively environmental support for theatral forms — masques, operas and ballets — in which instrumental music had a large role.

projected and "consumed." Over millennia, their evolutionary development has been symbiotic. Fifth-century Greek drama developed step by step with the perfecting of the roofless Greek theater (Fig. 46). The polyphony of early Christian church music was made at once possible and necessary by the long reverberation period of the Romanesque basilica: intelligibility being impossible, it was relinquished as an esthetic criterion. The reverse was necessary when the evangelical necessities of the Reformation required a new vessel in which the sermon could be clearly heard, the prayer book easily read. The rise of secular music led to the courtly operas of the eighteenth century which was predicated on the small, acoustically brilliant Baroque theaters in which which it was performed (Fig. 47).

This equilibrium between sonic form and acoustical container endured for centuries. It was anything but static — as any survey of music, theater or dance will quickly show — but it led to a rich and stable empirical tradition which was good for all concerned. Theater lore is full of significant anecdotes, apocryphal though they may be. Thus when he was told that he had a half-filled house in his rented London theater, Handel is supposed to have exclaimed, "Good! My music will sound the better." (Here he understood that fewer overdressed patrons would reduce the absorptive capacity, and hence extend the reverberation period, of the vessel — which, for his music, he must have considered desirable.) And Richard Wagner, touring the opera houses of Europe before designing his own new vessel at Bayreuth, reputedly told an Italian impresario, "I cannot hear your chorus over the surf of your orchestra." To avoid this error at Bayreuth, Wagner both submerged his orchestra pit and pushed it well back beneath the apron of the stage. Thus, he made it act as a "mixing chamber" to modulate the volume and direction of orchestral sound.

Electronic technology has quite truncated this long empirical tradition. The modern architect now has at his disposal the theoretical tool of mathematical acoustics and the extraordinary audiovisual equipment of electronic technology. Unfortunately, it has not followed that his new buildings are better instruments of communication. On the contrary, we find a disappointing record of acoustical malfunction in some of our most prestigious theaters, lecture halls and churches. All of which suggests that architects should master the lessons of preindustrial acoustical practice before dumping them in the trash bin of history.

THEATER — TEST TUBE OF ACOUSTIC THEORY *

In creating vessels for the performing arts, the architect is intervening in one of the most complex of all esthetic processes. The painter or the poet, for all the public nature of his creations, works in private. For this work, he needs one sort of environment; but the viewer of his canvas or the reader of his poem may require quite another. But in the theater the work of art is created anew with each performance, right in the presence of its consumers. Live actors, dancers, musicians confront the living audience. Action and reaction are to all intents and purposes simultaneous: the contact is electric and yields an emotional climate which is specific to the theater. It is the product of a *triangular* relationship (not a two-way one, as is commonly assumed): the actor's impact upon the audience as a whole; the collective response of that audience; and the effect of that response upon the individual playgoers who make it up. This three-way feedback is what has always made the theater the most electrifying of all the forms of art.

Until modern times, it was always understood that each theatral form — play, opera, concert, dance — had its own special environmental requirements and own inherent scale. When the Greek city of Eretria in Euboea made attendance at the theater compulsory for its citizens on certain high holidays, it was acknowledging the potency of the form. The theater was a major instrument whereby its citizens were inculcated with Greek values — where, in sober fact, they learned to be Greek. The form of the play and the form of the theater that held it had symbiotic origins, in whose development the playwright and the architect took equal and mutually supporting parts. Lacking the technical means for amplification of word or

---

* A fuller theoretical development of the following material will be found in the author's paper, "For the Theatrical Experience, An Architecture of Truth," in *Arts in Society*, vol. 4, no. 3 (1968), pp. 491–501.

gesture, the authors developed a characteristic set of formal conventions — the shouted lines and exaggerated, stylized gestures; the tragic and comic masks; most of all, the chorus. Placed midway between the cast on its raised stage and the audience in its roofless bowl, the chorus was a remarkable invention. It acted both as interlocutor for the audience *(Why, oh why, must Oedipus kill his father at the crossroads?)* and as interpreter for the playwright *(Patience, patience, you will see, the gods have willed it so)*. Pulsing back and forth between the cast and the audience, the chorus welded the two into one communion. Catharsis through pity and terror was the result.

Understanding both the importance and the fragility of this emotional climate, Greek architects exercised great care in designing the ambiance in which the play was to be experienced. Because artificial illumination was inadequate, performances were held in daylight. With the genial Aegean climate, the roofless theater was practicable; but without any technical means of visual or aural amplification, sight lines and acoustic behavior had to be exactly calculated. The Greek theater building was thus a vessel perfectly shaped to contain the Greek play.

Because of this experiential totality, its physical union of actors, audience and individual playgoer, the Greek theater can never become "obsolete." It represents a prototypal form *which cannot be manipulated without fundamentally altering the theatral experience itself*. Even to enlarge the auditorium is to push the outermost seats beyond the scanning range of good vision and hearing, thereby reducing the potency of the actors' projection. These limits are established by the physiology of the eye and the ear and they cannot be violated without a qualitative diminution in the experience itself.

American architects, like Americans generally, have accepted without serious challenge the proposition that technology has made obsolete or inoperative all these ancient relationships. Yet it should be obvious that when, for example, a play is transposed from the stage to the movie screen, it has already been divested of its most magical property — that feedback which enables the spectators not merely to receive the play but to modify the very quality of the actor's projection by the intensity of their response. In the movie, the audience no longer has a direct line of communication with the actor. Modern audio-visual technology gives the audience an acceptable facsimile of multidimensional reality of live theater; and as long as it is projected before the living audience of the movie theater, it maintains some of the central elements of theatral experience. A viable art form results. But when this same movie is projected upon an outdoor screen and the individual members of the audience are isolated in the sealed compartments of their individual automobiles, the situation is further compromised. Perception itself is fragmented. The visual image is reduced in size, distorted by curved glass, dimmed by condensation, wipers, etc.; the sound, robbed of dimension, direction and depth, issues from one little box; heated or cooled air from another. The entire experience is converted into a travesty of the technical virtuosity which makes it possible.

And when, finally, that same cinematic facsimile is projected across the indecent privacy of the TV screen, the process of electronic attrition is complete. With the radical alterations of both the intrinsic properties of the form itself (grotesque distortions in size, scale, color and length as well as the periodic interjection of extraneous advertising) and the radical change in the ambient circumstances under which it is projected, the play has been reduced to an impoverished simulacrum of the original. Removed from its special container of public exposure, the form has been mutilated and the climate demolished. Now, indeed, man has been reduced to the one-dimensional role of passive spectator. Instead of being submerged in the rich and stimulating theatral experience, a participant through all his senses, he views it as if through a knothole.

It would be nonsense, of course, to argue that electronic facsimiles (films, recordings, tapes) are without esthetic value or cultural utility. But it is equally nonsensical to argue that they are identical or interchangeable with their prototypes. Yet this is just the position assumed by many critics, including one who writes:

. . . almost any recording studio is acoustically superior to all but half a dozen halls in which orchestral music is played to audiences; and it is preposterous to think that a third-rate orchestra in a second-rate hall is closer to the prototype (what the composer intended) than a great orchestra, using the most modern equipment, in a studio.[6]

But the conditions under which the record is cut or the video taped are not the decisive factors in the experience: *it is rather the experiential circumstances under which they are projected and received.* These are literally never "superior" in the noisy bar or across the static and flicker of the living room TV, or in the parked car or the picnic grove. It is preposterous not to recognize this fact. Indeed, one could easily argue that it might be much more preferable actually to hear the live performance of a third-rate orchestra in a second-rate hall. (Though why must we assume, with this critic, that we must content ourselves with third-rate men playing in second-rate architecture?) To insist upon these distinctions is not to assume an "undemocratic" posture, as this same critic has charged: it is rather to establish and define the critically important categories of experience in a period when the tendency is to vulgarize them all.

It seems necessary to recapitulate some of these cultural and esthetic consequences of electronic technology, because the architect has become as much disoriented by them as the public generally. This is demonstrated by the fact that many theaters and concert halls (like much modern architecture) abound in the frivolous, the idiosyncratic and the arbitrary. Despite the fact that the technical means at the disposal of the architect are incomparably higher than ever before, he is producing new theaters whose overall performance is less satisfactory than many built centuries ago. This paradoxical state of affairs is due to his having uncritically accepted the pretensions of technology, on the one hand, and indulging himself in subjective, formalistic design decisions, on the other. He shares the field with a broad range of specialists — acoustical, illuminating, air-conditioning and structural engineers. Their very presence on the scene permits the architect to work in broader and more daring terms than hitherto, since responsibilities formerly his alone can now be delegated to these specialists. But these experts lack a common conceptual approach to what I have called the experiential aspects of architecture. The environmental requirements of the playgoer may be studied, but studied piecemeal, each by the appropriate specialist. These components are not often reintegrated into a satisfactory total environment.

The modern architect has a critically important responsibility here — and too often fails. One reason for this failure is that, in his work, *the appearance of things* tends to carry a weight in decision-making which is quite disproportionate to its objective importance. Since every architect is a visual artist, this bias in favor of vision amounts almost to an occupational disease. Whatever complex manipulation of environmental forces he may have in mind in a given building, his principal means of communicating his intentions are in pictorial and plastic terms — i.e., by means of drawings, sketches and models. Like heliotropism in certain flowers, this bends the design in the direction of *what it will look like* to the detriment of other values equally important but much harder to visualize: what it will *sound* like, what it will *feel* like, what it will *smell* like. Thus the temperature and ventilation of a theater during a performance will play a much more critical role in the audience's response than the color of walls or upholstery or the shape of the proscenium. However, it is easier to conceptualize the curve or the color than the temperature or air movement. Hence our theaters are full of devices aimed primarily at pleasing the eye (though not necessarily aiding it in perceiving the play itself) while other channels of perception are given only token attention: sight lines violated, ventilation skimped, acoustics poor, seating uncomfortable, etc.

There is no automatic congruity between "good looks" and good acoustics, any more than there would be between the taste and nutritional value of a dish of food. Of course, on the other hand, there is no necessary incongruity either. Many a room that is beautiful to look at is also beautiful to listen in. But any architectural vessel designed primarily for aural communication must first comply with those factors which determine acoustical behavior. These are the size and shape of the vessel and the physical characteristics of the enclosing surfaces. Only then, and only by respecting these acoustical parameters, can the vessel be manipulated for purely visual effects. Thus it will be irrelevant acoustically whether the theater seating is upholstered in red or green; but it will matter very much whether the seating is surfaced in velvet upholstery or enameled metal; or whether it is empty or occupied during any acoustical analysis.

Fig. 48. Philharmonic Hall, Lincoln Center, New York, N.Y. Harrison and Abramowitz, architects. Seen here in its original form, this concert hall proved so unsatisfactory that it has been repeatedly reconstructed. The parameters of shape, size and volume as originally recommended by acoustical engineer were ignored in order to increase seating capacity. Result: acoustic dysfunction so acute that both audience and performers rebelled. In present reconstruction, performance is now satisfactory.

This paradox, overvaluing the visual and undervaluing the aural behavior of auditoriums, has been very obvious in both the design and the critical reaction to the new theaters in New York's Lincoln Center for the Performing Arts. At the end of 1969, five had been completed: Philharmonic Hall (Fig. 48); New York State Theater (Fig. 49); Metropolitan Opera (Fig. 50); Vivian Beaumont Theater (Fig. 51); and Alice Tully Hall (Fig. 52). The critical reaction to the five auditoriums was most revealing. The architectural critics tended to discuss them in almost completely formal or esthetic terms — that is, as visual phenomena. There was some disagreement (mostly over the patent vulgarity of the interior décor of the Opera), but generally speaking, all five received favorable critiques in the architectural press.

Music and drama critics, on the other hand, were much sharper and more specific. They pounced on the atrocious acoustical behavior of Philharmonic Hall with such continuing force that it has been completely rebuilt internally *three* times. While the architectural critic of the *New York Times* was rhapsodic over the white

Fig. 49. New York State Theater, Lincoln Center, New York, N.Y. Philip Johnson, architect. Faulty acoustical conditions in many seats and poor lines from side balconies combine to render this theater unacceptable for drama; moderately satisfactory for opera; ideal for dance with its modest requirements for visual, aural acuity.

Fig. 50. Metropolitan Opera, Lincoln Center, New York, N.Y. Harrison and Abramowitz, architects; Cyril M. Harris, acoustical engineer. The uniformly excellent acoustics of this theater go far to compensating for its visual vulgarity. Following classic opera form, the house has good sight lines except side boxes.

and gold color scheme of the lobby of the State Theater, the music critic of the same paper could observe that:

The sound is excellent in the rings and galleries but very bad in the orchestra, where a strange bounce places the sound just where the loud speakers are located in the proscenium sides.[7]

At the opening of the Metropolitan, the *Times* architectural critic found it to be "a curiously resolved collision of past and present . . . a sterile throwback rather than a creative Twentieth Century design." She concludes her critique by ruefully observing that:

. . . since the new opera promises to be an excellent performing house, with satisfactory acoustics, it may not matter that the architecture sets no high water mark for the city.[8]

The music critic, reporting the same event, reported that, since the entire stage was being used without backdrops, the singers found their voices going about as far back as forward. Reports from the upper parts of the house were favorable but the $250 ticket holders found the sound vaulting over their heads.[9] But he also added that, at an earlier preview using normal stage sets, the house "turned out to be an acoustic dream." Neither critic felt it necessary to comment upon the atrocious sight lines from the side boxes, perhaps because that is the well-known shortcoming of the traditional opera house form.

Tully Hall, newest of the Center theaters, was inaugurated in late 1969. With an emphasis on performance rather than appearance (an emphasis which architectural critics might do well to emulate), the *Times* music critic Harold Schonberg writes:

It seats 1,096, is handsome and produces a nice, clear sound. It is what can be described as a modern sound. That is, clarity rather than warmth is its main characteristic. Its reverberation period seems short and — pending further acquaintance with the hall — there seems to be a slight loss in energy from front to rear. But there is a strong bass characteristic and plenty of presence. Musicians have already reported that they feel comfortable and happy playing from the stage. They can hear one another, they say. One of the complaints about the stage of Philharmonic Hall is that they cannot.[10]

Of the five theatrical vessels at Lincoln Center, the geometry of the Beaumont is the purest, most consistent and least idiosyncratic.

It follows quite closely the Greek parameters (diameter 130 feet; seating 1059 to 1140; shallow, stepped auditorium). It makes no use of any of the pseudo-historical decorative devices which mar the interiors of both the State Theater and the Opera (e.g., chandeliers, swags, cartouches, upholstered walls, etc.). But these visually conspicuous characteristics are only the end result which was shaped by the reach of the spectator's eye and ear. They are not decorative devices superimposed upon an abstractly conceived, anti-aural form — as is the case of the Philharmonic.

The architect of the Philharmonic is reported to have said, after the full dimensions of its acoustical dysfunction became apparent, "If we have learned anything from all this, it is that acoustics is still an inexact science." But this is to place the blame upon the acoustical engineer when, in fact, the failure seems due to fundamental architectonic misconceptions. The acoustical engineer had personally visited all the world's leading concert halls before beginning the design of the Philharmonic. From this survey, he found their average seating capacity to be around 1400, their average volume to be under 600,000 cubic feet. Yet, for economic reasons, the management tossed aside these parameters and the architects agreed to double the seating capacity (to almost 3000) and greatly increase the volume (to 850,000 cubic feet). The acoustical consultant went along, apparently feeling that such a change in size and scale was merely quantitative, and hence subject to purely technical manipulation. This miscalculation proved disastrous; only after three complete reconstructions, each by a different acoustical consultant and at a cost of several million dollars, has the hall been brought up to reasonably satisfactory standards of acoustical behavior.[11] It is a sad and costly confirmation of an old truism: what the trained architectural eye accepts, the musically trained ear may reject out-of-hand.

Even so, in America today, acoustical expertise tends to be concentrated on those building types which are specifically aimed at facilitating communication — telecasting facilities, theaters, auditoriums, classrooms, etc. Little comparable attention is paid to sound control in housing or places of work. Yet with the mechanization of industry, office work, transport and housework, the level of internally

Fig. 51. Vivian Beaumont Theater, Lincoln Center, New York, N.Y. Eero Saarinen and Associates, architects. Conforming quite closely to Greek parameters in both shape and seating capacity, this 1200-seat vessel has uniformly excellent acoustics. Sight lines are excellent from every seat when thrust stage is used.

Fig. 52. Alice Tully Hall, Juilliard School of Music, Lincoln Center, New York, N.Y. Pietro Belluschi and Associates, architects. Newest and smallest of the Center theaters, this 1096-seat vessel is designed exclusively for vocal and instrumental concert performances. Its wood-lined surfaces and acoustically balanced seats afford good support.

generated noise is constantly rising. This constitutes a serious environmental hazard: one authority estimates that anywhere from 6,000,000 to 16,000,000 workers may be subjected to noise levels which are hazardous to health.[12] Dr. Arain Glorig concludes that "the potential cost of noise-induced hearing loss is greater than for any other occupational disease."[13] Yet the reduction of noise in places of work and living is, technically at least, a simple problem. It involves a greatly expanded use of absorptive insulating materials and isolation devices to confine noise to its place of origin.

POLLUTION OF THE SONIC ENVIRONMENT

The acoustical design problem of the individual vessel (whether it be a room or an entire building) can thus be seen as entirely soluble — even though, as too often occurs, many solutions fall far short of the optimal. In any case, manipulation of the sound generated *within* a given building is the responsibility of the architect. But the control of noise in the environment is incomparably more difficult and complex. The sources of pollution are disparate and widely scattered; legal means of protection against them are almost nonexistent; and technical means of suppression are complex and costly. Two of the greatest sources of sonic pollution in the typical American city today are multilane highways and jet airports. Adequate control of them obviously implies cooperation of many agencies at municipal, regional and national levels.*

Recognition of this form of environmental degradation is rapidly growing, even though it has been slower to command professional attention than the exactly comparable pollution of air, soil and water by chemical agents. Today, there is no question but that environmental noise now constitutes a major threat to health and well-being.

The impact of environmental noise upon the individual can be observed at several different levels. The most familiar one is simple interference with conversation or with purposeful activities such as

---

* Comprehensive treatments of noise control problems are to be found in Cyril M. Harris, ed., *Handbook of Noise Control* (New York: McGraw-Hill, 1957); and R. D. Berendt, C. B. Burroughs and G. E. Winger, *A Guide to Airborne, Impact and Structure-Borne Noise in Multifamily Dwellings* (Washington: U.S. Government Printing Office, 1967).

studying or writing. At this level of environmental stress, we are normally aware of noise only as being an annoyance ("It's so noisy here I can't hear myself think!") Nevertheless, even at the level of casual exposure to such noise levels as obtained on most city streets, conversation for pedestrians becomes difficult if not downright impossible. Much more serious, from the standpoint of health, is exposure to noise levels high enough to interfere with rest and sleep. Such stress is now recognized as contributing to psychophysiological disturbances which, if extended across time, will have a deleterious effect upon the individual's health. This is a very common form of stress for millions of city dwellers, especially in hot weather when windows are open for ventilation. A survey of 1400 London households revealed that sleep and relaxation of 82 per cent were disturbed by noises originating outside the building and 16 per cent by noise coming from adjacent apartments. Only 1 per cent were disturbed by noise originating within their own apartments.[14]

But now environmental medicine is producing indisputable evidence that high levels of noise lead directly to physiological disturbance and degeneration, both of the ear itself[15] and of the body as a whole. A leading authority says "normal" city noises not only "get on the nerves" but can do permanent damage to the auditory system, negatively affect the heart and blood pressure and eventually "disturb every bodily function."[16] Loud blasts will send pulse and heartbeat skyrocketing, as will the effort to talk or be heard in presence of continuous, high-level noise. A study of German steelworkers, exposed to severe noise conditions, showed them to have an unusually high percentage of abnormal heart rhythms. Similar studies of Italian textile workers, also exposed to high noise levels in their places of work, showed abnormal brain wave patterns, some of them actually suggestive of personality disorders. Noise-related illnesses are clearly reaching epidemic proportions.[17]

EAR "HEALTH" AND SONIC STRESS

Like all the organs of the human body, the hearing system deteriorates with age. But there is mounting evidence that the onset of such hearing loss occurs earlier, and is much more severe, in the noise-

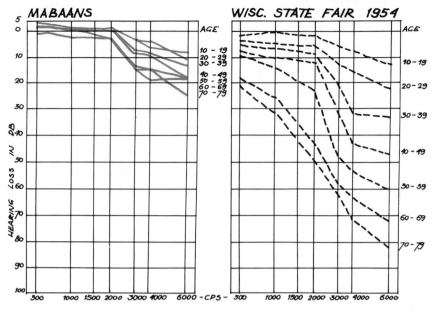

Fig. 53. Hearing acuity of men of Mabaan tribe (left) is strikingly superior to that of American men of all ages (right). Mabaans spend their lives in a sonic environment which is markedly less stressful than the American with its high levels of noise.

ridden environments of the Western world. To study this phenomenon, a group of specialists under the leadership of Dr. Samuel Rosen of Columbia University decided to study the hearing of a population living in a noise-free environment. The culture selected was that of the Mabaans, a people living in a remote region of southeast Sudan, some 10 degrees above the equator and 650 miles below Khartoum.

The investigators found the natural sonic environment almost entirely unpolluted by the noises of human activity. They found that:

In general, the sound level in the villages is below the 40 db on the C scale of the sound level meter except occasionally at sunrise or soon thereafter when a domestic animal such as a rooster, lamb, cow or dove makes itself heard. During six months of the year, heavy rains occur about three times a week with one or two claps of thunder. A few men engage in some productive activities such as beating palm fronds with a wooden club. But the absence of hard reverberating surfaces — such as walls, ceilings, floors and hard furniture, etc. — in the vicinity apparently accounts for the low intensity levels measured on the sound level meter: 73–74 db at the worker's ear.

The highest noise levels encountered during our stay occurred when the villagers were dancing and singing. One recorded group consisted of ten young men and ten young women. Stanzas of a song were sung by a very soft-voiced male who also played the five string lyre. [He was] followed at the end of each stanza by the chorus of twenty. The recorded levels of 20 singers in chorus were 100–104 db, topped by hoots and shouts at the end, yielding levels of 106–110 db. Such festival singing apparently occurs about one to three times a week and lasts from one to three hours.[18]

This analysis of the sonic environment of an African village was based on studies made in 1961–1963.[19] But it could perfectly well describe that of any preindustrial village in Periclean Greece, Shakespeare's England or the Illinois of Abe Lincoln's childhood.

Existing in this largely undisturbed and unpolluted natural environment, the Mabaans were found to enjoy a hearing capacity which was remarkably superior to that of Americans: and this superiority increases with age (Fig. 53).

The difference becomes quite marked in the age group 30–39 years, when the Mabaans hear better by 19.3 decibels, and at 40–49 years by 29.6 decibels . . . In the 70–79 year old group, we find 53% of the Mabaans responding to [sounds of] 14,000 c.p.s. as compared to 2% for persons of the same group in New York, Cairo and Dusseldorf.[20]

The Mabaans seemed spectacularly more healthy according to other indices as well. Blood pressures were much lower throughout life, hovering around 115 systolic from 15 to 75 years, while for Americans it rose from 115 at age 20 to 160 at age 70.[21] The Rosen group also found little arteriosclerosis, greater elasticity of the small arteries; no

Fig. 54. Comparison of mean blood pressures of apparently healthy Americans with those of the Mabaans confirms the known correlation between loss of hearing and cardiovascular diseases. Many factors are probably involved in Mabaans' better health, including diet, relaxed life style, etc.; but quiet sonic environment is important.

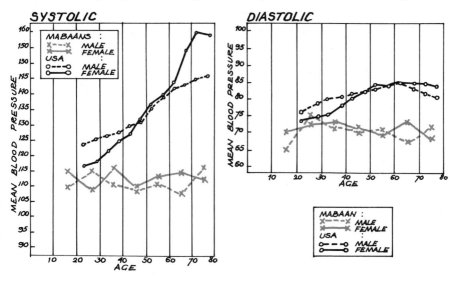

varicose veins or thrombosis; no bronchial asthma.[22] A decrement in hearing is associated with many of these vascular conditions, since an adequate supply of blood to the capillaries of the inner ear is essential to good hearing (Fig. 54).

Although the exact line of cause and effect remains to be traced out in greater detail, the Rosen report is epochal for establishing the fundamental relationship between environmental degradation and damages to health and hearing at an epidemiological scale. While modern industrial society cannot hope ever to re-create the sonic environment of a pastoral village, this relationship can serve as a bench mark for noise-control policy in the Western world.

Even today, most rural areas will have a sonic environment which, with minor exceptions, has remained much the same for centuries. Near the highways there will be the roar of diesel trucks; freight (if not passenger) trains still clatter down the tracks, though most planes fly at too high an altitude to be heard. But these sounds are merely superimposed upon a natural environment which remains largely unpolluted. For long intervals and over large areas, noise levels may sink below the threshold of hearing. To the sound-shocked city dweller, such a sonic environment will seem idyllic. And there is little doubt that the farmer and his wife move in a less stressful sonic environment than the machinist at his lathe, his wife at home or their children on the street.

Since, away from the highways, the rural environment is unpolluted, the problem of noise control is still fairly simple. Not one farmer in a thousand will need a soundproofed bedroom. No neighbors' TV sets are near enough to constitute a hazard. If he owns a tractor or power tools, the chances are that the noise they make is psychologically satisfying; in any case, he will seldom be exposed for long periods to noise levels which are injurious to his health. Nor is the farmer's wife apt to object to the swish of clothes, and the dishwasher, or the periodic thump of the water pump. If she is old enough to remember farm life before the appearance of gasoline and electric motors, their sound will pleasantly connote work done by energies other than her own.

There is, of course, an obverse to this idyllic condition of rural silence — boredom. Radio, record player and television are commonly assumed to have brought to the farm home an exact equivalent of the theater, cinema, concert and ballet actually available to the city dweller. But, however much better than the nineteenth-century rural vacuum these audio-visual facsimiles may be, they are very much less than the multidimensional reality of their prototypes. In any case, the steady drift of farm youth to the city — in the U.S.A. no less than in Latin America or Africa — seems to suggest that a mere freedom from noise does not compensate for the rich and stimulating environment of the city. Once they become conscious of these urban alternatives, even the Mabaan youth are apt to set off for Khartoum or Cairo, sonic pollution or no.

The city dweller finds himself at the other end of this spectrum. Here sound levels run a full gamut from the absolute (and synthetic) silence of the broadcasting studio, through the hubbub of street and tenement life, to the concentrated clatter of a printing plant or the ear-shattering clamor of punch press and foundry. The city dweller has lost the peace and quiet of the countryside but his sonic environment is, at the same time, infinitely more varied than that of the farmer. He has access, at least in theory, to a range of productive sound — concert, lecture, drama. He has greater access to all forms of electronic propagation (as does, of course, his neighbor). He dwells in a man-made sonic environment which is hostile to his physical well-being, however nourishing some aspects of it may be intellectually. He may have access to a thousand forms of productive sound. He has no refuge from noise.

A socially and physiologically satisfactory sonic environment will not be achieved in our cities without radical changes in their design and management. For here the natural environment has been destroyed. It can never be literally re-created; and it cannot be restructured along new lines until we are prepared to accept new and higher levels of control.[23] Noise is a sign of social dysfunction; the criteria for its elimination coincide at all major points with those for the elimination of all forms of environmental pollution.

7.
THE ARCHITECTURAL
MANIPULATION OF SPACE, TIME,
AND GRAVITY

Human experience, through its metabolic and sensory perceptual systems, occupies its own "habitat" in the external world. Indeed, for the purposes of fruitful architectural and urbanistic analysis, *each* of its component systems must be conceived of as having its own private habitat. Each of these can be described topologically in terms of modalities of stimulus and response. But each of these habitats must also be described in spatial and temporal terms as well, since all of them have dimension (heighth, width, depth) and all of them are experienced across time.

Spatially, these habitats may be visualized as being of three scales, microcosmic, mesocosmic and macrocosmic, nested one inside the other with interfaces between each. For the human body, the interface between micro- and meso-environments is delimited by the continuous, three-dimensional envelope of the epidermis. For architecture, the interface between meso- and macro-environments is delimited by the walls of the room or the walls of the building. Along both interfaces we commonly install artificial membranes to modulate the flow of forces across them — clothing along the body line, insulated walls along the building line.

Though they occupy the same space, however, the spatial characteristics of the habitat of the metabolic system are quite different from those of the perceptual systems. Only the actual thermo-atmospheric conditions along the body's surfaces play any role in the heat exchange across the epidermis. Only the air, water and food actually ingested through the mucous membranes of the body's cavities afford the fuel required for the whole metabolic process. Thus we can say that, though the habitat of metabolism has extension, it has no significant depth or thickness at all. Boundary, interface and habitat are one and the same. Heat, oxygen, water and food may exist in plenty around us, in either the meso-. or macro-environments. Our sensory scanning systems (sight, smell, hearing) may bring us information about their distribution in space. But they will have no significance for metabolic process until actual body contact with them is achieved. Moreover, *such a relationship between metabolism and its habitat exists independently of any perception of it.** (Thus, for example, the heat exchange across the epidermis will always critically affect the body's metabolic posture, even if for some reason — sleep, coma, anesthesia — the body's perceptual systems are unable at the time to perceive it.)

This dual nature of animal existence is the source of most of the fundamental paradoxes of architecture. In order for the building to be experientially satisfactory, it must afford a good "fit" for the body — the metabolic system and its habitat, on the one hand; the sensory/perceptual systems and their special habitats, on the other. These latter will have altogether different spatial characteristics, varying greatly in cross section: from microns (for the velvet we touch), to inches (for the rose we smell), to feet (for the painting we admire), to miles (for the church bells we hear or the distant view we admire), to interstellar space (for the stars we gaze at). Well-being, amenity, ultimately beauty itself, depend upon the architectural manipulation of all these environmental factors, with their varying scales and dimensions.

The boundaries of all architectural volumes are delimited by surfaces (floors, walls, ceilings) which constitute the second interface between man and the macrocosmic world of nature. These bounding surfaces play a decisive role in the way we respond to and behave in the spaces they enclose. Thus a wall may, at a given moment, be acting quite effectively to insulate us against the mechanical force and bitter cold of a winter gale. Together with the

---

* This proposition cannot, of course, be reversed — i.e., that perception can exist independently of its metabolic base. The metabolic process constitutes the platform of consciousness, as we have seen in Chapter 1.

heating system, the building may thus afford optimal thermo-atmospheric conditions for our metabolic well-being. But this same wall, at the same time, may have an inner surface whose color or brightness is an outrage to the eye or whose acoustical response is an insult to the ear. Similarly, a given room ("intimate" café, class-room) may be equipped with comfortable chairs and tables, prop-erly organized in spatial terms to support a successful luncheon meeting or seminar; but the same room may well have too low an illumination level, too high an ambient noise level or too poor a ventilation system (the "smoke-filled room") to permit satisfactory interpersonal communication. In short, the problem of a good fit between the occupant and the room extends from his skin right out to the walls and beyond, and implies the satisfactory manipula-tion of every habitat requirement simultaneously.

THE THREE DIMENSIONS OF "ENVIRONMENTAL FIT"

The design of any architectural component thus becomes a problem of successful adjustment between the organism and its environment — the buttocks and the chair seat; the eye and the lighting system; the student and the classroom; the pedestrian and the city street. In each case, we deal with a set of spatial parameters which describe the contours of the special vessel or container they require. How-ever, this vessel must be understood as not merely containing a given action but also as actually generating a specific mode of behavior (chair makes for sitting, light makes for reading, classroom makes for study, sidewalk makes for walking, etc.). Thus, as Raymond G. Studer has aptly expressed it:

The designed environment can be analyzed as a *prosthetic* phenomenon. It functions prosthetically in two distinct, but interrelated modes: 1) it is *physiologically* prosthetic in that it supports behavioral goals through maintenance of required (behaviorally correlated) physiological states, and 2) it is *behaviorally* prosthetic (Lindsley, 1964) in that it intention-ally configures specific behavioral topographies.[1]

The architectural fit, in order to support and/or elicit the desired behavior, must therefore be analyzed from several distinct but in-timately related points of view:

1. *ergonomics:* the study of the expenditure of physical energy required to occupy space and to overcome the gravity, friction and inertia implicit in all physiological work;

2. *anthropometrics:* the study of the spatial patterns which the body describes in the performance of work — walking, sitting, reaching, lifting, pulling, resting, sleeping, etc.;

3. *proxemics:* the study of the behavioral consequences of spatial relationships for interpersonal relationships of all scales and types.

Man has often been described — especially in the Puritan tradition — as being fundamentally a "lazy" animal. The term is pejorative, involving an ethical judgment on a simple fact — man's compelling need to husband his limited supplies of energy. There may indeed be such a thing as a "lazy man"; but there is no doubt at all that all animals, including man, are compelled by circumstances to expend large amounts of energy just to stay alive. Resisting the forces of gravity and inertia, of atmospheric pressure and environmental heat, is of itself stressful, as the Canadian physiologist Hans Selye has established. All animals develop characteristic modes of behavior in response to this circumstance. Thus cattle grazing on a hillside will follow the isoplethic contours so consistently that paths will be developed there. In just such fashion, college students will leave the formal patterns of paved walks to take diagonal shortcuts across the quadrangles. Cattle or college students, the trajectory of their movement represents a resolution of all the vectors of force acting upon them at that time. Some of these forces are exogenous (change of level, choice of sun or shade, mud or dry paving, etc.) and some are endogenous (late for an appointment, desire to be seen or not seen, etc.). Both sets of forces are equally "real," of course; and consciousness often compels men to take the less easy or more hazardous path (to jump into heavy seas to save a drowning child, to attack across an open field in battle, etc.).

Each trace or path represents the end result of a complicated process of cost accounting. It is largely an unconscious (or at least subconscious) process, in which we are continually weighing advantages against disadvantages, costs against possible returns, of this or that method of achieving our objectives. Exactly how this process is effectuated in human behavior is a complex and not fully understood question. All movement in space involves work, whether physiological or societal. (A two-hour set of tennis — "play" — may easily involve the output of as much energy as eight hours at a typewriter — "work.") Since movement is costly of energy, all animals have developed monitoring systems to aid in its conservation. In all higher animals, and above all in man, this is expressed in an extraordinary capability for orienting one's movements with reference to the outside world. It involves all the body's sensory perceptual systems but it clearly goes far beyond mere perception to include an ordered response. It gives the body the capacity to discriminate between movement and non-movement, or between its own movement and that of other bodies in the exterior world. Such capacity is critically important to survival — too important, as J. J. Gibson has put it, to be entrusted to any single set of sensory receptors.

There are many kinds of movement to be registered. There is articular kinestnesis for the body framework; vestibular kinesthesis for the movement of the skull; cutaneous kinesthesis for the movement of the skin relative to what it touches; and visual kinesthesis for perspective transformations of the field of view. In all these perceptions the sensory quality arising from the receptor type is difficult to detect but the information is perfectly clear. Kinesthesis is the registering of such information without being sensory; it is one of the best examples of detection without a special modality of sensation.[2]

The operation of these various forms of kinesthesis is quite apparent in the behavior of people in architectural or urbanistic space. Articular kinesthesis will be expressed in the way we sit in a chair or lie in a bed. If either is a bad fit, it will be expressed in the way we twist and squirm in an effort to find a more comfortable resolution. Vestibular kinesthesis determines our behavior on ramps and stairs. The spiral-ramped galleries of the Guggenheim Museum, for example, force a continuous disequilibrium on the visitor which stresses his vestibular apparatus. Cutaneous kinesthesis governs our response to surfaces — e.g., whether we follow the path or cut across the lawn will depend upon whether the grass is dry and resilient or wet and muddy. Visual kinesthesis enables us to anticipate, and hence to avoid, hazardous discontinuities in surface: it is at the base of our tendency to draw back from floor-to-ceiling glass walls in high-rise buildings. Of course, vision overrides all other forms of perception with its capacity for transmuting other forms of sensory input into visual data. Thus, it is thanks to visual kinesthesis that we can avoid mud without stepping in it; or steer clear of rough walls before we scrape an elbow on them; or avoid falls down unprotected changes in grade; or discriminate between soup and salad without having to taste either.

Every time the architect or urban designer erects a wall or paves a street, he intervenes in the behavioral modes of the population of that space. The consequences of his intervention may be major or minor, benign or malignant; they will always be real. Malfunction will be expressed in incidents or accidents among the population — in other words, *by their not behaving the way they were supposed to.* Conventionally, these are always blamed on the individual: he "wasn't looking where he was going"; he "slipped on the pavement"; he "stumbled on the stairs"; "tripped over the chair"; "got dizzy and fell out the window"; etc. But accident statistics alone are enough to suggest that this is a simplistic explanation of events, since different types of accidents are associated with specific sets of spatial configurations. It is true that the inner nature of accidents connected with buildings often seems inexplicable, because they involve movement. Careful research, especially time-lapse and slow-motion photography, is necessary to explicate even the simplest incident, since cause and effect are too entangled for the naked eye. But such research will usually reveal that despite the operation of articular, vestibular, cutaneous and visual kinesthesis, the user could not adapt his actions to the spatial set involved. In other words, the architectural element could neither support nor elicit the sequence of motions it was nominally designed to expedite (Fig. 55).

Hence the environmental designer must understand, far better than he presently does, what the consequences of his design decisions will be. To explore these fully will require the development of new concepts, new methods of measuring input-output factors, new means of resolving thousands of variables into comprehensible parameters for the designer. For, as Christopher Alexander has put it:

Today, more and more design problems are reaching insoluble levels of complexity. This is true not only of moon bases, factories and radio receivers, whose complexity is internal, but even of villages and teakettles . . . their background of needs and activities . . . is becoming too complex to grasp intuitively . . . The intuitive resolution of contemporary design problems simply lies beyond a single individual's integrative grasp.[3]

ERGONOMICS: THE COST ACCOUNTING OF
WORK AND FATIGUE

What, specifically, does the animal body require of architectural space? Not at all that it provide a controlled environment of absolutely uniform or unvarying qualities, as is so often assumed. To the contrary: the requirements of the animal body vary constantly as it goes about its various tasks. For optimal well-being, it requires equilibrium, dynamic balance between internal needs and external means of meeting them.

Although this is true for all environmental components, it is most easily demonstrated for the thermal since, as Winslow and Herrington have put it, "the whole life process is a form of slow combustion." The body is only about 20 per cent efficient in the conversion of fuel into work; it must therefore always dissipate a great deal of "waste" energy in the form of heat. And since it is very sensitive to its accumulation, this heat must be dissipated at the appropriate rate. The rate will vary with each level or type of activity — how widely is clear from Table 3.[4]

type of activity	calories per hour
sleeping	65
sitting, at rest	100
typing rapidly	140
walking (2.6 mph)	200
walking (3.7 mph)	300
stone working	400
swimming	500
walking up stairs	1100

Table 3. Effect of physical work on metabolism of men. Even under constant thermal conditions, heat production rises with increased activity.

It is obvious that we deal here with ratios, not fixed quantities: hence the building should be regarded as a flexible instrument for maintaining these ratios at levels established by the body. How important these ratios become not merely to human well-being and efficiency but ultimately to life itself may be seen from Table 4, showing the correlation between temperature, work and physical condition:[5]

effective temperature	*total work in foot-pounds*	*increase in rectal temp. degrees F per hour*	*increase in pulse rate beats per minute per hour*
70	225,000	0.1	7
80	209,000	0.3	11
90	153,000	1.2	31
100	67,000	4.0	103
110	37,000	8.5	237

Table 4. Effect of temperature on body processes. As temperature rises, body's ability to perform work begins to drop — moderately up to 80° effective temperature, rapidly thereafter. Such increasing stress is reflected in rising body temperatures. Pulse rates also soar as blood is rushed to body surfaces in effort to dissipate heat.

These illustrations, drawn from the relationship between the body and the thermal component of its environment, have analogies in other areas of existence. Thus we can be sure that any task involving critical acuity in seeing (classroom study, fine machine work, microsurgery) will require a luminous environment precisely structured to that end; and we can be certain that both work and worker will suffer if it is not so structured. Similarly any activity demanding critical discrimination in hearing or communication (concert listening, airport control, radio broadcasting) will require its own special sonic environment and will suffer qualitatively from the lack of it. The proper task of good architecture, in short, is to organize space and environment in which the eye, ear, tongue or hand can accomplish its task or activity — seeing, hearing, speaking, tasting, touching and lifting — with the greatest ease and precision, subject to the least interference or friction from extraneous factors.

But other factors, equally "real" but much harder to isolate and define, are also involved. "Work itself seldom leads to the chronic condition we call fatigue," says one researcher. "It is axiomatic that worry, not work, [is what] kills."[6] Moreover, there is growing evidence that the very process of living, quite apart from environment and work, produces measurable stress which leads in turn to measurable fatigue. Though it is only under laboratory conditions that we can observe man at rest and even partially isolated from external stimuli, it is clear that even here the body is still under stress — the heart and muscles resisting gravity and atmospheric pressure, etc. Hans Selye has gone so far as to try to isolate and measure such factors, giving them the status of a syndrome, "the stress of life."[7]

In this complicated field, the architect can never be more than one of many specialists, nor can his contribution ever be expected to solve it alone. But this is no justification for his abdicating responsibility. Indeed, by the very terms of his profession, he *cannot* abdicate, since his every act, whether ignorant or informed, constitutes an intervention in the field. Hence he must have a general comprehension of the problem and assume a measure of responsibility for its solution. Yet the contemporary architect displays a strange diffidence toward the whole subject. It is one of the paradoxes of American life that our architecture, like our technology generally, has always sought to lighten human toil and ameliorate the conditions of human life; but it has simultaneously distrusted both the labor-saving mechanisms whereby this was to be accomplished and the leisure time that was to be thereby won. The Puritan ethic links work with goodness, idleness with sin. Social Darwinists on the other hand (Puritans under the skin), equate survival with genetic superiority, economic stress with good muscle tone. Both thereby introduce extraneous elements (irrelevant if not fallacious) into an equation already sufficiently complex.

The Puritan's fears are, in the truest sense of the word, physiologically groundless: only in outer space will men ever confront a physical state so free of stimulus as to be degenerative. The task of architecture is not to "eliminate stress" or "abolish fatigue." It is rather to eliminate or at least minimize those environmental pressures which are peripheral, tangential or only accidentally associated with the task at hand. Then stress will be the by-product of productive work and fatigue will come from the accomplishment of human tasks and not from mere animal exertion. Good architecture, by this standard, would be that which permits man to *focus* his energies on whatever he is doing, whether running a lathe or listening to a concert, writing an essay or recovering from surgery. The ultimate criterion would be not lack of stress but optimal well-being under concrete conditions.

It is obvious that we deal here with complex equations in which variables of time and energy are involved. As a control instrument, the building should aim at a *qualitatively constant* set of environmental conditions, and not some merely quantitative uniformity of temperature, illumination, or ventilation. The criteria for this constancy can only be derived from the human body itself in action. It never asks for some abstract condition (72 degrees Fahrenheit, 50 per cent relative humidity, 10 foot-candles); it always demands instead that precise balance of forces dictated by the actual task.

As we have seen, a man at hard work has a metabolic rate some sixteen times as high as when he is asleep. The implications for the thermal environment of his place of work and his bedroom are obvious. Actually, for situations of protracted stress at the same task, it is likely that environmental conditions should be altered during the course of the work day. Much research is needed in this area but it is clear, in any case, that the criterion of building performance would be that it contribute fully to the maintenance of this dynamic equilibrium between man and his task.

Another and most important variant in this equation is the status of the individual himself — age, sex, health, emotional and intellectual attitudes. Just as the young man at rest has different thermal requirements from the young man at hard work, so a young man at hard work will have different needs from those of his father at the same task. In just such a fashion, women will have different reactions from men to the same task in the same set of environmental conditions. There are always idiosyncratic individuals whose requirements will vary from the norm. Their variations are real and cannot be ignored in the design of buildings involving them. But they should not obscure the fact that human response to heat, cold, glare, noise and stench are generally quite uniform. When plotted on a graph, all of us will lie on or quite near the general curve of humanity. The architect should accept this — as the physiologist and the psychologist do — as the basis, the point of departure, of his designs.

It goes without saying that the degree of precision of environmental control which will be required of a building will vary with its purpose. We demand a much lower order of performance from a bus shelter than from a bus terminal, from a circus tent than from an opera house, from a hospital waiting room than from the surgical theaters of that same hospital. The "margin for error" in architectural design is in inverse ratio to the criticalness of the process to be housed.

Most of what we know about fatigue comes from the factory. Yet research in the field has been complicated, in a sense, by the one-sided investigations of its external or objective aspects. This was perhaps the natural result of research largely subsidized by the manufacturers themselves as a means of increasing productivity. However important this approach may be, it is far from complete. For one of the most puzzling aspects of fatigue is its duality: it is at once objective and subjective, physiological and psychological. Thus, if we observe and measure it from the outside only, from the standpoint of management alone, we are ignoring the fact that the relationship between the two halves is not merely complex: it is dialectic.

It is obviously an entirely "natural" phenomenon, part of the basic physiological cycle of impairment and recovery in the living organism. But that, after all, is not saying much. More specific questions remain. Precisely how does fatigue affect production? How much fatigue can you endure this week without suffering later? How is it that modern building with all its labor-saving mechanization often seems to accelerate fatigue? What is the relation between types of fatigue and health? Although an analysis of the various types of fatigue may reveal a wide divergence in details, there is one fundamentally common factor: disturbance of the balance between wear and repair. We all get tired when we work. The longer we work, the more tired we grow; and the heavier the work, the less we can do of it. If overwork continues beyond a certain point, it begins to affect our health. The *temporary disturbance* between wear and repair becomes *permanent damage*. Where regular intervals of rest and recreation might have cured the first, long periods of medical or hospital treatment may be necessary to undo the latter:

The human nervous system, in common with the nervous systems of other animals, behaves as if it were a storehouse of potential energy. When its store becomes depleted symptoms of exhaustion make their appearance. In a person subjected to long-continued mental fatigue, recuperative processes do not have the opportunity fully to restore the nervous energy that has been utilized, so that the person is forced to rely on a special reserve store . . . which is intended to be used only for emergency.[8]

Nor do we all tire at the same rate. Joe seems to thrive on work that would kill Jim. Fatigue in one industry will differ sharply from that in another; while two offices doing exactly the same type of work will also vary widely as regards fatigue rates. Obviously many factors are involved in this problem and it would be an error to assume that the building and its equipment is any more important than half a dozen others. In the triangular relationship between the task, the organism and the environment, the building affords the "working conditions" under which work is done. A well-designed building will, unit for unit of work, cause less fatigue than a badly designed one. But the length of the work week, the rate at which work is performed, the character of the work itself are also of decisive importance, as are the health, morale, and adaptability of the worker himself.

Common sense should tell anybody — especially anybody who works for a living — that a 60-hour work week is detrimental to both the individual and society as a whole. Industrial experience amply confirms this: beyond given limits, increasing the length of the work week does not bring corresponding increases in production. Indeed, over a period of time, it results in a net drop. (A World War II report of the British Ministry of Labour cites an instance in which a group of men at heavy labor had their hours reduced from 66.7 to 56.5 hours: their total output increased by 22 per cent. The same report cites a machine which turned out 250 units per day when operated on three eight-hour shifts but only 192 units per day when operated on two twelve-hour shifts.)

Fatigue affects production in another important way: the quality of the product tends to deteriorate along with decreasing quantity. An excessively long week results in a sharp increase in "rejects" on the one hand, and in accidents on the other. Here an interesting psychological phenomenon is observed. Toward the end of the day, after a period of declining productivity, the worker gets a "second wind." From a mood of depression he will spiral into a sudden excess of exhilaration and confidence. He works rapidly again and, as it seems to him, accurately. Objectively, however, he is careless. His judgment of dimension and timing — essential in industrial operations — becomes noticeably impaired. Workmanship deteriorates rapidly. In one English factory, cited in the above report, accidents were two and a half times as frequent in a twelve-hour shift as in one of only ten hours.

The character of a specific job has a lot to do with fatigue. Modern serial or mass production involves careful analysis of the process, breaking it down into its component parts, organizing them in efficient sequence, and assigning specially trained men to each phase. The manufacturing process is thereby atomized. This often leads to a similar atomization of the worker's movements and mental processes, as Ruskin so shrewdly remarked a century ago. His job may require only a portion of a man's muscular and mental capacities: but it requires that portion all the time, and with sometimes horrifying monotony. Such routines skyrocket fatigue: they can actually cause psychological trauma, as Chaplin showed with such bitter wit in his movie *Modern Times*.

We are constantly reading in the newspapers of some new production method which "cuts in half the time formerly required" to make something — a house, a car, or a plane. Such advances do not necessarily imply a speed-up in the *rate* of work. (For example, a big riveted bomber had as many as 45,000 rivets, each of which took twenty seconds to drive or a total of 2500 man-hours. By changing the fabrication technique to automatic multiple welding, this time was reduced by approximately 30 per cent. Assuming that environmental conditions remain the same, none of these savings in time necessarily means that the men are more fatigued at day's end, even though production per man has been increased.)

It is intense rationalization *within* a given process which raises the danger of the "speed-up" or "stretch-out." Here the process itself is not altered. Instead, corners are cut, waste motions eliminated, men shifted, materials and tools rerouted. The time-and-motion expert studies each worker at his task, often by slow-motion photography. On the basis of such analysis, the expert can often show the worker a quicker and simpler sequence of motions which enables him to go through the same operation with a smaller expenditure of energy. Thus, if a given operation is redesigned so as to take 10 per cent less time and 10 per cent less energy, the worker can increase his output per hour by 10 per cent with no increase in fatigue. But if the savings in time outstrip the savings in effort, net fatigue will be increased unless the working day is proportionably shortened.

The simple and unadorned speed-up is the most obvious and most common technique of increasing the rate of work. Here neither time-and-motion experts nor labor-saving devices are employed. The work is simply piled on the workers and forced through at an accelerated rate. A high "norm" is established; the "best" workers hit the pace; and the rest have to keep up or else. This type of speed-up is, unfortunately, very common — especially among small, technically backward manufacturers attempting to meet the competition of the great streamlined monopolies. It has done much to prejudice the working public against work in mill and factory.

Of course, many of these issues are being made obsolete by the rise of the new technology of mechanization, automation and computerization. It is significant that, in the last decade, there has been a steady decline in the literature dealing with fatigue, labor-savings, time-and-motion studies, etc.; and a complementary rise in that dealing with cybernetics, computers, feedback, etc. Processes which once were studied by the experts either to save the energy of the worker or to increase his productivity (the two are by no means the same, as we have seen) have been leapfrogged. Now the process is automated and computerized and the worker is either reduced to a minor role in production or eliminated altogether.

None of this, of course, is an argument against the historical necessity of modern electronic technology. For the first time in human history it is possible for us to contemplate freeing workers everywhere from noisome, dangerous or exhausting labor. (It also raises, for the capitalist countries, the specter of a large and permanently unemployed body of labor.)

However, though this may be a perfectly valid line of development for many linear industrial processes, it has little direct application to many complex, nonlinear activities which are little subject, or not subject at all, to such forms of rationalization. Theaters, schools, hospitals, libraries, courtrooms and residential types of all sorts require a wide range of furniture, equipment and tools to facilitate their respective processes. All of this could stand vase improvement in terms of both design and manufacture. But the interface between the worker and his task (housewife — housework, teacher — teaching, actor — acting, student — study, etc.) requires the closest and most sophisticated scrutiny if efficiency, amenity and safety are to be improved. Unfortunately, both the scope and quality of research in areas such as these seem actually to have deteriorated. In fact, the neglect of problems of fatigue in industry has been reflected in a comparable neglect of functional problems in the design of consumer furniture and equipment.

ANTHROPOMETRY: SPATIAL MENSURATION OF MOVEMENT

Just as, in everyday experience, we equate intellectual comprehension with the sense of sight (I *see* what you mean), so emotional response is equated with the sense of touch (He has no *feeling* for the needs of others). This is no mere accident of language but describes rather a fundamental distinction. In many ways, the sense of touch is the most vivid capacity which the individual has for interaction with the world immediately outside his own body. It not only plays a central role in the satisfaction of sensual appetites (e.g., the sexual act); it is also the source of absolutely indispensable factual information about the qualities of the spatial environment. For the shape, size, texture, density and temperature of surrounding surfaces is perceived first of all by that marvelously complex system of nerve endings in the skin and muscles which furnish us with tactile, haptic and kinesthetic sensation.

Thus, our knowledge of the special properties of a material like marble derives largely from our tactile-haptic exploration of it. We learn its cold smoothness from stroking it; its hardness from sitting on it; its density and weight from trying to lift it. Only its color and pattern are visually perceived at this initial stage of exploration and discovery. After a quite limited experience with marble, we are able to transmute this tactile information into visual terms. We say: "It *looks* like marble to me"; we forget that the blind man would, each time, have to stroke it, punch it, lift it before he could safely conclude it was marble.

The capacity of vision to metamorphose other sorts of sensory data — data which are not primarily or even not at all visually derived — is vision's most splendid characteristic. It is a great time-and-energy-saving mechanism, especially in the design fields. It enables us to retrieve quickly from memory that particular combination of sense-perceptible properties which goes to make up "marble." It enables us to say: "I don't need to see a sample — I remember quite clearly what it looks like."

Nevertheless, this same syncretic power of vision has inherent dangers for all designers, and most of all for architects. For in real life vision is only one channel of perception among many and often of no greater importance than others. Many architectural problems involve the manipulation of phenomena which are literally invisible (e.g., poisonous gases, high noise levels, high temperatures). Many environmental hazards are not perceptible by any sensory means (e.g., carbon monoxide, a structural member just before collapse). But neither working drawings of the proposed building nor photographs of the finished one give any visual information about the possible existence of such factors or their relative seriousness. Because they are hard to visualize, many such problems are given low priority in relation to those which are easily visible. In short, the architect has a built-in bias in favor of the visually perceived; and it must be rigorously examined if his buildings are to be authentically successful. Nowhere is this more true than in the habitat of touch.

The sense of touch has a more complex perceptual capacity than those other scanning senses of vision or hearing, depending as it does upon several types of neural sensors in the skin and muscles.* These sensors, working in various combinations, bring us an astonishing range of information on the properties of the surfaces around us.

tactile information	smooth — rough
	blunt — sharp
	wet — dry
pressure information	hard — soft
	elastic — plastic
	pressure — suction
spatio-tactile information	shape
	volume
	dimension
	size
haptic-muscular information	weight and mass
thermal information	hot — cold ("pregnant center point")

Table 5. Types of information transmitted by tactile perception. Specialized sensors in skin, joints and muscles collaborate to pick up and transmit to brain a wide range of critically important data on states and properties of the objects and enclosing surfaces with which terrestrial space is furnished, subdivided and defined.

As in the case of other systems of sensory perception, that of touch can thus be described as occupying its own habitat. It is bounded by a lower threshold of perception (too little stimulation to be perceived) and an upper one of pain (too much to be endured) and centered by some "golden" zone of satisfaction. The analogy is only approximate, however, as the properties of matter explored by this sense are not strictly comparable with the others. For the thermal sensors, the habitat would extend upward (to intolerably hot) and downward (to intolerably cold) from a neutral centerpoint, the temperature of the body itself. For the pressure sensors, the limits would lie between the gentlest perceptible air movement and the crushing blow; or between the touch of velvet and the prick of a needle. Many other properties would produce tactile sensation without stress: a hard or a wet object is not, of itself, more stressful to handle than a soft or a dry one.

* Exactly how many types is still a matter of disagreement among neurologists and psychologists themselves. For example, it appears that some parts of the cutaneous system may be better for sizing of a stimulus than others, which serve as warning areas for eliciting visual attention or reflexive action. Cf. *The Skin Senses*, D. R. Kenshalo, ed. (Springfield, Ill.: Thomas, 1966).

Thus, in general terms, we can describe the topography of the habitat of touch. It has upper and lower limits of stress or lack of stimulation; and some central zone of optimal stimulation. But here again, the limiting factor is that of movement and change in position along time. To discriminate between velvet and paper, it is not enough merely to touch; one must also stroke. Any tactile-haptic experience, no matter how pleasurable initially, will cease to be satisfying if extended beyond its own built-in limits. Indeed, it will tend to cease to be perceptible at all. Here, as everywhere in the domain of the senses, change and variety is essential to perception itself.

An understanding of these tactile-haptic phenomena should be an integral part of the designer's expertise. For the boundaries of architectural and urbanistic spaces consist of surfaces — man-made or man-modified — which, by their very presence, affect tactile-haptic sensation in important (and often in unanticipated or ambiguous) ways. Much of the reason for success or failure of any space lies in the impact of its bounding surfaces. We have already seen how our behavior is affected by the way in which a wall reflects light or heat or sound; analogous relationships between us and the wall exist in the field of tactile-haptic stimulation and response. Surfaces which appear smooth, polished or velvety to the eye will often lead us to stroke them, as if to confirm the tactile pleasure they promise. Very rough surfaces, on the other hand, cause us to shy away from them, irrespective of how handsome they may be in purely formal (i.e., visual) terms.*

The tactile-haptic properties of floors and pavements have a similarly powerful influence upon the behavior of the people who traverse them. We have already discussed the effect of gross changes in level or direction: the effect of such surface characteristics as texture, resilience, cleanliness, wetness/dryness is equally profound. Highly polished pavements (marble, terrazzo, faience tile) may be handsome visually and pleasurable emotionally because of their connota-

---

* Thus, the corrugated, bush-hammered concrete walls of such recent buildings as the School of Architecture at Yale University are very handsome indeed *when experienced from a safe distance.* But their rough texture is too obviously hostile to the human epidermis to make a person feel safe at close quarters. The natural tendency of persons moving along them is to maintain a safety zone of empty air between the wall and themselves.

tion of wealth, ceremony, urbanity. But they *look* slippery and often *are* slippery; a duller matte finish would not only look safer, but from this point of view would actually be safer. Contrariwise, rough-textured pavements of gravel or cobblestones are so uncomfortable to walk on — and for women in high-heeled shoes so dangerous — that they must be considered as non-walkable, "anti-pedestrian" surfaces.

Resilience is another critical factor in paving materials, especially in buildings like museums and art galleries, where the preambulating picture-viewer is subject to unusual skeleto-muscular stress. In such situations, marble or terrazzo flooring materials would be least desirable from an ergonomic point of view (even though, for formal reasons, they are very commonly used). Cork or plastic would be better than lithic materials; carpeting on wood flooring installed on wood sleepers would perhaps be best of all. An inevitable experiential aspect of all these flooring materials is their acoustical behavior: since silence is a requirement in museums, galleries and libraries, the absorptive capacity of carpeting makes it a suitable material. The feeling of "hushed luxury" of carpeted spaces is thus as much an acoustical as a tactile-haptic phenomenon.

The exact way in which pedestrians behave on floors and pavements is subject to a number of environmental variables. Indoors, these are subject to very precise manipulation — light, heating, air movement, humidity, noise, etc. But out-of-doors, a host of climatic variables affects the comfort, usability and safety — and hence the patterns of use — of the pavement. While predictable, these variables are only predictable in gross terms — e.g., monthly precipitation, sun and shadow patterns, average wind directions and velocities, mean temperatures, etc. The maintenance of amenity in outdoor spaces is therefore very complex, involving dozens of meteorological phenomena varying in intensity with time and space. The successful manipulation of these phenomena constitutes one of the most challenging and least explored aspects of landscape design. Perhaps because of its very complexity, the problem is evaded: instead of designing outdoor spaces to meet at least the gross impact of the seasons, architects conceive of them as though for some ideal Platonic climate. It is always sunny and summer: there is no rain or snow, no dust or mud; no extremes of heat or cold; no wind; no cloudy days or stormy nights; no noise or fumes from the automobile traffic which is built into the design.

Fig. 55. Analysis of behavior-eliciting properties of stairs of varying proportions: kinesthetic research project by James Marston Fitch and José Bernardo. In an effort to isolate comfort and safety factors in different stairs, four actual stairways were replicated. Male and female models, ascending and descending, were photographed in time exposures under strobe light (below) and normal light (center and bottom). Photographs reveal that "easy" stairs (below) have a spatial configuration which imposes awkward gaits upon both male and female users.

Fig. 55a. Wide tread (25 in.) and very low riser (3.375 in.) impose culturally unfamiliar and kinesthetically awkward gait upon all users. Too wide for one normal male step (below) and too narrow for two female steps (center), stairs elicit erratic movement, especially in descent. Note irregular gait and arm swing.

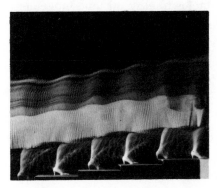

Fig. 55b. Steeper stairs (6-in. riser, 15-in. tread) elicit more-regular gait from female user in both ascent and descent (bottom). Males can adjust by shifting horizontal trajectory. Ascent is more comfortable despite greater energy expenditure.

This tendency to regard outdoor spaces as purely esthetic constructs, voids empty of microclimatic reality, is nowhere more apparent than in the big urban plazas which are increasingly a feature of urban redevelopment. This conceptual error is obvious not only from their malfunction in real life. It is also revealed in the architect's presentation drawings and models, which always subsume optimal climatic conditions. Obviously, it would be difficult for the sketch and impossible for the model to replicate a snowstorm or downpour, a cold wind or a blistering sun. There is nothing wrong with *presenting* the project under ideal conditions; the error lies in *conceiving* it as though such conditions were typical.

In experiential reality, there is no spot within the continental U.S.A. in which some or all of these meteorological factors will not, for some part of the year, combine to render these handsome and costly plazas literally uninhabitable. They thus fail in their central pretension — that of eliminating gross differences between architectural and urbanistic spaces, of extending in time the areas in which urban life can freely flow back and forth between the two. For much of the country and for part of the year, rain, sleet, snow and/or ice will be the principal obstacles to easy, urbane movement across these plazas: under any combination of them, they become unpretty, unpleasant or unsafe. Soiled snow accumulates; improvised pathways, alternately icy or water-logged and bearing little relation to the formal patterns of the plaza, are plowed or shoveled out. Trash becomes embedded in the snow and accumulates in the empty fountains. There is, in short, a great decline in overall amenity in bad weather; and the behavior the plaza elicits from its pedestrians reflects this fact (Fig. 56, Fig. 57).

Yet technically it is entirely possible to minimize or eliminate many of these phenomena at the microclimatic level. Scale models could be tested for aerodynamic behavior; cumulative shade patterns for cold-weather months could be simulated; and the whole complex adjusted to minimize winds and shading, maximize exposure to sun. Drainage patterns could be correlated to snowplow paths, areas allocated for mounding surplus snow. Snow melters embedded in paved surfaces would obviously be optimal. Since many of these

Fig. 56. University of Illinois, Chicago, Ill. Skidmore, Owings and Merrill, architects. Designed and built as a unit, this visually striking new campus is fundamentally a "fair weather" construct. In winter (intense cold, high winds, heavy snow cover) it fails as a life-support system, becoming unpretty, uncomfortable and unsafe.

Fig. 57. City Hall and plaza, Boston, Mass. Kallmann, McKinnel and Knowles, architects. Highly photogenic, the red-brick-paved square offers pleasant environment for strollers on an early spring afternoon. But shadeless paving produces high midsummer temperatures: numerous steps prevent effective snow removal in winter.

plazas are actually the roofs of underground areas, heat loss through the roof slab could be accelerated enough to melt the snow automatically, either by reducing thermal insulation or by employing radiant heating panels in the ceiling. In climates without snow or ice but with heavy rainfall (e.g., Florida, Gulf Coast, Puget Sound) the main problem becomes one of effective shelter along the lines of high pedestrian traffic.

The problem of year-round viability in open urban spaces has its obverse side — protection from excessive insolation, with the resulting heat and glare, during hot-weather months. As we shall see in Chapter 9, all pavements tend to be much hotter than the natural surfaces they replace, because of their heat-absorbing and heat-holding characteristics. Unless adequately shaded and ventilated, they will create desert-like microclimates, often with astonishing extremes of heat or glare. Thus, the urban plaza must be analyzed just as carefully for summertime amenity. Plant material of all sorts — trees, vines, lawns — are more desirable shade makers than architectural constructions, since they maintain low surface temperatures, converting much of the solar energy which falls upon them into other forms of energy. Whatever the devices employed, however, hot-weather viability implies reduction of ambient heat and light.

It is in the highest degree ironic that contemporary design has abandoned so many of those architectural and urbanistic devices which gave beauty *and* amenity to earlier cities (Fig. 58). The covered sidewalk, the loggia and arcade, the courtyard and gallery — all aimed at facilitating movement through urban space by modifying the impact of environmental forces upon it. The time is overdue for an objective analysis of all such features, on a functional and not a formalistic basis.

PROXEMICS: SOCIAL CONSEQUENCES OF
HUMAN DEPLOYMENT IN SPACE

The senses of vision, touch and hearing bring us vital information about the objects which furnish, and the surfaces which enclose, terrestrial space. These sense data are so important, in fact, that we are apt to think of them as being the exclusive source of information as to where, at any given moment, we "are." But the neural sensors embedded in our joints and muscles give us an altogether different type of spatial information — i.e., our kinesthetic-proprioceptive orientation in space itself. These sensors afford us a marvelous control both of our overall posture with reference to gravity and also the disposition of our various bodily members in relation to each other at any given moment. This kinesthetic-proprioceptive capacity is what makes bodily movement possible in higher organisms. But it does not explain, except in purely mechanical terms, why and how we move as social beings.

Any movement in space requires an outlay of energy and we have an easily understandable tendency to conserve it. However, this energy cost is only one factor in the complex equation of our physical movement in space. The actual pattern or trajectory which we trace in any given action must be viewed as the resolution of a whole system of vectors of force acting upon us, the algebraic sum of which determines that pattern or trajectory. Some of these forces are subjective, or internally generated, and some are objective:

Fig. 58. Piazza San Marco, Venice. In this classic example of the Italian town square, formal and functional requirements are resolved to make an admirable fit with a difficult climate. Unbroken indoor-outdoor pavement plane facilitates year-round pedestrian movement. Perimetric loggias provide shelter from hot summer sun, heavy winter rains.

Psychological — the motivation of the individual, his incentive to accomplish the action in question;

Physiological — the physical condition of the individual with reference to the energy required for the action;

Sociocultural — the type of behavior which the space is designed to elicit (playing field, work place, place of study or worship, etc.);

Microclimatic — the actual environmental conditions obtaining on the site (rain or snow, sun or shade, temperature, wind, etc.);

Topographic — the contours, textures and shape of the surface on which the action transpires.

The relative value of these various kinds of force, all of them simultaneously acting upon the individual, will vary with the circumstances actually obtaining. Thus a man in a desperate hurry will cut across a muddy field or run up a steep flight of stairs which a casual stroller would circumnavigate or reject. Social convention forbids the male to use the women's toilet, no matter how great the physiological pressure, just as it requires him to walk slowly and quietly in churches, libraries and museums. A bargain sale or an accident may pull pedestrians to the sunny side of a street, which otherwise would be deserted because of heat and glare.

The precise fashion in which architectural and urbanistic space is to be organized, and the way in which furnishings and equipment are deployed within it, should be determined by a clear understanding of vectors of force described above. Unfortunately, architects and planners have had to rely upon a quite primitive theoretical approach to these complexities and a quite eclectic methodology for handling them. Now help is coming into sight from unexpected quarters. Ecologists, ethologists and behavioral psychologists have increasingly turned their attention to the study of animal behavior in its wild or natural condition. The result has been a startling increase in our understanding of the impact of spatial organization ("territoriality") upon animal societies. Lessons learned here have obvious applications for an analogous approach to the more complex problem of human communities.

The behavior-eliciting function of architectural space is being explored by many investigators, from many disciplines and from

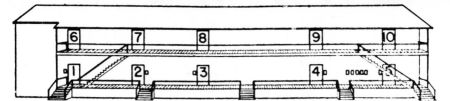

Fig. 59a. Diagram of married-student housing where friendships were studied.

(1)	(2)	(3)	(4)
Units of approximate physical distance	Total number of choices given	Total number of possible choices	Choices given (2) / Possible choices (3)
S	14	2×34	.206
1S	39	6×34	.191
2S	20	8×34	.074
3S	14	7×34	.059
4S	4	2×34	.059

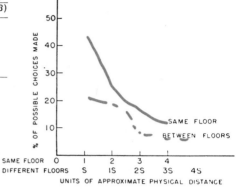

Fig. 59b. Spatial ecology of group formation. Leon Festinger, Stanley Schacter and Kurt Back made a study of the impact of physical distance on friendship formation in the context of fluid university populations. Statistical chance of friendship based on casual meeting (above) drops sharply with horizontal distance and even more abruptly with vertical separation (right).

many points of view.* For example, one group of experimental psychologists has studied the effects of spatial organization of certain housing projects upon interpersonal relationships which developed among the inhabitants.[9] The psychologists established a dramatic distinction between what they call physical and functional distance. In the projects under study, they found that two apartment houses might be only thirty feet apart (*physical* distance); but if their entrances faced in opposite directions and gave out onto different streets, the chance of interaction (and hence of friendship) between the tenants of the two houses was as radically reduced as if thousands of feet intervened. The *functional* distance may be the equivalent of miles (Fig. 59).

Such investigations should have a sobering effect upon the architect, indicating as they do the sociocultural consequences of *all* his spatial sets, large or small. He cannot erect a wall or enclose a room or pave a path without affecting some of those vectors of force which play a role in modifying the behavior of the occupants of his

* The literature, especially in periodical form, is vast and increasing. No brief summary is possible. Even bibliographies become quickly obsolete. A recent collection of papers of special significance to architects and planners is *Environmental Psychology: Man and His Physical Setting*, edited by Harold M. Proshansky, William H. Ittelson and Leanne G. Rivlin (New York: Holt, Rinehart and Winston, 1970).

space. But there are subjective forces here too — internally generated forces over which he has little or no control. These he can only
try to understand and respect. The anthropologist Edward Hall has
explored this aspect of human behavior.[10] Hall attempts to quantify
the spatial dimensions of various levels of human interaction. He
visualizes each individual as centered in a concentric series of "balloons" or "bubbles" of private space, a sort of territorial extension of
his own body in which he moves through space. These concentric
spheres represent optimal distances for a hierarchy of interpersonal
relationships: *intimate,* up to 1½ feet; *personal,* 1½ to 4 feet; *social-
consultive,* 4 to 10 feet; *public,* 10 to 30 feet and beyond (Fig. 60).
Any violation of these optima by other individuals will, according to
Hall, be reflected by a stress upon that relationship.

The scale of this hierarchy is partly a mere quantification of our
powers of perception — how well we can hear the words of the
actor, how clearly we can see the face of a friend, whether or not
we can touch the person we love. But the governing factor is not
only one of acuity of perception. We want contact with the actor,
the friend, the lover: but we do not want to be as close to the actor
as to the friend, nor as close to the friend as to the lover. (The
reverse is also true, of course: the lover wants to be closer than the
friend, the friend than the actor, and so on.) Even these spaces are
not absolute, according to Hall: they will vary somewhat with
culture, each society establishing its own norms. Thus male friends
in the Middle East will want to be able to touch each other while
in England such close contiguity would be considered distasteful.
In just such a fashion body odors might be considered attractive in
one cultural milieu (e.g., Elizabethan England) while in another
they would be a social liability (e.g., contemporary U.S.A.).

Technology, too, has made it possible to modulate some of these
spatial balloons. The telephone permits verbal contact between
lovers across miles of space. The footlight and spotlight extend the
radius within which we can clearly see the actor's facial expression,
just as the microphone has extended the distance across which we
can hear the political speaker. And the air-conditioned, floodlighted
arena has extended in time and in space the number of people who

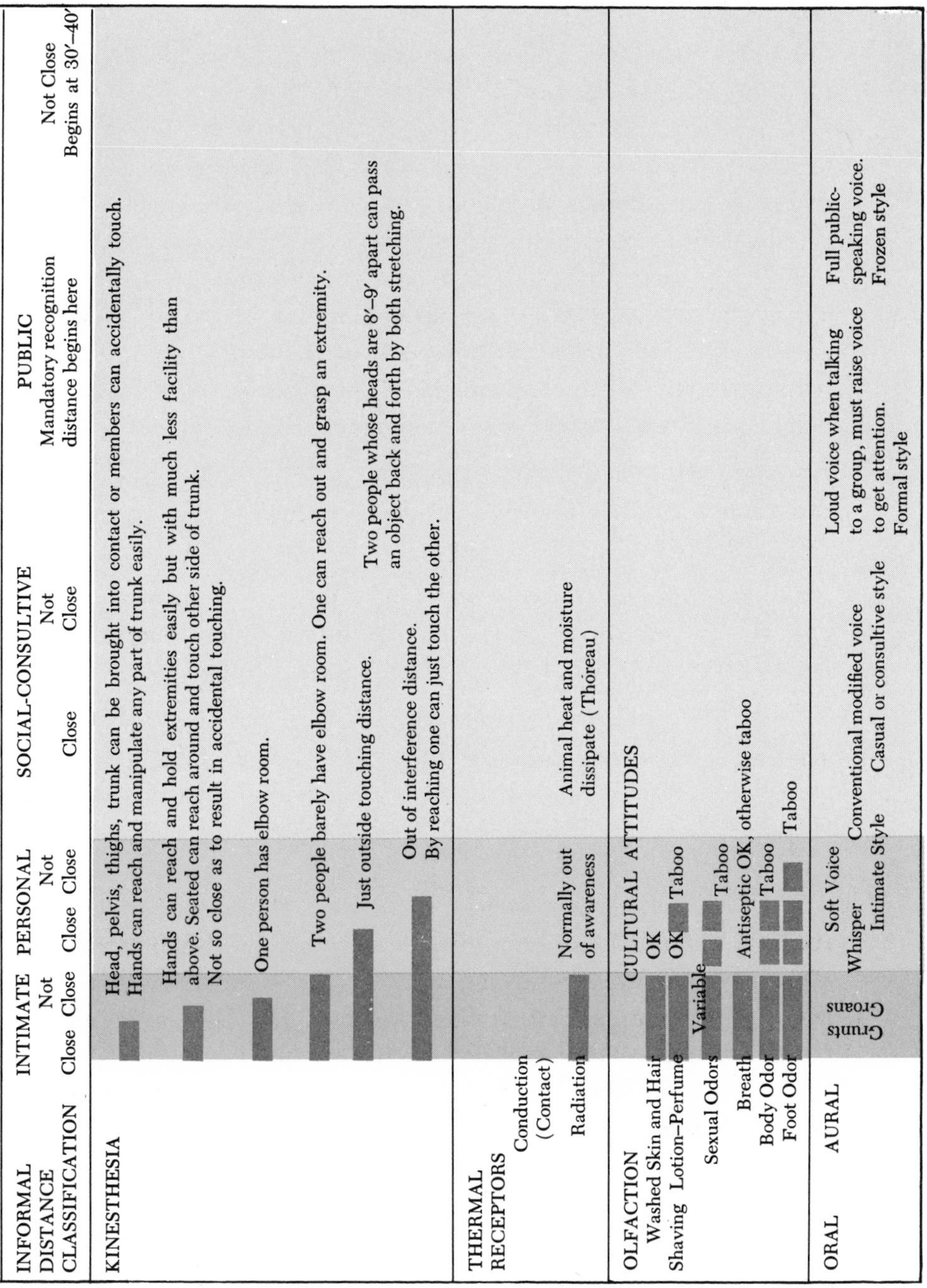

INFORMAL DISTANCE CLASSIFICATION

FEET	0 1 2 3 4 5 6 7 8 10 12 14 16 18 20 22 30
	INTIMATE — Not Close / Close **PERSONAL** — Not Close / Close **SOCIAL-CONSULTIVE** — Close / Not Close **PUBLIC** — Mandatory recognition distance begins here **Not Close** — Begins at 30'–40'

KINESTHESIA

Head, pelvis, thighs, trunk can be brought into contact or members can accidentally touch. Hands can reach and manipulate any part of trunk easily.

Hands can reach and hold extremities easily but with much less facility than above. Seated can reach around and touch other side of trunk. Not so close as to result in accidental touching.

One person has elbow room.

Two people barely have elbow room. One can reach out and grasp an extremity.

Just outside touching distance.

Two people whose heads are 8'–9' apart can pass an object back and forth by both stretching.

Out of interference distance.

By reaching one can just touch the other.

THERMAL RECEPTORS

Conduction (Contact)

Radiation — Normally out of awareness   Animal heat and moisture dissipate (Thoreau)

OLFACTION — CULTURAL ATTITUDES

Washed Skin and Hair	OK
Shaving Lotion–Perfume	OK Taboo
Sexual Odors	Variable Taboo
Breath	Antiseptic OK, otherwise taboo
Body Odor	Taboo
Foot Odor	Taboo

ORAL   **AURAL**

Grunts   Groans

Soft Voice   Whisper   Intimate Style

Conventional modified voice   Casual or consultive style

Loud voice when talking to a group, must raise voice to get attention. Formal style

Full public-speaking voice. Frozen style

Fig. 60. Impact of distance on proxemic perception as formulated by Edwin T. Hall. There is a striking correlation between interpersonal relationships and their physical deployment in space. For each type of relationship there are spatial parameters violation of which will negatively affect the quality of the relationship itself.

can follow the hockey game or volleyball game within acceptable limits of perceptual acuity.*

The express purpose of many types of architectural spaces (classrooms, offices, stores, workshops) is to expedite or facilitate interactions, contact or communication between certain groups of people engaged in certain types of activity. But privacy and isolation are desiderata in other types of spaces (bedrooms, toilets, libraries). In an interesting study of how university students actually use library reading rooms, significantly called "The Ecology of Privacy," the behavioral psychologist Robert Sommer reports that:

Of those students who entered the room alone, 64% sat alone, 26% sat diagonally across from another student, while only 10% sat directly opposite or beside another student.[11]

He found that chairs at the end of the table were invariably most popular because this automatically gave the student one protected flank. Moreover, elaborate stratagems were employed to reinforce this privacy:

The seats alongside a person or directly across from him were rarely occupied except at times of high density. Individual readers marked out territories in various ways, using personal belongings (books, purses, coats, etc.) and positioning their own chair.[12]

At the same time, the students did not want absolute isolation while reading. Some felt more comfortable near people, although avoiding direct eye contact. Most of the reported distractions, however, came from human sources rather than deficiencies in the environmental control systems — illumination, ventilation, heating, etc.

The Sommers study indicated a number of fairly simple measures aimed at ensuring the privacy which students require in library work, suggesting that attention to size, design and arrangement of library reading tables would go a long way toward meeting these requirements.

---

* But as we have seen, especially in Chapters 5 and 6, these attenuated spatial relationships will be reflected in an analogous diminution in the experiential potency of the contact. No phone conversation can replace the face-to-face talk; no musical form can be amplified without distortion; no cinematic facsimile is a full surrogate for the multi-sensory reality of the live theater.

Partitions between reading areas at a table [should] insure that no more than, for example, six individuals occupy one side of a table. These barriers [should] permit two people to sit side by side at very close distances without physical contact. By permitting greater physical closeness without psychological discomfort, barriers increase the upper limit of comfortable room density. Such barriers need not be ponderous or weighty objects. A small raised strip down the center of the table can effectively serve as a barrier and increase feelings of privacy by defining individual territories . . . it can serve as a resting place for the reader's eyes when he looks away from his books. These "study breaks" are major sources of accidental intrusion.[13]

Of course, the design and arrangement of furniture in a room can be used to bring people together as well as to separate them. In a now famous study of the behavior of patients in mental institutions, Dr. Humphry Osmond found that certain seating arrangements in the day rooms tended to "bring people together" (*sociopetal*) and others that tended to "keep them apart" (*sociofugal*). In spaces where interaction and communication were themselves therapeutic, Osmond urged the use of sociopetal designs.[14]

One factor which is of great significance for architecture and urbanism emerges from these studies of spatial and territorial behavior. *For each type of social activity or process, there are upper, lower and optimal limits of size and density appropriate to that activity.* This is partly purely quantitative, though it assumes qualitative aspects. As Osmond says:

Among ten people there are 45 possible two-person relationships; among fifty people there are 1225 possible relationships. The complexity of society has gone up by a factor of 27 at least.[15]

Four persons are required for a game of bridge, no more, no less: easy access to and recognition of the cards dictates a table no more than 42 inches across; tables should be at least 8 feet apart; but there is apparently no optimal number of tables. A regional shopping center also has a minimal (and almost certainly, a maximal) size and requires for its economic existence 50,000 people within a radius of 20 miles. In urbanistic terms, there is clearly a "critical mass" below which that form of social invention and innovation which characterizes the city simply cannot occur. A village of 1000 souls can neither produce nor support a symphony orchestra or a repertory theater. And yet, it is also clear that this state of "critical mass" creates only the preconditions, the sociocultural climate for social creativity: it is, by itself, no *guarantee* of it. Neither Periclean Athens nor Medicean Florence was as large as Chattanooga, Tennessee. Parameters of size appear to be relative, not absolute. Optima seem to vary with culture and especially with technology.

Optimal levels of density, on the other hand, appear to be relatively fixed, regardless of the size of the city. These density optima are functions of the physical limits of pedestrian range and personal contact. Such density factors have a decisive effect on the *quality* of life afforded by the city. The catastrophic drop in the effectiveness of American cities is due to, among other things, the fact that density has dropped in inverse proportion to rising size. One of the major factors here is technology — specifically, mechanized transportation by rail and, most recently, by private automobile. The sheer *presence* of large numbers of autos, in urban spaces which were calibrated to pedestrian speed and reach, has a negative impact on pedestrian behavior. The climate of social intercourse is at once diluted and polluted by the presence of these foreign bodies; the number, ease and frequency of face-to-face contacts is diminished; the sites of such contacts are more thinly dispersed in space; the minimal critical density necessary for self-propagating social intercourse is not achieved.

REDESIGN OF THE TOOLS FOR A BETTER FIT

The building, of course, can only establish the general environmental conditions in which space, time and gravity can be manipulated to expedite a given social process. The building affords the preconditions under which that process can occur (classroom for study, operating theater for surgery); but a range of furnishings and equipment are required to make it actually possible (desks, chairs and blackboards; operating table, surgical instruments, oxygen tanks). A century ago, a few desks, stools and ledgers were all that was required for bookkeeping: nowadays, the volume, complexity and speed of modern accounting demands a wide range of furnishings — desks, chairs, tables, filing cabinets and shelving — and electronic equipment for typing, dictating, recording, reproducing and computing. For all their superficial dissimilarity, these must all be regarded as tools for manipulating space, time and gravity in favor of the work; links in a chain for reducing the time and/or energy required to complete a given unit of work.

In view of this fundamental similarity of function, the disparity in design between these components is startling. The criteria which govern the design and fabrication of what is usually called "furniture" (e.g., the typist's chair) and those which operate in "equipment" (e.g., the dictaphone or electric typewriter) are light-years apart. It is obvious that the behavior of an electrical impulse in a circuit now seems simple in contrast to the problem of the fit between the human buttocks and the chair seat. But the point to be made here is that the behavior of electricity seemed equally obscure until scientific criteria were applied to the study of electrical phenomena. Precisely because it is incomparably more complex than electrical circuitry, the design of the typist's chair implies the highest levels of scientific theory and technological method.

Aerospace medicine is currently deeply involved in the investigation of the "weightless state" of man in space. Whatever the consequences for the colonization of extraterrestrial space, such investigations have profound implications for the weighted state of man on earth, for they mark the first systematic attempt to formulate a holistic concept of the optimal fit between man and his tools and equipment. As one recent researcher has put it:

The human body can be thought of as a structure composed of several masses, each with its separate weight and center of gravity, linked together by a system of joints, and held in balance with the help of muscles and ligaments. The motions of the various systems of linkages are extremely flexible and the end members or masses — i.e., the hands and feet — may assume a wide range of positions. When the body interacts with external objects (such as a tool), the system of linkages becomes increasingly complex.[16]

Just how complex these interactions are, in even a simple action, becomes clear if the action is carefully analyzed. Thus

... when a seated person operates a foot pedal, the closed chain (of the action) involves the shoe sole, the soft tissue of the foot, the foot and limb links, the pelvis, the non-rigid buttock tissues (and) the chair seat, the floor and the pedal.[17]

All furniture is, in the last analysis, a tool for intervening in this situation, for relieving the stresses of gravity on one or another of these linkages. In even such activity as resting — e.g., sitting or lying down — a number of variables are involved. If a chair were only a problem in anthropometry, for example, design would involve only adjusting all its dimensions to those of the sitter's anatomy. But physiological and physical factors are also involved. The exact degree of resistance or resiliency of the seat in response to the pressure of the buttocks will vary with material (marble or feathers, coil springs or leather straps). Ease of movement when seated will vary both with the friction between the sitter's clothing and upholstery (velvet is difficult to slide across, leather very easy) and with the shape of the seat. Thus the popular sling or hammock chairs of the 1950s tended to concentrate the body's weight in such a way as to make any change in position difficult.

Another ergonomic aspect of seating is the thermal response of the chair to the sitter. As we saw in Chapter 3, the human body must dissipate about four-fifths of its heat to its environment: and a large portion of its heat-exchange surfaces are in the thighs and buttocks. Chairs upholstered in conventional fabrics will slow down this rate of dissipation and are thus often uncomfortably warm. Many of the new molded plastic chairs are made of materials which act as radiant reflectors which reflect body heat back onto thighs and buttocks: the result is a "hot seat" in actual fact.

Today, there are many types of specialized seating situations which simply cannot be satisfied by "intuitional" design: posture seating for airline pilots and bus drivers; theater seating where, in addition to normal requirements for postural comfort, the acoustical response of the chair should be identical whether occupied or empty; or operating chairs for the dentist, where comfort requirements of the patient must be balanced against muscular-skeletal strain on the dentist. It is significant that only in such specialized areas as the above, where quantifiable and discrete actions occur, do we find any effort to solve the problem of optimal fit. Though contemporary chairs often boast of a "new look" or of employing "miracle" methods and materials, their design remains fundamentally idiosyncratic and their performance consistently poor.

Much the same situation obtains throughout the furniture field — in beds and bedding, for example. Current research into sleep and sleeping has served to discredit many old theories. One of the most widespread misconceptions is that a "good night's sleep" will be "deep and dreamless"; and that the proper equipment for eliciting this state will be a mattress upon which one floats as upon a cloud. Clinical studies now make it clear that dreaming is a necessary function of sleep; and motion picture studies of sleeping subjects show that, actually to rest all its parts equally, the body must "twist and turn all night"! Since it is a linkage system of semi-independent weights and masses, the body best accomplishes this while supported by a fairly firm surface.

Similarly, it has long been held that it is "healthy" to sleep in a cold room "with all the windows open." Proof of this was supposed to lie in the fact that it led to a big appetite at breakfast. But the accelerated heat loss from this exposure, from a metabolic point of view, would be the equivalent of a night-long walk at two or three miles per hour! And conventional bedding sufficient to reduce such heat loss to acceptable levels might well be so heavy as to *increase* fatigue, as anyone will remember who has spent a winter night in an American farmhouse under homemade quilts!

This type of malfunction, the consequences of a poor fit between the tool and the user, still goes largely unobserved in the design field. It is not only that we do not as yet have modern methodologies for isolating and measuring these complex experiential relationships, as a necessary prelude to the redesign of the object. We do not even have an adequate terminology for describing them. Fragmentary and discontinuous research has been carried on in the anthropometry of bathing and dressing;[18] kitchen equipment;[19] and furniture design.[20] But most of this work occurred decades ago and there is little evidence that these promising beginnings have been understood or followed up by the architectural and design professions. As in the automobile industry, lip service is paid to such performance characteristics as comfort, efficiency and safety but superficial appearance remains the dominant criterion.

A notable exception to this attitude is to be found in some of the early work of the architect Frederick J. Kiesler, who published a remarkable theoretical paper in 1939, "On Correalism and Biotechnique: A Definition and Test of a New Approach to Building Design."[21] In this paper Kiesler first formulates a theory of the morphological development of the tool in history; and then publishes a prototype designed according to the theory. He sees the tool as being the result of the continual interaction between tool and user, always strictly conditioned by the culture in which the interaction takes place. The rate and direction of this development is a function of the evolution of the culture as a whole. Thus a given tool-form might survive in a primitive culture relatively unchanged for millennia, since neither the *need* for a change nor the *means* of changing it is present. Until even the comparatively recent past, the rate of change was slow, so that the basic type survived with only modest modifications. But in contemporary industrial society, with its accelerating rates of change, the life span is radically reduced. Minor modifications are no longer adequate; a new tool might become obsolete in a decade. But its redesign could not be successfully accomplished without a fundamental re-examination of the problem in its context.

To demonstrate his theory, Professor Kiesler and his class at the Columbia University School of Architecture set to work to design and fabricate a prototype. Proceeding on the assumption that the design of even the simplest and most prosaic item of furniture was subject to radical revision and improvement, Kiesler's class chose the bookcase as a subject of analysis. It did not require much research to discover that historically the bookcase had reached its present form a long time ago and had seen little if any improvement since. How well did it meet the requirements of the user? And how well those of the books? History offered little in the way of intelligent answer. More and more books had been published, and bigger and bigger libraries built to hold them. But if it were the task of a book storage unit to take the load off the user, then it had clearly fallen far short of its objective. On the other hand, if it were the task of the unit to provide the books themselves with an optimal environment, here too its success had not been spectacular (Fig. 61).

Beginning with the human body, where Kiesler felt all building research — to be productive — must begin, Kiesler's group came upon a major discrepancy. The first criterion of a bookcase would obviously be easy recognition of and access to the books themselves. Since the sweep of both the eye and the arm is circular, the limits of both recognition and access are also circular in the vertical as well as the horizontal plane. All existing bookcases were rectilinear in both planes, so that between the user and the tool there was only one point of actual tangency — immediately in front of him at a point between shoulder and eye level. To read or reach any other point, the user had to stretch, squat or move sideways.

The ideal solution would be a hollow spherical bookcase, with the user at the center and the interior radius approximately that of

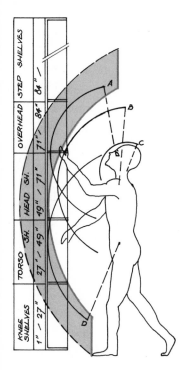

Fig. 61. Frederick Kiesler's formulation of user-tool relationship in book storage. Skeleto-muscular access and visual recognition of standing man to objects in space is spheroid. Books and book-storage equipment are rectilinear. Interface between man and book-storing tool is tangent, placing maximum strain upon user. To shift load, tool should be redesigned. Theoretically, man should stand in center of hollow sphere of book shelves; in reality, tool must meet other requirements — stability, use in rectilinear architectural space, etc. Interface should therefore take the form of concave segmental arc scaled to vertical and horizontal reach of the user.

his arm. Other considerations would immediately modify this initial concept. The user would not want his books directly overhead nor immediately underfoot: so the sphere would be truncated top and bottom. The center of the sphere should be somewhere near eye level: so the truncated bottom would be well off the floor. To enter or leave the unit, the user would not want to climb over or crawl under: so the unit would be built in spheroid sections, like the outer surface of the lobes of an orange, one of which would be omitted. But only the inner surface of the sphere would be accessible to the user when he was inside it: hence each of the sections would pivot upon its vertical axis, so that both surfaces would be equally accessible. And since capacity would vary with the needs of the individual user, each section should be complete in itself: as his library grew, he could add sections to complete the sphere.

What of the books themselves? Had they any properties which importantly affected this schematic solution? They were, first of all, rectilinear in form, and there was little prospect of that property's being modified: hence the unit could only *approach* the spherical by means of small chords. Books were comparatively heavy: so construction of the case would have to be strong and the center of gravity low. They varied in size, so the shelving would be adjustable. The whole unit should be easy to move: hence the individual sections should be mounted on noiseless casters. Easy recognition implied good lighting. Hence each unit would have its own fixture — a fluorescent tube with adjustable reflector — mounted on a universal joint.

Had books any special environmental requirements? Information was scanty here, but it was agreed that excessively dry air was as bad for paper as excessive moisture. Moving air of moderate temperature and humidity would be a satisfactory norm: so glass fronts were omitted and the shelves would be slotted. Dust was bad for books, however: so transparent plastic flaps would hang from the outer edge of each shelf, mounted on friction hinges which would stay put at any angle.

Only now was it possible for Kiesler's students to produce actual working drawings. And this involved a realistic survey of industrial resources. What materials were best suited to the design? What modifications would be imposed upon it by available fabrication methods? How could cost be held to a minimum without sacrifice of quality? These and many other questions were answered in the construction of a pilot model (Fig. 62). The result bears little resemblance to the standard bookcase because, as a tool, it has been redesigned from the ground up. It is not the only (and may not even be the best) possible solution to the problem of book storage. Its significance here lies in the *methodology* of its design. The user, the task, the tool: each has been analyzed, free of historic precedent and prejudice, to discover the best solution in terms of modern scientific knowledge. A much more productive tool is the result. (Kiesler, incidentally, thirty years ago already noted that knowledge had not always been stored in books. At one time we used clay tablets, at another papyrus rolls; and the time might not be far off when microfilm, tape and computer cards would replace the book. The storage method for such new units would have to be correspondingly revised.)

Fig. 62. Mobile Home Library, designed and built by Frederick Kiesler and his students, Columbia University School of Architecture. The basic module (left) has double face, pivots on vertical axis, stores 250 books. It can be assembled in circle (above) for 3000 books.

In an excellent research project completed some three decades after Kiesler's pioneering work, Alexander Kira analyzed the bathroom from much the same point of view — although apparently unaware of Kiesler's theoretical formulations. Beginning with the notorious inadequacies of the modern American bathroom (high cost, great weight, complex fabrication; deficiencies with reference to physiological function; unsafe conditions, etc.), Kira points out that:

The development of design criteria for the major personal hygiene activities (body cleansing and elimination of body wastes) must be based on the analysis of each of these activities in terms of: first, the complex cultural and psychological attitudes surrounding the subject — attitudes which influence our hygiene practices and our reactions to equipment;* second, the basic physiological and anatomical considerations; and lastly, the physical or "human engineering" problems of performing the activity.[22]

Basing his research upon these premises, Kira first established the performance criteria suggested by medical and public health authorities. Then he photographed live models of both sexes, acting against calibrated backgrounds. By this means, he was able to record the anthropometrics of personal hygiene (washing the hair, face, hands, body as a whole) and elimination of body wastes (urination and defecation). This first stage employed conventional fixtures (lavatories, tubs, showers; water closets, bidets, urinals) to measure the correspondence — or lack thereof — between the activity and the fixture supposed to serve it. The second stage involved "mock-ups" of conventional fixtures, modified in size, shape and location with reference to the floor. The final stage was the design of new prototypes whose configurations were based upon an optimal resolution of physiological, anatomical and physical factors (Figs. 63, 64).

---

* An objective analysis of the bathroom is no simple matter, since it does indeed collide with a whole nexus of cultural restraints and taboos. The fate of the bidet at the hands of the American plumbing industry is a case in point. Although the bidet can be merely a basin to facilitate feminine hygiene, the European form usually includes a jet of water. This jet is an extremely effective aid to cleansing the vaginal area. But it also has contraceptive potentials; and this has led to its being blacklisted on the American market for decades. Of course, the same jet is also a great aid to cleansing the anorectal areas of both sexes; and this fact has finally led the plumbing industry to place it on the open market under the name "*Mister* Bidet"! (my italics: JMF).

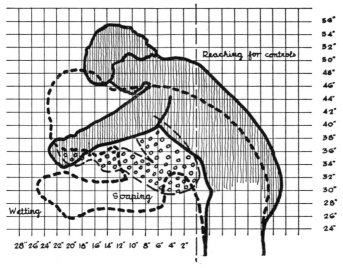

Fig. 63a. Ranges of body and arm movements while washing face, plotted without reference to equipment. Diagram is based on photos of models moving in front of calibrated backgrounds.

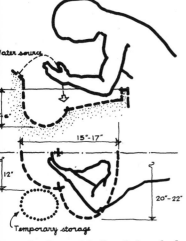

Fig. 63b. "Spatial balloon" described washing face, plan and section above). Comparison between space required and that afforded by available lavatories (below) shows wide deficiencies of current models.

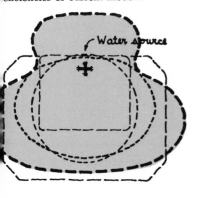

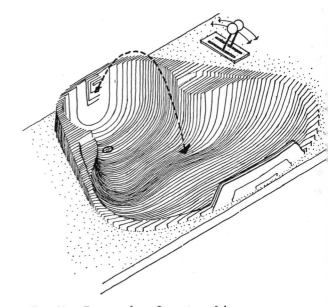

Fig. 63c. Prototypal configuration of lavatory designed by Alexander Kira. Size, shape and location of bowl, as well as location of water jet, respond to spatial deployment of body in washing face and hands. Bowl now represents optimal fit between user and tool; despite radical reshaping, however, bowl can be fabricated out of conventional metal, ceramic or plastic materials currently in use.

The Kira prototypes do not depend upon any radically new developments in technology; on the contrary, they could easily be manufactured with existing materials and fabrication methods. Yet they promise a whole new level of performance because of the experiential fit achieved between user and tool. And the Kira study itself represents a model demonstration of how new methods of research and design can be applied to the re-design of all types of architectural furnishings and equipment.

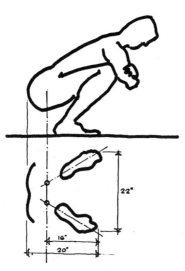

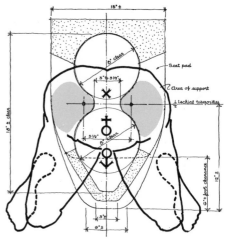

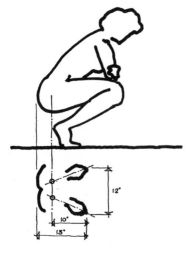

Fig. 64a. Natural postures for defecation.

Fig. 64. Prototypal unit (below) designed by Alexander Kira combines functions normally associated with water closet with those of the bidet. In addition to flushing action to carry away feces, new unit has two water jets for cleansing of genital and anal regions of both sexes. Height and configuration of seat (left and above) are derived from analysis of physical and physiological aspects of act.

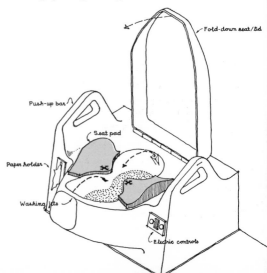

8. SKELETON AND SKIN: THE MORPHOLOGICAL DEVELOPMENT OF STRUCTURAL SYSTEMS

Although for thousands of years and in all parts of the world, many cultures have shown a superb grasp of one or another aspect of the spectrum of structural possibilities, a comprehensive and universal — i.e., scientific — *theory* of structure has only been established in the last century or so. The marble porticoes of the Parthenon and the articulated wooden skeletons of the Ise Shrine in Japan; the plastic concrete vaulting of Diocletian's Palace and the stone-ribbed vaulting of the High Gothic in England or Bohemia; the mud-walled skyscrapers of the Moroccan oases and the monumental rubble masonry of the Mayans — each of these is the end product of a self-contained process of experimentation and refinement. Each represents a summation of one specific aspect of structural experience, developed within one specific set of objective conditions — cultural, technological, geographical. But, encapsulated by the accidents of history and lacking both the internal coherence and external applicability which only modern mathematics could afford, none of these could yield a universal theory. The planful accumulation of structural knowledge, the systematic exploration and development of applied mechanics, the standardized testing of natural materials and the deliberate search for new synthetic ones — all of these essentials to a scientific theory of structure had to await the maturation of the Industrial Revolution* (Figs. 65–69).

* A lucid exposition of the present state of this theory is to be found in Mario Salvadori and Robert Heller, *Structure in Architecture* (New York: Prentice-Hall, 1964).

Fig. 65. Temple of Hera Argiva, Paestum, Italy. This fifth-century-B.C. Doric temple, now roofless, clearly reveals its phylogenetic origins in articulated wooden skeletons, subsequently transmuted into marble. Most of the decorative devices of the Doric order also derive from the requirements of carpentry and joinery in woodworking.

Fig. 66. Hall of Rites, Kamingano, Japan. Skeletal wooden construction has been raised to the highest level of sophistication in the monumental architecture of Japan.

The history of American structural development coincides with the last phases of this historic process. Moreover, as we have seen in the first volume of this work, this process has always been superimposed upon the special conditions of American life — a rapidly growing and polyglot population, inheritors of many specialized building techniques; a society which was constantly meeting new climatic and geographic conditions; a country which was, for almost three centuries, always partly settled and partly wilderness, partly agrarian and partly industrial, and — for most of its history — partly slave and partly free. Under such conditions, it is not surprising to find that neither our structural theories nor our structural practice has remained static for long. Rapid and violent change, uneven and undisciplined, replaced that slow, almost imperceptible accumulation of experience which characteristically preceded the sudden flowering of the great schools of building of the past. For this reason any discussion of contemporary American structural theory and practice must seem simplified, diagrammatic and misleadingly symmetrical.

In the preceding chapters, we have seen something of the enormously complex problems of contemporary architecture — first in understanding and then in solving man's requirements for shelter, his need for the "third environment." It must at all times be remembered that two factors in this complex equation are constants and have been throughout his history: man himself and the terrestrial environment in which he is submerged. These constants are virtually the same as they were 500; 50,000; 500,000 years ago. The factors which *have* changed, and radically, are: our increasing understanding of man's experiential requirements; our increasing technical ability to manipulate environmental forces; and the increasingly complex institutions and processes required to sustain social life under these new circumstances. Together, these new factors have at once required and made possible a whole new order of building performance.

It is evident that the environmental forces which play upon a building are numerous and complex. They result in two kinds of stress upon the actual fabric or structure of the building. One set of stresses is *mechanical* — the loads to which gravity, wind and earthquake subject the structure. The other is *chemico-physical* —

Fig. 67. "Temple of Venus," Horti Sallustiani, Rome, Italy. Plastic potentialities of mass masonry were brilliantly exploited by Roman architects after second century A.D. as seen in this daring 12-sided segmental vaulted dome of the Hadrianic period.

Fig. 68. Entrance hall, house in Telč, Czechoslovakia, late sixteenth century. The flamboyant expertise of late Gothic vaulting survived as a vernacular idiom until 1700.

the remorseless attrition represented by the action of heat, light, atmosphere, precipitation upon the structure. The response that we require of the building is, of course, that it resist both these sets of natural forces. The roof must not collapse under the snow load, the walls must resist anticipated winds, the structure should not burn, rot or rust. Expressed in purely experiential terms, however, the main requirement that we make of the structure is that it manipulate the flow of these forces between inside and out. It should act as a selective filter between the natural and the man-made environments.

Generally speaking, these two tasks are mutually exclusive for any single building material. That material whose molecular configuration makes it strong in resistance to tensile or compressive loads — steel, for example — will, by the same token, offer little resistance to the transfer of heat. A vibrated concrete panel will be structurally strong but acoustically poor; a foamed-concrete panel, on the other hand, makes an excellent acoustical barrier but will have no load-bearing capacity. Marble floors are waterproof but not resilient; cork floors will be resilient but not impervious. Glass is transparent to light, bronze opaque; one shatters, the other corrodes. And so it goes: the properties of matter are contradictory and intractable. The task of structural design has always been that of untangling and isolating them, so that they can be better exploited for the specific task at hand.

The accomplishment of this historic task, in the century since the Crystal Palace, has led to an unprecedented flowering of structural theory and a parallel proliferation of structural systems and building materials. In general terms, this specialization has taken the form of a separation of structural tissue into supporting frame and enclosing membrane — that is, into skeleton and skin.* Such an evolutionary course of development has obvious analogies with a comparable specialization of tissue in the animal kingdom, a development which made possible the appearance of the higher vertebrates and of man himself. And, as in animal evolution, it has had comparably significant consequences for architectural performance.

* Of course, this same expertise has made possible new developments in endoskeletal structures, where the skin is at once supporting member and enclosing membrane. Such are the stressed-skin shells in metal or reinforced plastic and the tension and inflated structures whose potentials are discussed in this chapter.

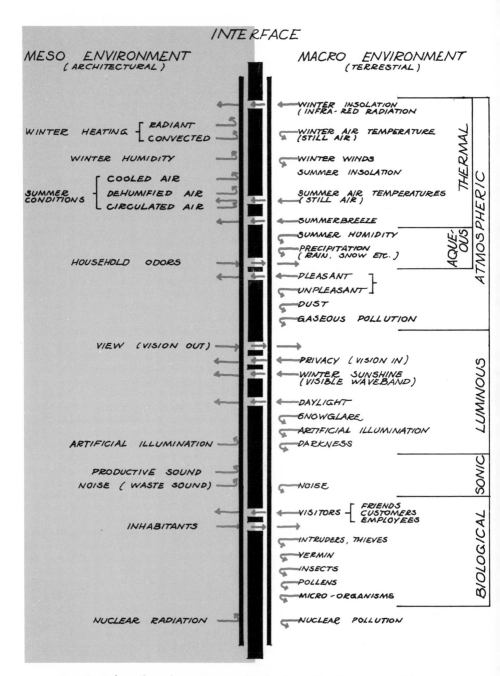

Fig. 69. Only with modern science and technology did it become possible to separate load-bearing task of architectural structure from environmental-control function of enclosing membrane. Only then could the wall be conceptualized as a selective filter, acting as interface between natural macro-environment and man-made meso-environment. This technical capacity can yield higher levels of environmental control.

Modern engineering theory and technological expertise have permitted us to project this process of analysis and synthesis to new levels undreamed of even a few decades ago. (The manned mooncrafts are the most advanced examples of this new capacity.) And yet the ultimate architectural implications of these new structural potentials are by no means clearly understood. This is quite obvious from the behavior of new buildings all around the world: employing the most advanced design and fabrication techniques and the most sophisticated materials and equipment, they often have an overall performance which is qualitatively lower than some of their preindustrial prototypes. In fact, it is one of the paradoxes of the present state of architecture that the vernacular buildings of the folk cultures of Western civilization, not to mention the architecture of primitive, preliterate peoples, often display a more precise understanding of experiential reality than does our own.

THE FUNCTION OF STRUCTURE

The building is a sum total of two components: those structural elements which we employ to create a container for the meso-environment; and that mechanical equipment required to hold meso-environmental conditions at the desired level. Building is thus a specialized instrument which may range from the comparatively simple case of a bandstand (where the curved shell merely distributes the sound in the desired pattern and the sloping floor organizes the spatial relationship of the audience so that all may see) to the enormously complex building type required for telecasting (where the building is called upon to furnish whole environments without any precedent in the natural world).

Conventionally, capacity for perceptible — or at least measurable — transfer or conversion of energy is the dividing line between structure and equipment. This is a necessary oversimplification. The compressor which removes excess heat from a room is classed as equipment. The steel truss which absorbs and then distributes the earthquake shock, in such a fashion as successfully to resist it, is called structure. Yet both are engaged in a transfer of energy. In the last analysis, all of the building is dynamic. The air conditioning apparatus which forces cool air into the room is no busier controlling its thermal environment than is the insulation in the wall, which inch by inch and molecule by molecule, slows down the transfer of heat from the blistering outside. Thus the difference between structure and equipment is largely one of passive versus active function.

In previous chapters we have seen how various types of equipment are employed to modulate the various properties and components of the meso-environment. Here, we are concerned with structure — i.e., the physical envelope or container whose function it is to enclose, support and protect the environments so created. Modern structures are characterized by a high degree of specialization, usually expressed in a clear separation between skeleton and skin, framing and surfacing, support and enclosure. Nature subjects all man's constructions to a complex process of attrition. When moisture corrodes steel, it is chemical; when winter cold penetrates the wall, it is physical; when snow load collapses the roof, it is mechanical. Such complex attack requires specialized response; the undifferentiated tissue which attempts to do everything at once will do none of it very well. Hence modern structural theory assigns to the skin the primary task of resisting chemical and physical attack; to the skeleton is assigned the task of resisting the mechanical forces of gravity, wind, snow loads, earthquakes, etc.

The frame or skeleton is subjected to two sets of forces:

1. *vertical*　weight of the structure itself
weight of people, equipment and goods inside it

2. *horizontal*　wind pressure
earthquake

In its simplest terms, the task of the skeleton is to absorb these forces and convey them safely to the ground. When the house shakes before the blast of a winter gale, its frame is busily resolving such loads, breaking them down into their component parts and dispatching them to the ground along the members designed to handle them. The building skeleton thus converts "raw" natural forces into characteristic stress patterns called *normal* (compression, tension and bending) and *tangent* (shear and torsion).*

---

* There is another type of loading — vibration — in which the critical factor is time and not force. All materials have some elasticity, depending upon their molecular

There are dozens of different structural systems for accomplishing this load-bearing task: and hundreds of permutations and combinations of these basic systems, adapted to different building materials, construction techniques, etc. But in terms of geometry, all structural elements, assemblies and systems may be said to derive from four primary forms: the rigid stick, the rigid slab, the flexible filament, and the flexible membrane.

The stick is the basic element of all endoskeletal structures, from the most primitive post-and-beam trabeation to the most complex space-frame or geodesic dome.

The slab (which, in geometric terms, is generated by the stick when moved along a given plane) is the basic element of all exoskeletal structures, from the rubble masonry vault to the most complex of reinforced concrete folded plates or hyperbolic paraboloids.

The filament is the basis of all net-like structures, from the rope ladder to the suspension bridge or bicycle roof truss.

The membrane (which is generated when the filament is moved along a given plane) is the basic element of all endoskeletal tensile structures like the tent and of all exoskeletal pneumatic structures like the balloon.

In recent decades, thanks to the rise of modern mathematics and technology, these have been cultivated and refined, crossed and re-crossed into a whole spectrum of specialized systems, each with its own inherent advantages and inherent limitations. Generally speaking, they can be classified morphologically from "lower" to "higher" forms, as indicated in Table 6.

Historically it had been possible (indeed, before modern mathe-

---

structure. Up to a given limit, each will deflect under a given load and snap back into original shape when the load is removed. Beyond this elastic limit is a second stage of resistance to load in which the material deforms — i.e., supports the load but is permanently misshaped as a result of the strain. Beyond this point of deformation lies that of ultimate failure: the material ruptures under the load. But under certain circumstances, the cumulative effect of a series of even small loads, rapidly applied, can telescope this process. Certain types of vibration can alter the crystalline structure of metal and radically modify its properties. Sound waves at a certain pitch will set up vibrations in a water glass which will shatter it. Soldiers marching in lock step across a bridge can set up an oscillation which can literally destroy it, though the same men — walking out of step or standing still — would not approach its load capacity. And the dramatic failure of the then new Tacoma Narrows suspension bridge in 1940 has demonstrated the dangers of aerodynamic instability in structures that were very strong from any conventional point of view.

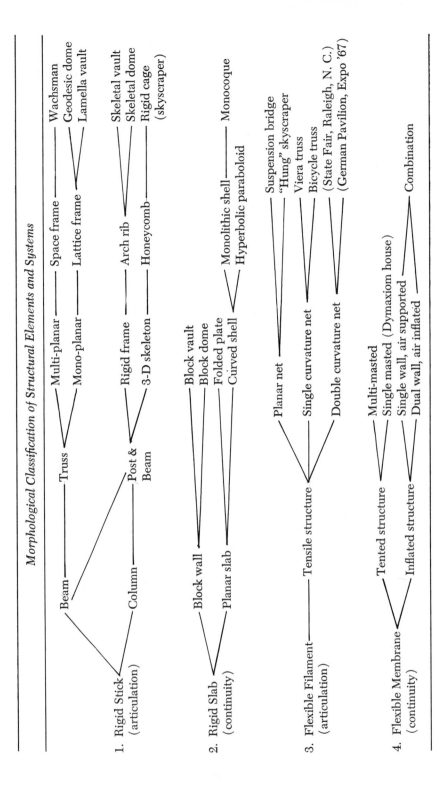

Morphological Classification of Structural Elements and Systems

1. Rigid Stick (articulation)

Beam ────── Truss ─┬── Multi-planar ─── Space frame ─── Wachsman
                   │   Geodesic dome
                   └── Mono-planar ─── Lattice frame ─── Lamella vault

Column ─── Post & Beam ─┬── Rigid frame ─── Arch rib ─┬── Skeletal vault
                        │   Skeletal dome
                        └── 3-D skeleton ─── Honeycomb ─── Rigid cage (skyscraper)

2. Rigid Slab (continuity)

Block wall ─┬── Block vault
            └── Block dome

Planar slab ─┬── Folded plate ─── Monolithic shell ─── Monocoque
             └── Curved shell ─┬── Hyperbolic paraboloid

3. Flexible Filament (articulation)

Tensile structure ─┬── Planar net ─── Suspension bridge
                   │   "Hung" skyscraper
                   ├── Single curvature net ─── Viera truss
                   │   Bicycle truss (State Fair, Raleigh, N. C.)
                   └── Double curvature net ─── (German Pavilion, Expo '67)

4. Flexible Membrane (continuity)

Tented structure ─┬── Multi-masted
                  └── Single masted (Dymaxiom house)

Inflated structure ─┬── Single wall, air supported
                    ├── Dual wall, air inflated
                    └── Combination

Table 6. A morphogenetic classification of structural systems. All man-made constructions can be visualized as ultimately deriving from four basic components. Modern technology has made possible an unprecedentedly wide crossbreeding and proliferation of variants.

matics and physics, inevitable) that the building wall be conceived of as a barrier pure and simple; an element which held up the roof, kept out the cold, and offered maximum resistance to the attacks of rot, rust, rodents and robbers. But modern scientific knowledge has forced the modification of such concepts in many fundamental respects. In the first place, to raise the efficiency and performance levels of the building, clear distinctions had to be made between the functions of *support* and *enclosure*. This was necessary first of all for analytical purposes: since environmental stress was manifold and complex, structural response had to be correspondingly specialized. Then it became clear that "barriers" were only relative, not absolute; no single material was literally impervious to all environmental forces. Finally, it became clear that all concepts of "permanence" were relative; no material was permanently resistant to all forms of chemical, physical or mechanical attrition.

These specialized structural forms are thus to be understood as the direct response to the above discoveries. They represent the invention and exploitation of whole species of means of structural support; the enclosing function is largely incidental to most of them. But, as we have seen in preceding chapters, there has been a comparable florescence in means of enclosure. The selection of any one of these structural support systems for any given project will generally be determined by the given requirements for enclosure. Thus for building types in which transparency or permeability to environmental forces (heat, light, sound, breeze, etc.) is a desirable quality, endoskeletal support systems are apt to be most suitable — e.g., shops, houses, schools, office buildings. If, on the other hand, maximal opacity or resistance to movement of environmental forces across the interface is desirable, then exoskeletal support systems are more suitable — e.g., concrete shells for exhibition halls, museums, warehouses, etc.

All of man's constructions are peculiarly vulnerable to another form of attrition: fire. In a certain sense, fire merely telescopes the ordinarily slow and often imperceptible processes of physical, chemical and mechanical attack into a single cataclysm — a process which makes up in intensity for what it lacks in time. With its threat to life and property, fire has always been an important consideration in building design. But with the growth of modern urban society, the demand for fire-resistance (the term "fireproof" is seldom employed now because the genuinely unburnable building is almost an impossibility) has increased.

The first iron-framed buildings were widely hailed as fireproof, but a few disastrous fires sufficed to prove the fallacy of this assumption. Metal frames were then encased in concrete and ceramic sheaths, thus making possible the multistory skyscraper. But this has not prevented a series of very serious conflagrations. Thus, the La Salle Hotel in Chicago was a "fireproof" building on the June night in 1946 when fire swept through it, taking the lives of sixty-one persons; and it was probably *structurally* as sound the day after as it was the day before. Actually, the fire had fed upon the contents of the building, not the building itself — curtains, carpets, furniture, even the accumulated paint on the walls and the grease in the elevator shafts. As a result of these varied combustibles, the smoke from the fire was complex and toxic, so that many of the deaths were due to asphyxiation, not burns. This was true, to an even more marked degree, in the famous Cocoanut Grove nightclub fire in Boston in 1942, in which 492 persons died. Subsequent investigation revealed that the principal cause of death was the presence of noxious fumes from the flammable artificial shrubbery. Deaths directly due to flame and trampling were secondary — i.e., had the victims not been overcome by the gases, they would have been able to escape unharmed.

Hundreds of thousands of fires occur in this country each year, mostly in structures which, being wholly or largely of wood, are as flammable as their contents. In 1969, some 12,100 persons lost their lives in fires, and property losses ran to $1,952,000,000* for the year. It is probable that no more than 10 per cent of all American buildings reach even minimum levels of firesafeness. Yet the fires which occur in even this upper 10 per cent of "fireproof" buildings indicate that the problem is only partially a matter of incombustible structure. As long as the contents are flammable, a fire hazard exists. Realization of this has served to widen greatly our concepts of fire prevention

* Figures do not include losses in U.S. government properties.

and control. The field now covers a range of measures in planning, building codes, fire-fighting equipment (both inside the building and out) and the training of building inhabitants in fire safety precautions. Only by the most careful control of all these factors can the incidence of fires be measurably reduced.

Many purely architectural problems remain to be solved, however. For example, current trends in "open planning" reinforce the natural tendency of halls, stairways and shafts to act as flues which can rapidly fan a small fire into a disastrous conflagration. (The fire which all but wrecked the building and threatened the collection of the Museum of Modern Art in New York in 1966 was of this type.) Hazards like these are implicit in modern buildings and it is difficult to see how they can ever be completely eliminated. Hence, even the most advanced buildings must be assumed to have some hazards and to require secondary lines of defense. Fire extinguishers, sprinkler systems and alarm systems all have inherent limitations. In many buildings, where contents may be very valuable (libraries, museums) or fragile (department stores), conventional water sprinkling systems may easily cause more damage than the fire itself. A most promising variant here has been the development of a sprinkler system using carbon dioxide instead of water. This smothers all fires, including many types which water does not affect, with a foam instead of a liquid, thereby greatly reducing risks of damage to goods and furnishings. Perhaps the most important single advance has been the development of extremely sensitive electronic alarm systems: these are designed to react to very small rises in temperature or to increases in smokes or gases in the atmosphere and thus summon firefighters at a very early stage in the fire.

STEEL, THE MATHEMATICIAN'S MATERIAL

From a purely structural point of view, the walls of the pyramids are the least efficient structures in the world, occupying all but the merest kernel of the total space they displace. From the same narrow viewpoint, the molded plywood or laminated fiber-glass boat hull is probably one of the most advanced. "Efficient" and "advanced" are, however, relative terms: that structure is most advanced or efficient which most closely corresponds to the configuration of its own stress patterns. To put it another way, that structure is best which does the most work with the least material; or — as the engineers put it — whose strength-weight ratio is highest.

The first great demonstrations of this principle were the Crystal Palace, the Brooklyn Bridge and the Eiffel Tower. All three were remarkably efficient structures. But two of them were not buildings at all, and the Palace itself was a very special sort of showcase, with few of the complexities of plan or function which characterize the ordinary five-room house. Of greatest significance about all of them, however, is the fact that they were built of iron. The historic accomplishment of their designers was their demonstration of a new structural concept: the achievement of strength through precision instead of sheer mass. To accomplish such a task it was necessary to analyze the problem of structural efficiency theoretically — i.e., mathematically. Only thus could one determine in advance precisely under what circumstances a given amount of a certain material would support the greatest load. Such theoretical investigations were scarcely possible until the development of structural iron and steel. Steel is a mathematician's material because it is almost perfectly isotropic — that is, its physical characteristics are such as to make it react identically in all directions from a given point of stress. Natural materials such as timber or granite do not react in this fashion because of their cellular, crystalline or fibrous construction; nor do they react with predictable consistency, because of their natural flaws and impurities. Steel was the first building material to display the fabulous potentials of isotropism.

Structural theory fed chiefly on steel during the latter half of the nineteenth century. Because it was equally strong in compression and tension, it could be fabricated in either stick or filament form: the tower and the bridge gave dramatic evidence of the structural implications of this fact. For American experience, the steel stick and steel filament had a special appropriateness. The primeval forests of North America made it inevitable that our construction would be primarily wooden. Thus when steel structural shapes began appearing in quantity around 1850, the transition from wooden to metallic members was rapid and easy. Heavy-mill construction of timber; the wooden truss; and the frame house, with its light skeletal cage and thin stiffening membranes of sheathing and plaster — these had long been basic structural forms. They had channelized American technique and it was entirely logical that iron or steel columns and beams be at first treated as merely improved replacements for the wooden prototypes. It was only gradually that the concept of a complete metallic skeleton was evolved and the skyscraper appeared. Even here, a great debt was owed the earlier wooden structures, for it was in such systems as the balloon frame that a clear differentiation had been made between supporting skeleton and enclosing skin.

Once this distinction had been made, the wall ceased to have much structural significance, despite its visual importance. The sleek walls of Chicago's Monadnock Building gave it the appearance of a true skyscraper (vol. 1, Fig. 163). By dint of solid masonry walls, seven feet thick at the sidewalk, it reached sixteen stories and visually challenged the genuine steel cage of Le Baron Jenney's Home Insurance Building nearby. In reality, there was a great morphological gap between the two: the Monadnock was the old, exoskeletal masonry pushed to its uttermost limits; the Home was the newer, articulated endoskeleton with its more highly specialized tissue. As with the evolutionary appearance of the higher vertebrates, it was the precondition to higher levels of performance.

The other great forcing bed for structural advance was transportation — first the canals and then the railroads, with their requirements for bridges and terminals of unprecedented clear spans. Here again, the metallic stick and filament took over from their vegetable predecessors. It will be recalled that it was to produce stronger, more uniform and longer-lived cables than the hemp and sisal ones then available that Roebling had developed his first machinery for making steel cables. After their successful use on the Pennsylvania Canal, he quickly went on to apply them to structural uses, producing that spectacular series of suspension bridges which culminated in the Brooklyn. Yet the enormous structural potentials of steel in tension (as in tensile or suspension structures) has never been fully exploited in architecture proper.

Of course, the steel cage was an important development for architecture, as the great skyscrapers of today bear witness. Yet the sheer overpowering mass of hundred-story towers like the Trade Center in New York or the Hancock in Chicago is apt to obscure the fact that, from a purely structural point of view, the first skyscraper was as advanced as the last. As a matter of fact, articulated "stick" constructions, which are morphological developments of the simple truss, represent a far more advanced exploitation of the metal, whether they assume a monoplanar form, like the Lamella vault or Fuller's geodesic dome; or multiplanar forms, like some of the recent great space frames. In all such cases we find steel operating most efficiently in fundamentally compressive applications. In the one case, the lattice gets its great stiffness from being curved into a vault (Lamella) or a dome (geodesic). In the other case, the lattice is developed three-dimensionally: this gives the structure as a

Fig. 70. Cable-suspended roof, Municipal Auditorium, Utica, N.Y. Lev Zetlin and Associates, structural engineers. A two-layer prestressed cable-suspension system yields a 250-ft. clear span, with a minimum of material doing maximum work. System is entirely free of flutter despite dynamic and vibratory forces to which it is subjected. Entire roof was prefabricated, erected in three weeks from one central scaffold.

Fig. 71. Westcoast Building, Vancouver, B.C. Rhone and Iredale, architects; Bogue Babicki and Associates, structural engineers. A 12-story office tower is hung from a central mast. Floors are carried by high-tensile-strength steel cables looped over top of concrete core, which also contains elevators, stairs and toilets. Core was poured from bottom up, steel floors installed from top down. Method is said to have saved 20 per cent in material costs, 40 per cent in erection time. Curtain walls are of heat-rejecting insulating glass.

Fig. 72. West Gate Pavilion, 1970 International Exposition, Osaka, Japan. Kunio Kato, architect; Minoru Wakabayshi, structural engineer. Theoretical investigation of tented structures, pioneered by German engineer Frei Otto, makes possible safe, stable, flutter-free designs like this. Modern high-strength steels and durable synthetic membranes presage tented structures of unprecedented scale and complexity.

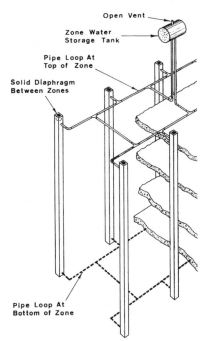

Open Vent

Zone Water Storage Tank

Pipe Loop At Top of Zone

Solid Diaphragm Between Zones

Pipe Loop At Bottom of Zone

Fig. 73. U. S. Steel Building, Pittsburgh, Pa. Harrison and Abramowitz and Abbe, architects. Two of steel's most dangerous enemies — fire and rust — are foiled in this design. Freestanding exterior columns are tubular, filled with antifreeze water to disperse heat from nearby fire (above). Exposed skeleton is fabricated of special steel which quickly develops a stable, self-protective coating of rust. The 64-story is framed so that 3-floor increments hang free of columns; each has self-contained pressurized water system (diagram below).

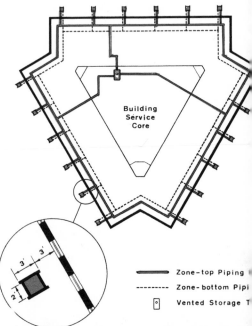

Building Service Core

3' 3'

2'

—— Zone-top Piping

- - - Zone-bottom Pipi

▫ Vented Storage T

whole the stiffness which permits it to be used in a single plane, for enormous spans and cantilevers (space frame).

Two environmental hazards — fire and corrosion — still restrict the use of exposed steel in most architectural applications. Building codes require that, in multistory buildings, all steel members be wrapped in a fireproof casing: this is bound to lead to reductions in the flexibility and efficiency of the steel skeleton. One obvious way to get around such limitation is to move the skeleton completely outside, and free of, the enclosed space. This device is being increasingly employed in low-rise buildings — notably in the John Deere office building at Moline, Illinois (Fig. 31). The architects of the sixty-four-story office building for U.S. Steel in Pittsburgh have gone much further (Fig. 73). Not only have they placed all columns outside the building envelope; but the columns themselves have been converted into hollow tubes filled with water. The design assumption here is that heat from any possible conflagration inside the building would be dissipated up and down the column of water so rapidly that it could not accumulate in the metal tube itself.

Corrosion is the other limiting factor on the exterior use of unprotected steel. Until recently, the only solutions to this problem were stainless steel or repeated painting; but stainless is difficult to fabricate, expensive, and in many locations, objectionably shiny; painting is costly, messy and endless. Recently a new alloyed steel called Cor-Ten has been developed which has the property of quickly establishing a solid, permanent coat of rust. Since this coat is itself chemically stable and physically unchanging, it affords permanent protection to itself thereafter. The final surface is a handsome red-brown matte finish which requires no subsequent attention. It was this new steel which made possible the exposed frames of both the Deere and U.S. Steel buildings.

CONCRETE, THE ORIGINAL PLASTIC

Although metals dominated the field of large and complex structures from the 1850s on — capturing the imagination of designers and public alike by the remarkable bridges, towers and skyscrapers they made possible — the eclipse of the other two basic structural materials, wood and concrete, was only temporary. Both have reappeared; and both have followed a line of morphological development analogous to that of steel and iron.

Of the two, concrete rose most quickly to prominence. The manufacture of true Portland cement preceded that of steel since it was being produced in large quantities, in both France and England, before 1850. But the concept of reinforcing concrete with steel, uniting the compressive strength of the former with the tensile strength of the latter, was later in its appearance and slower in its spread. The actual invention is attributed to a French gardener, Joseph Monier, who in 1867 hit upon the idea of embedding small steel rods in concrete fishponds he was building.

Prior to Monier's discovery, and for decades thereafter, the chief use of cement was as the binding element in masonry mortars. Perhaps because of this, the real identity of concrete as a distinctly new material was overlooked. And even after ferroconcrete emerged as a new structural medium, it was for a long time regarded as a purely utilitarian material — ugly, gross and inaccurate. Under the conditions of empirical design and on-the-job mixing, it was in fact often both ugly and inaccurate. But, once begun, the technology of reinforced concrete was rapidly perfected, especially in Europe. In the present century, it became unchallenged in such constructions as highways, dams and harbor works. Indeed, such masterpieces as the Tennessee Valley Authority system of locks and dams are inconceivable without it.

Concrete is by definition a plastic material: poured into any mold, it assumes that form and permanently holds it. It is all the stranger, therefore, to see how seldom this property of plasticity was exploited by American designers before World War II (bridge and hydraulic engineers always excepted). In architecture, its principal use was in rectilinear skeletal structures — that is, as a competitor of wood and steel. It even had certain advantages: it was its own fireproofing; it required somewhat less skilled labor; it could be used for floors and walls which would have been impracticable in wood or metal.

Yet all such structures failed to fully exploit concrete's peculiar properties. The mere fact that it could be poured into any shape or form did not mean that it was equally appropriate for all of them. Europeans were much quicker to grasp this fact than Americans. In his now famous bridges in Switzerland, the engineer Robert Maillart displayed a totally different conceptual approach to the material. By an exquisitely detailed knowledge of ferroconcrete, Maillart was able to achieve forms which no longer bore any resemblance to their steel or masonry prototypes. Basically, he used the reinforced slab and beam; but he used them in a revolutionary manner. He saw that by its homogeneity he was able to thin down the member without reducing its strength. In fact, to all intents and purposes, he reduced both slab and beam to a two-dimensional plane which he stiffened by folding or bending — sometimes vertically, sometimes horizontally, or both. In a series of brilliant bridges, he was able to isolate and exploit the special plasticity of the material in such a way as to indicate wholly new levels of structural efficiency.

There was little American work before mid-century to compare with Maillart's. The "monolithic" buildings so widely publicized by the Portland Cement Association were not significant structurally. They were derivative forms, absurdly imitating the mass-masonry Baroque of the Spanish American Southwest (vol. 1, Fig. 183) or late medieval English Gothic, where reinforced concrete vaulting was sheathed in a thin limestone veneer to imitate the original. Frank Lloyd Wright was one of the few Americans to use concrete as an *architectural* material — i.e., one with authentic esthetic qualities which put it on a par with marble or brick. But even he, in his early buildings, used it in fundamentally mass-masonry forms — e.g., Unity Temple (vol. 1, Fig. 176).

Fortunately, this unhappy phase is over and concrete is now being used in a bewildering range of applications. In fact, the new concrete technology has been brilliantly employed, not only where one might expect it (in "plastic" architectural forms like shells, domes, vaults and paraboloids); but also in most of the stick- and block-derived forms shown on page 221. Here, thanks especially to prefabrication and prestressing, one finds structural shapes (columns, beams, panels) as strong and as precisely dimensioned as any steel equivalent. Concrete has even been used in a suspension form by Eero Saarinen in the great catenary roof of the Dulles Air Terminal near Washington. Such virtuosity in a material so long assumed to be clumsy and inert is due to a wide range of technical developments: the use of computers in the design of complex, hitherto incalculable structures; precision control of chemistry, aggregate size and vibration of mixes; chemical additives to control setting time; prestressing; etc.

In these varied forms, modern reinforced concrete has most of the attributes of steel construction and lacks two of steel's weaknesses — susceptibility to fire and corrosion. (It must be observed, of course, that the so-called temperate climates subject concrete to severe attrition by repeated freezing and thawing, wetting and drying, expansion and contraction. In all but warm, dry climates, concrete shells and domes will require weatherproof membranes for protection.) Moreover, because of its versatility, concrete makes possible a wide range of structural systems, ranging from trabeation to shells, which would be almost inconceivable in any other building material.

But, aside from this astonishing versatility, which makes possible the fabrication of almost any structural form in concrete, it has another fundamental advantage: abundance. The cementitious stones, sands and gravels out of which it is fabricated are available anywhere on earth. This fact has long dominated the building picture in wood- and metal-poor countries and explains why concrete technology has reached such high levels in Japan, Brazil and Italy. With the imminent exhaustion of our own forests and iron ore deposits, it will make concrete increasingly dominant in the United States.

WOOD, THE UNIVERSAL MATERIAL

Wood has always been America's favorite building material. In some respects, it still is: over 80 per cent of the nation's dwelling units are wholly or substantially built of wood. The reasons are not far to seek: on the one hand, wood's unique structural and

Fig. 74. Field House, University of Virginia, Charlottesville, Va. Baskerville and Son, architects; Severud and Associates, structural engineers. Plasticity of concrete is demonstrated in this scalloped dome 282 ft. in diameter. The precast petals rest on precast arch ribs which are tied into a cast-in-place tension ring at perimeter and central compression ring to provide monolithic behavior for an arena for 8500.

Fig. 75. Prefabricated concrete skeletal system designed by David Geiger and Horst Berger, engineers. Advanced concrete technology makes possible skeletal systems previously associated with metal or wood. Control of mix and curing, prestressing and posttensioning of reinforcing steel yield members of refined and complex cross-section such as this system for use in large-scale multi-level housing projects.

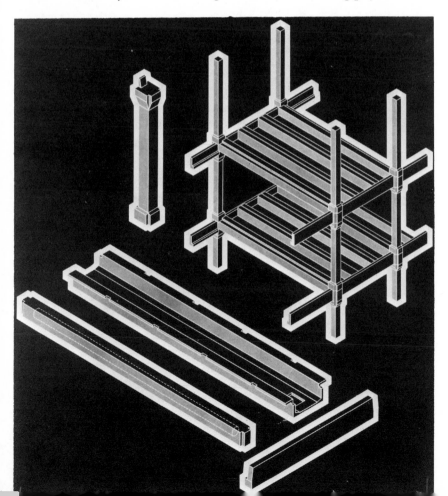

esthetic characteristics; on the other, its abundance and (until recent times) low cost. It is strong in compression and effective in tension and shear. Easily worked, even by unskilled workmen using simple tools, it can be chopped, sawn, bored, turned; mortised, nailed, glued and bolted; sanded, planed, polished, painted. Esthetically, it is one of the most ingratiating of all materials — endlessly varied in color and pattern, warm and silken to the touch, in many cases even fragrant. Such properties made it almost the universal building material of preindustrial America. In the form of sawn lumber, it lent itself naturally to skeletal use, either in trusses or in cages. Thus, for popular building, it was ideal — plentiful, easily worked, yielding relatively efficient structures with low costs. This made it applicable not only to simple domestic structures: it was also used in fairly large and complex structures like the great New England churches with their trussed roofs and daring steeples; in many remarkable covered bridges and railway trestles; and in heavy mine and mill construction.

Wood began to be eclipsed only after the Civil War, when the whole scale and complexity of American life began its escalation. This eclipse was due to wood's inherent limitations. Although relatively strong (2250 pounds per square foot), it could not compare with steel (18,000 psf and upward). It was combustible. Being a natural cellular material, it was not isotropic and hence could not be accurately calculated. It was not uniform in texture and strength; and, being organic, it was subject to attack by insects, fungi and microbes. Finally, it was a very lively material, responding quickly to changes in the moisture content of the atmosphere.

Nevertheless, significant new potentials lay hidden in wood, for nineteenth-century technology had neither the theoretical nor the technical means of isolating them. But with modern methods of manufacturing plywoods and laminated structural members, wood reappears in forms so novel as to be almost a new material. In multi-ply laminations, the characteristics as well as the form of wood are radically altered. It becomes relatively isotropic for, if the grain is placed at right angles in successive plies, tensile strength is equalized in both directions. By the same token, plywood becomes much more stable and uniform than natural wood — flaws or expansion and contraction in one layer being largely corrected by the other plies. The weakest aspect of earlier plywoods (they have been mass-produced for almost a century) had been the animal glues used as binders: soluble in water and subject to fungal attack, they had held plywood to the level of an interior finishing material. But with the development of synthetic resins as binders, plywood has emerged as a structural material. These new resins have great adhesive strength (under test, the individual plies will rupture before the joints between them); in addition, they can render the plywood resistant or immune to moisture, fire, fungus and insect attack.

From a purely structural point of view, the most significant development has been the perfection of plastic resins which permit the molding of all types of curved shapes under heat and/or pressure. Shells such as speedboat hulls, when molded in this way, have a very high strength-weight ratio — especially in resistance to impact blows and vibration. But the greatest significance of lamination is in the fabrication of skeletal elements such as hinged arches or rigid bents. Laminated-wood elements of this type are in many ways superior to comparable ones in steel or concrete — especially in single-story buildings of large span, such as churches or club-houses where the color and texture of wood are desired.

There have been limited advances in fabrication methods of conventional wood framing — e.g., so-called "engineered" nailing in light-frame structures, timber connectors in heavy mill construction, etc. Such technical improvements extend the structural use of wood products. But there are many informed persons who would argue that, with the nation's forests all but exhausted, *any* structural use of wood would be barbarous: because of its unique esthetic characteristics, its use should be confined to purely decorative applications in furnishings and interior design generally. Pulp and paper technologists could make the same sort of argument against the structural use of wood but for quite different reasons. From their point of view, wood is a chemical treasure trove of raw materials (resins, lignin, alcohol) and finished products (paper, rayon, film). Of course, these industries are now partly (and could in the future be wholly) supplied by fast-growing poplar and slash pine, raised as a commercial crop.

THE ROLE OF MASONRY

Though brick and stone have always dominated the urban landscape, there has never been an authentic masonry tradition in the United States. The masonry surfaces which seem so important are preponderantly only membranes stretching around endoskeletal structures. The reasons for this historical anomaly, which have been traced out in Volume 1 of this work, are peculiarly American: they are complex and interlocking; but the central one has been the abundance of skeletal materials, first wood, then iron and steel. Even in its heyday, the masonry building relied upon wood and metal for framing of floors and roofs. Our genuine masonry vaults can almost be counted on the hands. Even our most famous dome, that on the U.S. Capitol, is fabricated of cast iron and steel.

Nevertheless, as surfacing materials, stone and ceramic materials still have great merits. They are all relatively inert and stable and hence much less vulnerable to rot and rust than either steel or wood. They are nonflammable and their resistance to climatic attrition is relatively high (though marbles and some stones are attacked by atmospheric pollutants). Masonry has other merits of both functional and cosmetic nature. Brick, tile, stone and marble offer a matchless range of colors, textures and integral patterns; and these can be used in almost limitless combinations. They assemble into a surface of many joints, which gives the surface as a whole a degree of elasticity that is missing in sheet and panel materials. In climates with wide diurnal or seasonal temperature fluctuations, the masonry wall will have less crazing and cracking; such imperfections will be largely confined to the joints and hence less obtrusive. Because of mat finishes, natural irregularities and generally darker tones, small failures — which, in smooth materials like stucco or glass, would be disastrous esthetically — are effectively masked in masonry. Moss and lichens, capillary action and coal smoke have little cosmetic effect on most masonry. Moreover, this capacity to absorb thermal shock has functional significance as well. In far northern cities like Moscow, for example, it is notable how much better medieval brickwork has survived climatic attrition than either the stucco of Baroque times or contemporary reinforced concrete.

SYNTHETIC FILAMENTS AND MEMBRANES

The extraordinary development of the chemical industry during the past few decades has produced an enormous range of new synthetic fibers, fabrics and extruded membranes. Used singly or in combination, they display an equally wide spectrum of performance characteristics — high tensile strength, flexibility and elasticity; resistance to fire, intense cold and many chemicals and gases; immunity to attack by animal pests, fungi and microbes; transparency/opacity to light, heat and other forms of electro-magnetic energy; permeability/impermeability to fluids, gases; etc. The availability of such materials has, in turn, brought to the fore the much neglected family of suspended, tented and pneumatic structures.

Some of these forms, like the tent, have never been used by the urbanized Western world; some of them, like the suspension bridge and dirigible, have had great significance for transportation and the military. But, until recently, none of them has played any significant role in architecture proper — and this despite the fact that they are all extremely efficient structural forms, since they employ tensile materials almost wholly in tension. Part of this neglect has no doubt been due to simple prejudice: traditionally, Western society has always equated strength with rigidity. With its great emphasis on stability and permanence, it has relegated tented structures to carnivals, Gypsies and primitive nomadic peoples generally.* But neglect of these tensile-stressed structural types has been fundamentally due to the very real limitations of the fibers, fabrics and membranes hitherto available. Exclusively organic in origin, they were all too vulnerable to all forms of environmental attrition. The appearance of the new synthetics is changing all this. Tensile, tented and pneumatic buildings are among the most promising developments in the entire field of structural engineering. Pneumatic structures promise unprecedented means of enclosing very large areas (Fig. 76).

---

* Suspension bridges, of course, had flourished ever since the perfection of the steel cable by Roebling in the mid-1840s. But there has been no comparable flowering of suspended structures in architecture proper. This paradox was no doubt due to the fact that steel in trabeated forms was so cheap and abundant that no economic drive for its maximal exploitation in tensile structures developed. There are now signs that this is changing and we begin to see the principle applied to buildings.

Fig. 76a. U.S. Pavilion, Expo '70, Osaka, Japan. Davis, Brody and Associates, architects; David Geiger and Horst Berger, structural engineers. Enormous size of inflated dome is dramatized by scale of two men at lower right. It weighs less than 1 lb. psf.

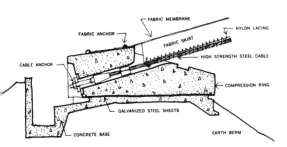

Fig. 76b. Cross section, compression ring.

Fig. 76. This air-inflated dome, 262 ft. wide by 460 ft. long, is held in shape by an internal pressure differential of only .03 psi. Yielding 100,000 sq. ft. of unobstructed floor space beneath a "roof" of unprecedented lightness, the structure consists of a diamond-pattern lattice of steel cables stitched to the vinyl-coated fiber glass membrane; this lattice is in turn anchored to a perimetrical concrete compression ring which rests on an earth berm. Designed to resist earthquakes and winds of 125 mph, the structure is safe even with air-pump failure, since it cannot sag low enough to injure visitors.

Fig. 76c. Technology of air-supported structures makes enclosure of entire towns entirely practicable. This cable-restrained, air-supported technique would be especially useful in Arctic and Antarctic climates, where an absolute deficiency of heat and light plus low temperatures, high winds and heavy snow cover restrict full development of urban life. For significance of such potentials, see pp. 274–277.

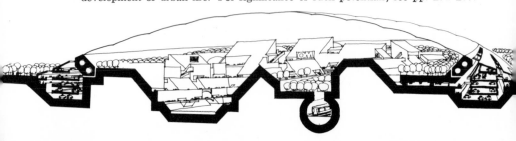

THE LINE OF INCREASING EFFICIENCY

Structural theory did not develop and could not exist in a cultural vacuum. We have seen that, in the light of the past century's accomplishment, it is possible to formulate the laws of structural development. All of man's structural forms, like those of organisms generally, belong morphologically to two broad genera: endoskeletal and exoskeletal. Within these two categories, some species are more advanced than others, either relatively (because of more intensive cultivation by a given society) or absolutely (because of inherent static characteristics). Finally, there has been an evolutionary progression toward more efficient forms — often, as in organisms, as a result of hybridizing and crossbreeding. But historically this development has been largely unplanned, pragmatic and hence asymmetrical. This is by no means a purely technological phenomenon; on the contrary, controlling factors have often been economic, geographic, even political or military. Thus the formulation of ferroconcrete theory was largely the by-product of the great burst of dam and highway construction beginning in the early years of this century. Similarly, the intensive cultivation of the steel truss and the steel cage was the consequence of the great periods of railroad and skyscraper building in the last half of the nineteenth century.

Each material had its characteristic potentials, each had its limitations. As a result, each became associated with certain types of structural forms or systems. This parallelism between form and material served to accelerate the development of some aspects of structural theory: but by the same token it often served to distort or stultify the development of other aspects equally promising. Here three factors are in constant interaction: structural system, material, and production or fabrication method. A change in one inevitably affects the other two and — consequently — the entire equation. But contemporary technology is dissolving most of these parallelisms, often with startling effect. By means of a new fabrication method (thermo-pressure molding) an existing material (plywood) can appear in a radically new structural form (semi-monocoque and stressed-skin shells). Materials which have been traditionally thought of as "sticks" are now the basis of latticed spheres (Fuller's geodesic dome). A plastic material like concrete, once thought uniquely appropriate for curved shells and vaults, is now prefabricated into skeletal components as precisely dimensioned as steel or wood "sticks." Such a state of affairs makes possible an unprecedented hybridization of structural systems.

But since this very plenitude of structural means has also led to unprecedented confusion in the selection of structural systems for various plan types, it might be appropriate to recapitulate their essential characteristics. Structural systems derived from "stick" or "string" lead to articulated constructions, while those derived from slab or flexible membrane employ the principle of continuity. In the first case, the integrity of the walling membrane can be interrupted at almost any point, since it is merely hung on the outside of the skeleton and contributes little or nothing toward resisting the mechanical loads of gravity and wind. Continuity structures, on the other hand, employ a shell which is at once enclosing *and* supporting; its integrity cannot be violated without serious or even disastrous consequences.

The significance of this for architecture should be obvious. Those activities which involve a great deal of traffic, movement, exchange across the interface between meso- and macro-environments are apt to be most easily contained in the exoskeletal structural systems, where nonstructural skins hung on load-bearing frames make provisions for penetration at any point a simple matter. In those types of buildings where movement across the interface is regular, limited in space or periodic in time (e.g., theaters and stadiums of all sorts, warehousing and storage facilities, etc.) the endoskeletal structure is more appropriate. This congruence of structural system and use is all the more marked since large and unobstructed spans are also indicated for spectator sports and theatrical performances of all sorts.

ECONOMIC ASPECTS OF BUILDING PRODUCTION

It is clear that modern technology has made possible an unprecedented range of structural possibilities. It is also very clear that they are only partially and sporadically employed in the mass of

American building. The most advanced technology on earth flourishes in a landscape filled with a preponderance of unsafe, obsolete and unattractive structures. The sources of this paradox lie largely outside technology itself, however.

The production of buildings is one of the most complex and difficult of all operations in present-day America. To assemble the capital, land, materials, equipment and specialized skills involved in the production of even a single-family house is a process proportionately more complex than the construction of a 100,000-ton tanker. Hundreds of separate items, made by different manufacturers and distributed through various channels, must be individually assembled from a host of entrepreneurs. The talents and skills of an entire hierarchy of trades and professions must be dovetailed together, and — with the present rate of technological development — this hierarchy necessarily grows larger. A network of building and zoning ordinances — often contradictory and almost always lagging behind the current technology — must be traversed. Finally, all the legal processes involving mortgaging, title search, deeds, etc., must be negotiated. As a result of this anarchic system of production, the prices of all building types are high, the quality often low and the output — especially in housing — quite inadequate.

These anomalies flow from a central fact of historic importance: the building field has never been fully industrialized as have most other major fields of production. It is not, in some senses, a homogeneous industry at all but rather an agglomeration of related interests, united in an awkward and uneasy truce. For, in addition to all the conflicts which characterize any American industry today — labor vs. management, big vs. little producers, producer vs. consumer — the building field has a deep vertical fissure in its economic structure. To the one side of this fissure lie the interests associated with manufacturing, fabrication and construction. The profits and wages of these interests derive from the production of new buildings. This fact naturally gives them a vested interest in high rates of production; hence in accelerated rates of obsolescence. Like the automobile industry, they would like to see accelerated rates of technical obsolescence.

But, on the other side of this vertical fissure lie the *rentier* interests — the realty, mortgage and lending institutions — who depend for their incomes upon the ownership of existing buildings. Since many a fifty-year-old building is still yielding good returns, the *rentier* shows an understandable tendency to restrict the production of new units to a minimum. This resistance to high rates of obsolescence is reinforced by the fact that these interests control the ownership of land upon which any building must ultimately stand. It constitutes a veto of not inconsiderable dimensions — the more so because land ownership is distributed among tens of millions of small owners.

It is this split between profit-through-production and profit-through-continued-use-of-existing-plant that has largely prevented that consolidation of capital and that centralization, mechanization, and automation of production facilities which characterize contemporary industrialism. This split has been perpetuated by two special aspects of the field: buildings are, by all odds, the largest, most durable and most expensive of all consumer goods; and land values, although socially created, are individually owned and exploited. As long as these conditions continue, the building field is apt to retain its peculiar characteristics and the potentials of structural innovation will not be fully utilized.

"Prefabrication" has always envisaged the volume production of completely shop-fabricated building units which would be delivered ready to be plugged in, like a dishwasher or TV. Such a production method would involve a transfer of labor from all the hazards of scattered, open-air field operations to the controlled conditions of the assembly line. If the problem were solely technical, the shift from field to factory would have long ago taken place. But, because of the above-mentioned economic contradictions, the process has only partially and unevenly occurred.

Rationalization, mechanization and automation have been widely employed by individual companies in the building field, both in factory fabrication and in on-site assembly. Such prefabrication of structural systems and equipment has seen its widest application in commercial and industrial buildings, especially in skyscraper construction. Here the wide use of skeleton-and-skin structural systems has permitted a relatively high degree of prefabrication. The components of the steel frame have, of course, always been "prefabricated"; and with the development of welding, on-site fabrication has been facilitated. Recent advances in concrete technology have, as we have seen, made the prefabricated concrete skeleton fully competitive with steel. Comparable developments have made possible the appearance of prefabricated curtain wall and interior partition in various combinations of glass, metal, concrete and plastics. But they have been largely confined to non-residential building types.

In the housing field, where the arguments for prefabrication have always seemed most persuasive, there have been decades of effort to unlock these economic paradoxes. Though there were many companies on the profits-through-production side of the field with adequate resources, few of them have shown any disposition to undertake the large-scale manufacture of prefabricated housing. The required investment was large, the risks not small and the resistance of the craft-oriented building field was enormous. Thus, by default, exploratory work fell to small, inadequately capitalized independents. Their background was generally industrial. Most of their products have reflected that fact — i.e., their designs and fabrication methods have sought to increase production and reduce unit costs by typically industrial techniques. These independents dreamed of producing a complete, ready-to-live-in house which could be bought from a showroom and delivered like an automobile.

However, if distribution, advertising and consumer financing were dismaying for the big companies, they were to prove all but insuperable for small independents. The only way in which they could hope to market their product was by using the facilities of the traditional house-building field. But to use these facilities, they had to have a product which involved no major threat to existing interests in that field. This, in turn, led the independent prefabricator into a maze of technical compromises which robbed his product of the inherent advantages of industrial mass production.

The bathroom, for example, could not be stamped out of one piece of metal or formed in one unit of reinforced plastic — not because it was technically unfeasible but because it threatened the vested interests of the locally dominant system of appliance and fixture dealers, master plumbers, and plumbers' unions. The structural steel could not employ advanced engineering principles because local lending agencies, material dealers, building unions and building codes would, for one reason or another, be opposed to it. Even the appearance of the completed house would be dictated not by functional requirements but by local esthetic standards, strictly enforced by local realtors and lending institutions. The attempt to meet limitations such as these established the lower limit of the spectrum of prefabrication — the so-called "packaged house." Here both design and materials are conservative, and work in a central factory is confined to those aspects which do not threaten the local *status quo*.

The history of prefabrication, at least as it applies to single-family housing, is a story of shuttling back and forth between these two extremes. An advanced technical solution was conceived; then it was measured against economic realities; it was then revised downward to meet those realities or it disappeared from the market. The halfway point between a genuine industrialized product and a packaged house was the trailer or the so-called "mobile home." This product had the great advantage of a mobility which permitted it to be parked on rented land or permanently installed on the purchaser's own land. It is not surprising, therefore, that in 1970, the mobile home industry produced some 401,190 units at an estimated retail value of $2,427,000,000.

However adequately American society has been able to keep production of nonresidential building abreast of its needs, its record in the production of housing has been uniformly inadequate. There has probably always been a housing shortage in the United States, especially in the cities; but in the past few decades, this shortage has become steadily more acute. The shortage naturally affects the poor most harshly and, among the poor, the racial minorities — Negroes, Puerto Ricans, Indians and Mexicans. And the deficit can be described in both qualitative and quantitative terms, as a recent authoritative survey clearly shows (Table 7).[1]

Some two-thirds of all substandard housing in the nation lies outside the standard metropolitan areas — where some 34,000 communities lack modern water facilities and another 44,000 are without modern sanitation facilities. The need for the decade 1970–1980

Construction of new standard units:	
Units for new households	13.4
Replacement of net removals of standard units	3.0
Allowance for vacancies	1.6
Subtotal	18.0
Replacement or rehabilitation of substandard units:	
Units becoming substandard during 1968–78	2.0
Replacement of net removals	2.0
Other substandard units in inventory 1966	4.7
Subtotal	8.7
Total construction needs	26.7

Table 7. Estimated U.S. housing needs for decade 1968–1978, expressed in millions of dwelling units. The large and growing deficit of housing meeting contemporary standards of amenity and health is conservatively estimated at over twenty-six million.

for this type of housing alone has been estimated at 13,500,000 units (new and rehabilitated). Of these, 7,000,000 must be subsidized.[2]

But annual production of housing units continues to lag far behind even the most conservative estimates of need. For the ten-year period ending 1968, average annual production hovered around 1,550,000 — just about half the number required to replace attrition and provide for new family growth.[3] When analyzed from the point of view of economic need, the picture is even more discouraging. In the decade ending 1968, only some 36,000 publicly owned low-rent units were produced each year. Yet in that same year the President's Committee on Decent Housing estimated that 7,800,000 families could not pay the market price for standard housing — i.e., housing that would cost no more than 20 per cent of their income.[4] 11.8 per cent of all white families fell within this category but for non-white families the figure was 29.2 per cent.[5]

There is thus little in its recent history to indicate that the building field can, unaided, and uncontrolled, give the American people the kind of housing to which their technical accomplishments entitle them. The field seems to have forgotten nothing and learned nothing. For, while it has bitterly resisted federal and municipal intervention, even at the points of most critical need, it has been unable to present a program of its own. Its internal contradictions remain unsolved. Here and there, it is true, it has produced well-designed, well-built houses and apartments, even occasionally entire neighborhoods. These have been within the reach, economically, of only the topmost layers of the population. There is a hoary thesis — currently popular again — that the housing field has only to produce new units for this stratum of the population. Their discarded housing units will in turn become available for the next-lowest income group and so on down the line until, according to the theory, everyone will be housed. While this "escalator" has always operated in American housing, it has never filled the need and never will. Statistically, the production of upper-class housing has always represented a portion of the national total so small as to be insignificant. Philosophically, this theory is even less defensible. If the American people were told that their society could offer them no better perspective than an existence in which they would wear only secondhand clothes, drive only secondhand cars, sleep only in discarded bedding, and read only hand-me-down books — in short, were to have access only to consumer goods handed down to them by the income group above — they would certainly reject it.

9.

THE INTEGRATION OF
ENVIRONMENTAL CONTROL SYSTEMS

The optimal control of all environmental factors within a given building, in the interests of the persons and processes housed in that building, is today technically more feasible and socially more imperative than ever before. Yet by and large, contemporary architecture does not succeed in discharging this task. The reasons for this failure are to be found in many different domains. There is, first of all, the architect's difficulty in formulating the program — in conceptualizing the exact behavioral topography which the building is supposed to elicit and support. Even when this part of the task is properly defined, he faces the task of effectuating it — of reconciling the many contradictory requirements of the various control systems he must employ. Thus some special problem in acoustics may render more difficult an optimal solution of the illumination system. Or some mandatory requirement for ease of access or exit may complicate the design of wintertime weatherstripping and thermal insulation. Or some local condition, such as earthquake or hurricane hazards, may dictate a structural system which is far from ideal for the plan suggested by the program. Finally, almost any building will be expected to satisfy the often divergent environmental requirements of the men and the processes which it shelters.

Such contradictions must be resolved at the highest possible level: yet they involve factors which are at once disparate and variable — biological and mechanical, subjective and objective, poetic and practical. Nevertheless, such considerations are fundamentally endogenous to the design; as such, they are subject to a fairly high degree to rational analysis and design control. In meeting them, the building becomes both the container for and the creator of the third environment, or "meso-environment." But the contradictions between this contained meso-environment and the natural macro-environment in which it stands submerged can be only partly resolved at the wall line, no matter how sophisticated the design of that walling membrane may be. The qualitative fluctuation of that macro-environment, across both time and space, is immense, and only in gross terms predictable. Such exogenous forces must therefore be dealt with by means of other techniques of environmental manipulation — i.e., landscape architecture and city planning.

Unfortunately, the coordination between these three levels of environmental design is ordinarily poor or nonexistent. As a result, the individual architect, acting for his own client, is compelled to adopt a defensive design policy. Thus, for example, the buildings which surround his own will obstruct the prevailing breeze. Unable to exploit this natural resource, he must install ventilating fans. Neighboring structures not only make no intelligent use of their own share of the sun's heat and light, they also prevent a normal distribution of sunlight on his plot. Thus, for him, insolation and daylighting remain academic questions: he has to install space heaters and fluorescent tubes instead. Surrounded by paved courts, masonry walls, and traffic-crowded streets, his plot is flooded with noise: he must rely upon sound insulation to make his building tolerably quiet. Having access only to polluted air, he must rely upon filters to cleanse it. His building is thus doubly on the defensive — against nature and against man. It has to overcome the natural deficiencies of its external environment without being able to exploit those features which are favorable. And, as if this were not bad enough, it has also to overcome the cumulative damage which its neighbors have already wrought upon the natural environment.

The ingenuity which American buildings display in overcoming such peripheral obstacles is little short of miraculous. By mechanical means, we can now create any set of environmental conditions we desire. Important as they are, however, the wide use of these techniques and equipments has inherent dangers. The contemporary designer runs the risk of accepting electrical air filters as a satisfactory substitute for clean, fresh air; of feeling that electronically operated louvers are preferable to natural foliage; of preferring sound insulation to plain ordinary silence. There are, as we have seen, many specific situations in which our synthetic environments are superior to nature's. But this is no adequate basis for the mechanistic conclusion that we "don't need nature anymore." On the contrary, with the complexity of modern building we need nature more than ever before. It is not a question of air conditioning versus sea breezes, of fluorescent tubes versus the sun. It is rather the necessity for integrating the two at the highest possible level.

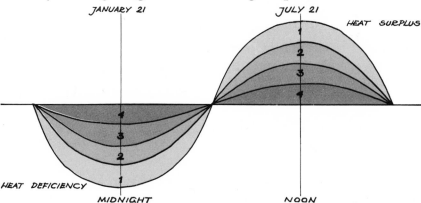

Fig. 77. Four stages of optimizing thermal "fit" between building and its environment (after Victor Olgyay). Instead of employing transparent walling membranes and then relying upon complex mechanical systems to compensate for high rates of energy transfer across interface, the design process should begin at other end of design-option process. (1) Site should be selected for microclimatic advantages and landscaped to maximize them. (2) Building's mass should be shaped and oriented to maximize desirable, minimize negative exposures. (3) Enclosing membranes should be selected for transparency or opacity to specific environmental forces. (4) Only then can mechanical systems operate economically while yielding better comfort conditions.

ON UNDERSTANDING THE TERRESTRIAL ENVIRONMENT

To intervene effectively in the situation in which we find ourselves — that is, to construct a truly effective "third environment" for individual and social life — both architect and urban designer require a much deeper understanding of the terrestrial environment than they commonly display. For the quality which most characterizes all contemporary architectural and urbanistic activity everywhere in the world today is a profound misunderstanding of ecological realities. This misunderstanding is, in turn, characterized by two sorts of error. One is a lack of comprehension of the absolute inter-relatedness of all the component elements of the natural environ-ment — an interdependence which makes it impossible to manipu-late one factor without setting in motion a complex chain reaction that usually extends far beyond the individual designer's sphere of action. (Thus it now seems possible that gaseous wastes from two centuries of fossil fuel combustion, accumulating in the upper atmos-phere, may irreversibly alter the climate of the entire world.) The other error is the consistent tendency of modern architects and engineers grossly to underestimate the magnitude of the natural forces of the environment; or, contrariwise, grossly to overestimate the magnitude of man-made capacities at their disposal. (Recent spectacular failures of the power grids in the American Northeast in December, 1966, and May, 1967, are two examples of such faulty estimates.)

The natural world in which we live and move is the result of the interaction of a vast number of forces acting upon the earth and upon each other. A bewildering network of relationships, primary and secondary, causal and resultant, interact to produce those con-ditions which we call climate and weather. While we cannot expect architects and urban designers to be also meteorologists and clima-tologists, we might at least demand that they have a general under-standing of the ecological systems which they are constantly called upon to manipulate in one way or another.

For the purposes of our analysis, the principal environmental factors may be summarized in this decreasing order of magnitude (*not* of decreasing importance):

1. meteorological   a. electromagnetic radiation
   b. air masses
   c. precipitation

2. geographical   a. latitude
   b. land mass–water surface ratio
   c. elevation above sea level

3. topographical   a. elevation
                             b. orientation to sun, prevailing winds
                             c. soil structure

4. biological   a. fauna (including micro-organisms)
                             b. flora

While the scale of these factors will vary enormously — the first being cosmic, the latter quite local in extent — they interact with each other at every level. A forest, for example, is the result of a given temperature and precipitation regime. This regime may be regional or sub-continental in extent. But this same forest, by its very presence, will in turn modify the regime which makes it possible in the first place. Every local factor will act upon regional norms to create local variations. Often these variations assume quite astonishing magnitudes and compel us to make the distinctions we do between *macro*climates and *micro*climates — the distinction being all the more important because the locus of all individual experience is obviously always the microclimate.

The sun is the prime mover of the entire terrestrial system. All meteorological phenomena — wind, rain, clouds, temperature; night and day, winter and summer; gravity, magnetism, the movements of the earth itself — are the results of the sun's actions upon the otherwise inert solids, fluids, and gases of our planet. But the sun, in addition to being the generator of all terrestrial activity, is itself a prime factor in the climates of the world. Insolation, the amount of solar energy falling upon the earth, is constant. Its variable impact is due to the complex motions of the earth itself (Fig. 78). This insolation sets in motion the whole great global system of air circulation. From this solar action upon the earth's atmospheric envelope comes the movement of equatorial and polar air masses whose collisions over land and sea bring the whole train of clouds, sunshine, winds and precipitation which make up local weather (Fig. 79). At both these levels, insolation is the most important factor in the thermal environment.

The principal geographical factor in environment is expressed in latitude, for it is distance from the equator which determines the amount of solar energy which any given point receives. (Longitude

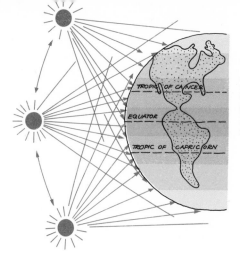

Fig. 78. Solar energy received annually at any point on earth's surface is function of angle of incidence times exposure length. Hence higher latitudes have colder climates than low ones.

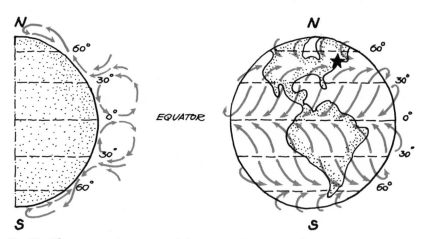

Fig. 79. The sun as prime mover of the terrestrial system. All meteorological phenomena — including wind patterns, cloud cover and precipitation — are the consequence of the sun's irradiation of the solids, fluids and gases of our planet.

Fig. 80. Temperature change with latitude. The earth's temperatures drop in proportion to distance north or south of equator. Annual average mean is about 5.6° F for each degree of latitude but actual differential between two points can vary widely.

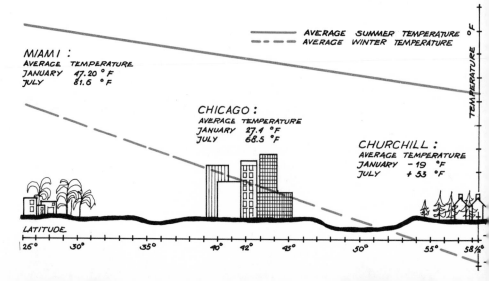

AVERAGE SUMMER TEMPERATURE
AVERAGE WINTER TEMPERATURE

TEMPERATURE °F

MIAMI :
AVERAGE TEMPERATURE
JANUARY   47.20 °F
JULY   81.6 °F

CHICAGO :
AVERAGE TEMPERATURE
JANUARY   27.4 °F
JULY   68.5 °F

CHURCHILL :
AVERAGE TEMPERATURE
JANUARY   - 19 °F
JULY   + 53 °F

LATITUDE

25°   30°   35°   40°   42°   45°   50°   55°   58½°

has no comparable significance: it is merely an index of location, never of climate.) Were the surface of the globe absolutely uniform in profile and material, the correlation between latitude and climate would be absolute. However, since the earth's surface is so widely varied, the climates along any given latitude will vary also. Thus Pompeii and Samarkand lie on the same latitude as Peking and New York; Leningrad is as far north as Churchill, Manitoba, while St. Augustine, Florida, and Lhasa in Tibet both lie near 30° N.

The main reason for this climatic anomaly along a given latitude lies in the differing heat-holding capacities of water bodies and land masses. Since water has much the higher specific heat, temperature accumulation and decay is much slower in water than on land. Thus the effect of any body of water upon its immediate environment is to reduce diurnal and seasonal temperature extremes: the larger the water body, the more pronounced this stabilizing effect. Honolulu, at 19° N, near the center of a great warm ocean, sees very little temperature variation between midnight and midday or January and July. Timbuctoo, in Africa, at approximately the same latitude (17° N) has much higher temperatures and much greater diurnal and seasonal variations because it is imbedded in the center of a great arid land mass (Fig. 80).

Land masses themselves have vastly different heat-holding capacities. Partly these are due to the physical characteristics of the earth itself — i.e., whether it is sand, silt, rock — and partly to the overlying ground cover or lack thereof. Thus the sands of the Sahara and the snows of Antarctica are the result of a set of primary climatic factors — very dry air and intense insolation in the one case; very cold air and weak insolation in the other. But the two materials are, at the same time, the cause of secondary climatic characteristics. Sand is a good absorber of solar energy while snow is a good reflector of it. Thus each tends to exacerbate still further the climates that caused them, rendering the desert still hotter and the Arctic tundra yet colder than they otherwise would be.

It is also apparent that the *ratio* between land mass and water body at any given point will have a characteristic impact on the climate of that point. For this reason, *continental land masses* produce wide regional variations even along the same latitude (Oregon and Maine, Copenhagen and Omsk in Siberia) and wide seasonal

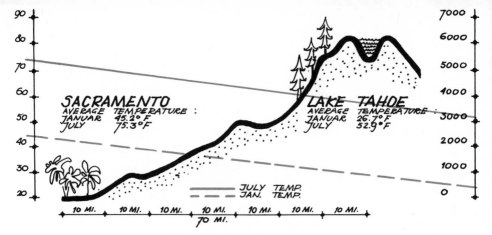

Fig. 81. Temperature with altitude. Air temperatures drop in inverse proportion to altitude at an average rate of 3.6° F per thousand feet. Local conditions can modify or even reverse this ("temperature inversion") but only for limited periods of time.

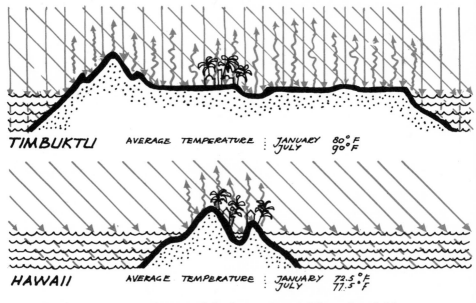

Fig. 82. Temperature change with land mass. Due to differing heat-holding capacities of land and water, higher temperatures will develop, and greater diurnal and annual temperature extremes occur in large land masses than in large water bodies.

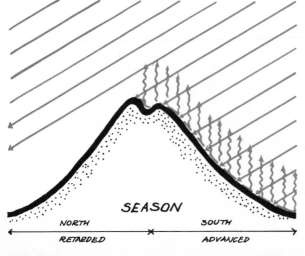

Fig. 83. Temperature change with exposure. On a local scale, microclimatic variations due to different exposure to sun can be as significant as if separated by hundreds of miles instead of a few feet.

extremes within a given region (e.g., the climates of the American-Canadian prairies and the Russian steppes). *Peninsulas and isthmuses* tend to yield climates strongly influenced by adjacent water bodies (Mexico, Italy), while *islands* will always show the steadiest climates and the least deviation from the norms of their latitudes (the Azores, Galápagos, Madagascar).

Elevation above sea level acts to modify climate in two important ways. The first effect is due simply to the fact that air temperatures drop at a constant rate as one rises — i.e., inversely with altitude. This temperature "lapse rate" amounts to 3.6° F per thousand feet of altitude. Thus a 1000-foot rise in altitude is equivalent to a horizontal displacement or change in latitude of 450 miles to the north or south of the equator. This elevational effect is what leads to such climatic anomalies as the Peruvian Altiplano or the Mountains of the Moon in East Africa. Despite an almost equatorial location, their altitudes (10,000 and 16,795 feet, respectively) give these regions the icy fogs and alpine flora of the tundra, instead of the tropical rain forest normal to such low latitudes (Figs. 82, 83).

But high elevations have an important climatic impact upon the lower lands around them. Thus the mountain ranges along the North American West Coast force the moist-air masses coming in off the Pacific to rise. In the process this air is chilled and condensation takes place. As a result, the air mass discharges most of its moisture (in the form of either rain, hail, sleet or snow) on the "upper-weather side" of the ranges. This effect, called an orographic uplift, produces a so-called "rain shadow" on the windward slopes and an "aridity shadow" to the leeward. In the American Northwest, this finds classic expression in the cool, rainy climates of coastal Oregon and Washington and the semi-arid regions of Wyoming, Nevada, and Utah (Fig. 84).

THE MICROCLIMATE AS HUMAN HABITAT

Such meteorological and geographical factors as the above are decisive in establishing the climatic regimes of continents and large regions, the macroclimates of the world. But for the average man, as for the average building, they are largely statistical abstractions.

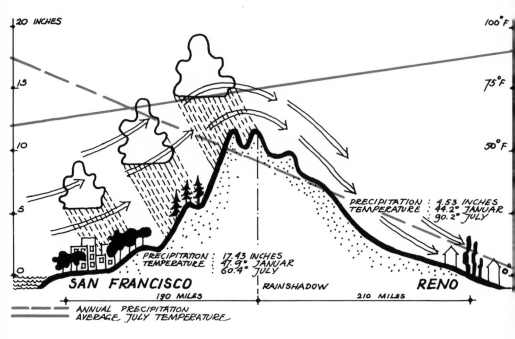

Fig. 84. Temperature and precipitation changes due to orographic uplift. Large climatic variations can occur within relatively short distances when precipitation occurs on windward side of mountain ranges. When this drop in precipitation on leeward slopes is severe, as in American Southwest, desert conditions can result.

They bear little relation to the experiential reality in which individual men are, at any moment of their existence, immersed. The microclimate — the milieu of the yard, the street or the neighborhood — is the only true measure of this level of human experience. Here, the play of larger forces upon the local landscape produces the weather in which men actually live.

The perspiring man in the street who doubts the Weather Bureau's 88° F when his own private thermometer shows 103° F in the shade; the irate citizen who chases his hat down a roaring street-wide gale while the instruments at the airport blandly register an eight-mile breeze; the gardener whose seedlings on the north side of the house were frozen despite an official low of 39° F; the puzzled housewife whose radio proclaims a visibility of nine miles when outside her window the smog is so thick that she cannot see across the street — all these people are the victims of experiential contradiction. There is nothing wrong either with their powers of observation or with the instruments at the weather station. It is merely that the same climate is being measured at two entirely different levels. The Weather Bureau is reporting on the macroclimate while the citizen is feeling on his own back the effects of his microclimate.

Meteorology has reached a high stage in this country, especially since World War II. But so far it has worked largely on a macroscopic scale, dealing in terms of continents and regions inside which important variations go largely unobserved. Historically this emphasis is not difficult to understand. Meteorology got its earliest impetus from such activities as agriculture and maritime shipping. In recent decades, aviation has enormously extended both its coverage and its accuracy. This is essential knowledge, but of scant use to the designer or consumer of buildings. For the rude and pressing needs of the individual deal with his immediate environment — conditions within his apartment, block, or place of work. Detailed knowledge at this scale is almost totally lacking in this country.

When homely observation christens a certain intersection as "the coldest corner in town," the chances are that a check with instruments would confirm the fact. Moreover, intensive research along accepted meteorological lines would reveal why it is the coldest corner and how it might be redesigned to correct the situation. It is the character and juxtaposition of air masses which determines the weather in a given locality at a given time. But the local behavior of these air masses is in turn affected by the particular configuration of the land: the height and depth of its hills and valleys; the shapes, sizes, and densities of the buildings upon it; its bodies of water, groves of trees, parks, and paved streets; finally, by the way the sun falls upon the whole ensemble.

It thus follows that every change we make upon the landscape — every house we raise or tree we cut down, each field we plow or street we pave — affects the microclimate. This change may be small: it will certainly be definite. It may be for the better: but the chances are that, with our appalling ignorance, it will be for the worse. We cannot say, with Mark Twain, that everyone talks about the weather but no one does anything about it. As a matter of fact, we talk about the weather all the time and are never conscious of how importantly we are changing it.

The microclimate of a given site will be largely determined by small-scale variations in the topographical features of the site:

1. elevation above sea level
2. exposure to sun and prevailing winds
3. size, shape and proximity of water bodies
4. soil structure
5. vegetation (trees, shrubs, meadows, crops)
6. man-made structures — buildings, streets, parking lots, etc.

It is imperative for us to remember that, although the spatial extent of any of these factors may be quite limited, their physical magnitude with reference to the people in that space may be very large. For example, a building may at noon cast a very small shadow on the adjacent sidewalks; but if the location is Miami and the month July, the condition of pedestrians in that shadow will be dramatically different from the condition of those in full sun a few feet away. From an experiential point of view, hundreds of miles and not dozens of feet might separate the two micro-environments.

We have seen the macrocosmic effect of elevation upon climate. Architects and urban designers seldom realize that changes in elevation play a comparably important role in the microclimate. Such phenomena are well understood by farmers and orchardists who know that a rise of a few feet may render the higher elevation frost free. In some marginal areas, like the northern edge of the Florida citrus belt, elevation becomes so important that weather forecasts and frost warnings are issued in terms of feet above sea level. (Incidentally, the heat-holding capacities of the many lakes and ponds in this district are very apparent after a night of frost: there will always be a band of undamaged vegetation around the edges of each water body.)

Orientation has comparably important consequences for the microclimate. A north-facing slope (in the northern hemisphere) may have a growing season shorter by several weeks than a southern slope at the same elevation on the same mountain. Knowledge of this phenomenon would be critically important to developers of a ski trail, who would find longer and more severe winters on the northern slopes. The vineyardist or orchardist would seek a southern orientation for the opposite reason — i.e., shorter, less severe winters and longer growing season. Colorado potato growers exploit this phenomenon at the smallest possible scale by planting the tubers along the southern base of east-west furrows cast up by special plows (Fig. 83).

By themselves, then, minor changes in elevation or orientation can produce significant variations within even small horizontal distances. Combined, the two effects can produce spectacular climatic anomalies. The Italian lakes (Como, Garda, Lugano) afford classic examples of this. The shores of these lakes on the same latitude as Minneapolis enjoy a subtropic climate, complete with bougainvillea and palm trees; yet only a mile or two inland and several thousand feet higher, the climate is literally alpine. This anomaly is the composite result of several factors. One factor is a location at the southern base of the Alps, which exposes them to low winter sun and protects them from the cold winds off Western Europe. Superimposed upon these warming effects are two others: the warm *foehn* winds which slip down the southerly slopes in winter, and the heat reservoirs represented by the lakes themselves (Fig. 85).

Fig. 85. Several meteorological and geographic phenomena coincide to produce microclimates around north Italian lakes which are much warmer than Alpine hinterland: (1) *Foehn* winds warmed by orographic air coming over the Alps; (2) low elevation of lake shores; (3) maximum exposure of northern shores to low winter sun; and (4) thermal reservoir of lakes with their slow rates of temperature decay. Result: semi-tropical microclimates in close proximity to true Alpine climate regimes.

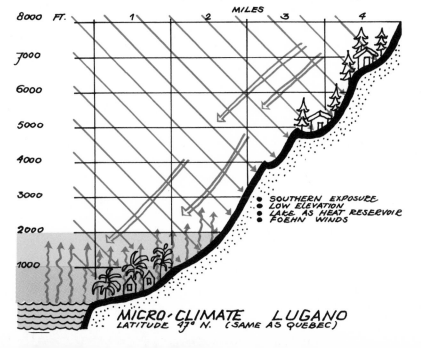

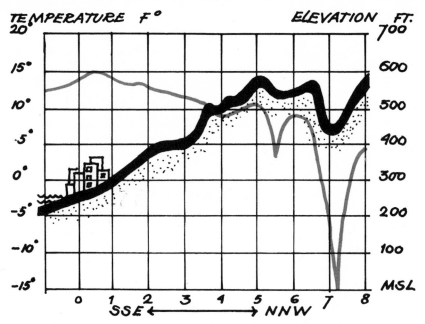

Fig. 86. Temperature distribution on a January night across Toronto, Canada. Warming effect of lake added to metabolism of heated urban tissue renders temperatures in central city some 30° F higher than hinterland seven miles inland. Note sharp drop in temperatures along floor of inland valley into which cold air of slopes has drained.

In varying degrees, such anomalies are to be found everywhere; and architects and planners should be much more attentive to them than they commonly are. This example is typical:

Tremendous microclimatic temperature differences [have been found] within the Neotama Valley of Central Ohio, based on four-year studies of 100 to 300 observational points within one square mile. The number of frost days varied from location to location between 124 and 276 per year; the dates of the last Spring frost from March 9 to May 25; those of the first Fall frost from September 11 to December 13. Differences between temperature minima amounted to about 40° F and those between maxima seem to be even higher.[1]

Nothing in the city layout or architecture of Toronto, for example, reflects the climatic realities shown in Fig. 86. Here, on a typical clear winter night, it will be 30 degrees colder seven miles inland than downtown at the lake front. This radical difference is due to three factors: (1) the heat-holding capacity of the lake; (2) the heated masonry fabric of the city itself, together with the "haze hood" of atmospheric pollution, which prevents much of the heat from escaping into outer space; and (3) the "frost pocket" effect of the little valley seven miles north-northwest of the city.[2]

Superimposed upon these natural microclimatic variations are an increasing range of man-made effects, the scale of which is rapidly approaching geographic or geological dimensions. The most important of these, from the standpoint of architect and urbanist, is the process of urbanization itself. By its substitution of a masonry landscape of paved streets and heated buildings for the vegetable cover of the natural landscape, urbanization automatically substitutes the micro-environment of the desert for whatever it replaces. This is characterized, first and foremost, by disturbances in the normal thermal cycle of the day — a disturbance due to the heat-absorbing and heat-holding capacities of masonry materials as compared to vegetal ones. Thus urban tissue absorbs heat all day and re-radiates it all night. This thermal effect is further accentuated by heat loss from millions of cubic feet of heated building space and by the "haze hood" to which we have already referred. For these reasons, the city is *always* warmer than its surrounding countryside, day and night, winter and summer. And this situation is commonly much more exaggerated than Weather Bureau data would indicate, since their measurements are always made inside instrument shelters and take no account of *radiant* temperatures, which play a critical role in human comfort (Fig. 87). Indeed, this phenomenon has now become so marked that it is necessary to regard the city as an organism with its own peculiar metabolism.[3]

Fig. 87. Temperature distribution at 1:00 A.M. on August night across Washington, D.C. Air temperatures in built-up central city are much higher than in wooded suburbs, reflecting slow temperature decay of sun-heated pavements and buildings. Effective temperatures are even higher, due to radiant temperature and high humidity.

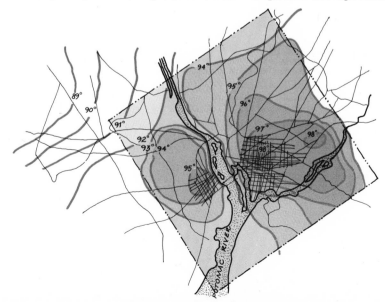

Even agriculture, in replacing virgin ecologies with plowland, alters pre-existing climatic conditions in real and significant proportions.* Indeed, it can be said with certainty that every time man plows a field or erects a building or paves a road, he alters the microclimate of that spot. Always, until very recent times, the architecture of each region displayed characteristic responses to the special climatic regimes with which it had to cope.[4] Indeed, this is the origin of many of the most distinctive features, in both plan and structure, of American regional architecture, as we have seen in volume 1 of this work. A close scrutiny of the meteorological data for these regions will show that preindustrial architecture was often more scientific than our own in its method of handling environmental stress.

Since, as we have seen, the animal body is first and foremost a "heat machine," the primary task of all building everywhere is always the control and manipulation of the thermal environment. In a highly advanced technology like our own, one might expect that contemporary American architecture would be characterized by a precise and elegant response to thermal stress. Unfortunately, this is far from true. American technology produces a splendid range of heating, cooling and ventilating equipment, as well as a wide array of thermal insulation materials. These make possible a level of thermal control which would have been inconceivable until the recent past — exemplified, of course, in rocket and space-vehicle technology. But, in normal architectural practice, this equipment and material is often less efficiently designed and more wastefully operated than were the much more limited resources available to our ancestors. The result is that our buildings yield far less satisfactory thermal environments than we have the right to expect; and they cost far more to install and to operate than they would if we paid as close attention to microclimatic reality as our ancestors were always compelled to do.[5] It is a vulgarization of technology to argue that, with modern potentials, such factors "do not matter anymore." The fact is, they matter more than ever: the air conditioner needs a cool roof even more than the man who lives under it.

* The German microclimatologist, Rudolph Geiger, has published many actual measurements of such variations in his epochal study, *The Climate of the Air Layer Nearest the Ground* (Munich: 1929). Fourth edition published by Harvard University Press, 1965.

In one of the few detailed examinations ever made of actual American climates, one striking characteristic emerges — i.e., the enormous variations in thermal regimes between one region and another and the large seasonal and diurnal fluctuations within a given region.[6] Such wide variations are characteristic of continental climates, and they subject all structures to enormously unequal stresses in both time and space. Minneapolis, for example, has a recorded range from 107° F down to —45° F; the city commonly sees a range of from 90° F down to —20° F (Fig. 88d). Spatially, the discrepancies are equally dramatic: in New York, on December 21, the south wall of a building will receive 107.7 times as much solar radiation as the north wall of the same building. Annually, the differential will amount to 72.8 times as much insolation on the south as on the north walls (Fig. 90).

The architectural consequences of such asymmetrical thermal stresses will be expressed at two different levels. (1) Wear and tear on the actual fabric of the building: nothing is so destructive of building materials as alternate freezing and thawing, wetting and drying, expanding and contracting. (2) Wear and tear on heating and cooling equipment to meet fluctuating external conditions. Such conditions clearly make the design of a building in Minneapolis a more difficult task than for Miami (Fig. 89). In the former instance, the building budget must be spread equally over a wide range of heat-generating and heat-dissipating devices, with redundant capacity inevitable in both. In Miami, on the other hand, the budget can be largely concentrated upon heat-dissipating devices and equipment. For this reason, also, a truly effective wall for Minneapolis is not likely to resemble a comparable one for Miami.

In the light of such considerations, the current tendency toward standardization of building form and building fabric to conform to a few international stereotypes does not in fact represent a truly scientific exploitation of modern technology. The visual poverty and monotony of the resulting architecture is merely one expression of overall dysfunction. Contrariwise, an esthetically rich and sensuously satisfying architecture can only be derived from the closest attention to and respect for its actual terrestrial environment — especially at the microclimatic scale.

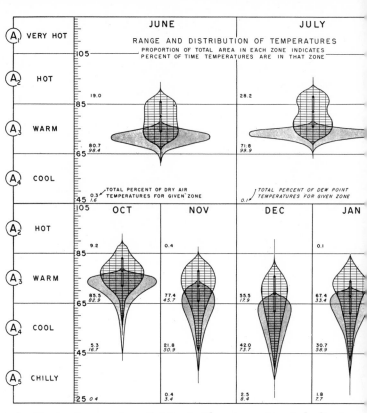

Fig. 88a (above). Temperature regime of Miami, Fla. A semi-tropical climate characterized by moderate air temperatures, high relative humidity and intense insola-

Fig. 88b (below). Temperature regime of Phoenix, Ariz. A true semi-arid climate characterized by high ambient temperatures, low humidity and very high radiant

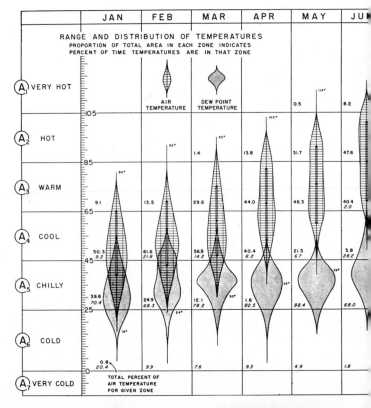

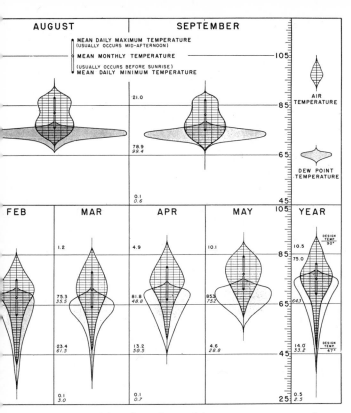

tion. Because of low latitudes and location on a peninsula surrounded by warm seas, there is a comparatively small diurnal or seasonal variation in temperature.

temperatures due to intense insolation. Because of clear skies and sparse vegetation, both diurnal and seasonal temperature variations are very large, as seen below at right.

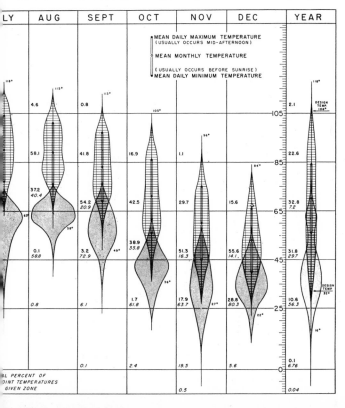

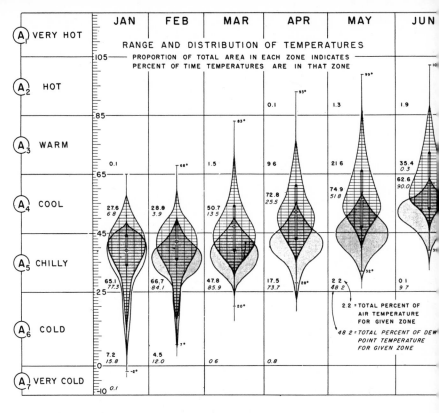

Fig. 88c (above). Temperature regime of Portland, Oreg. A truly temperate climate, characterized by moderate temperatures and modest diurnal and seasonal extremes.

Fig. 88d (below). Temperature regime of Minneapolis, Minn. Located at downwind rim of a continental steppe, this city has one of country's most difficult climates.

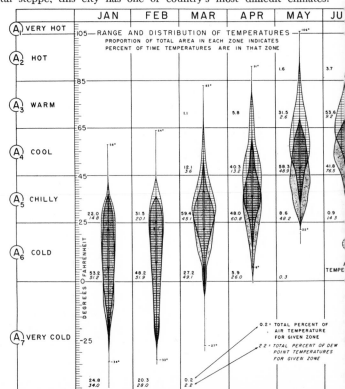

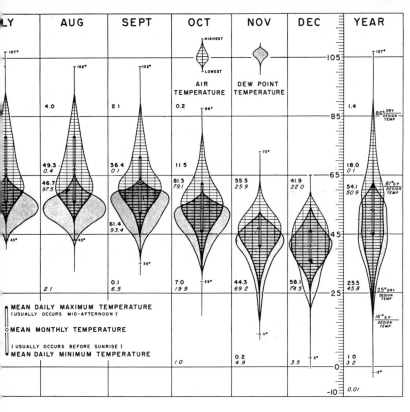

Because of prevailing winds off the Pacific and high mountain ranges to east, Portland is in a "rain shadow" with high precipitation, fog and cloudiness year round.

Extremely cold winters, with high winds and heavy snow cover, alternate with hot humid summers to make difficult a good fit between environment and architecture.

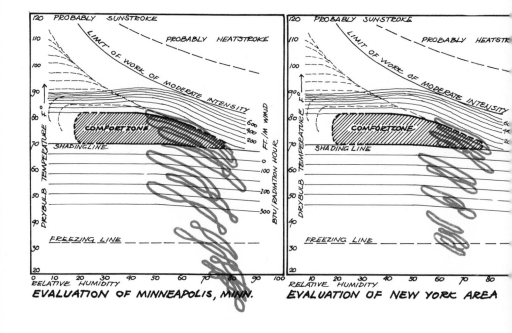

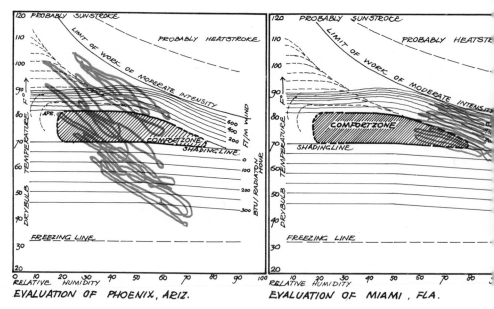

Fig. 89. Evaluation of four American climates relative to human comfort (adapted from Victor Olgyay). By plotting hourly temperatures at ten-day intervals on psychrometric chart two facts emerge: (1) none of these climates would be habitable without architectural intervention; and (2) an architecture truly responsive to the environmental reality of each would of necessity be very different, in both performance and appearance, from the limited stereotypes currently used by American architects.

ARCHITECTURAL RESPONSE TO CLIMATIC REALITY

To minimize stressful fluctuations across the interface between the building and its immediate environment, manipulation of all physical factors must be extended far beyond the building wall. This is carried on at two scales — that of the landscape architecture and that of urban design. Such manipulation of the landscape has obvious significance for the performance of the building. Yet recognition of the importance of landscape design to overall architectural amenity is, even today, of a peculiarly limited kind, being justified (even by landscape designers themselves) in largely esthetic terms. Streets planted with trees are now quite generally recognized as being more attractive than streets without them. Buildings are no longer considered completed until their surroundings are landscaped. Open areas add to the beauty of a neighborhood. Parks and playgrounds are important to the health of growing children. All of this is true. Yet it does not convey an adequate picture of the complex relationship between man, building, and landscape. It does not comprehend the real physical impact of the landscape upon us and upon the microclimate, nor of our every action upon it.

Fig. 90. Average solar heat absorbed by vertical walls at latitude of New York City. Curves indicate immense disparity of energy input at various times of year for walls of different orientation. At winter solstice, southwest wall receives 1400 times as much heat as north wall of same building. This asymmetry of the natural thermal environment, so hostile to an indoor thermal steady state, is inadequately recognized in design of walling membranes; buildings thus fail to give optimal performance.

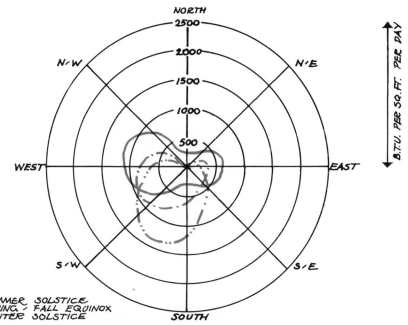

SUMMER SOLSTICE
SPRING - FALL EQUINOX
WINTER SOLSTICE

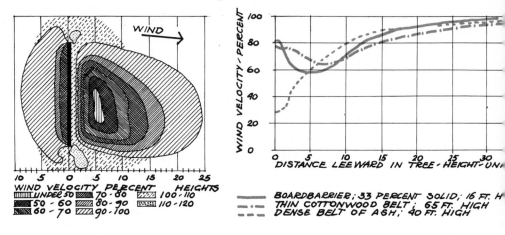

WIND VELOCITY - PERCENT

DISTANCE LEEWARD IN TREE - HEIGHT-UNI

WIND VELOCITY PERCENT   HEIGHTS
UNDER 50   70-80   100-110
50-60   80-90   110-120
60-70   90-100

BOARD BARRIER; 33 PERCENT SOLID; 16 FT. H
THIN COTTONWOOD BELT; 65 FT. HIGH
DENSE BELT OF ASH; 40 FT. HIGH

Fig. 91. Reduction of wind velocities by barriers. In cold climates, where an absolute deficiency of heat is a prime environmental problem, wind chill is an important cause of thermal stress. Thus all types of windbreaks, whether natural or man-made, should be considered integral components of overall thermal control systems.

Certain aspects of the landscape are susceptible to wide and flexible manipulation, the health and comfort potentials of which have scarcely been tapped by contemporary architects and landscape architects. Two examples will suffice: the functional use of trees and lawns in urban areas. Above and beyond their esthetic contribution, which is of course generally recognized, the scientific use of deciduous trees will accomplish any of the following environmental desiderata: (1) deflect, absorb and reduce solar heat; (2) reduce free air temperatures; (3) filter the atmosphere of particulates; (4) reduce light levels and glare; (5) increase visual privacy; (6) reduce transmission of airborne sound (Fig. 92).

In general, trees have a stabilizing effect upon their immediate surroundings, reducing all environmental extremes. Rudolph Geiger, in his pioneering study of the microclimate,[7] found that mixed forest growths of spruce, oak and poplar cut off 69 per cent of the sun's heat from the ground. He found that forests are cooler in summer and warmer in winter than cleared land; and that a belt of trees would reduce wind velocities in its lee by as much as 63 per cent. In this country, measurements have shown that a shelter belt of trees will reduce wind velocities by 50 per cent and reduce fuel consumption in farmhouses thus protected by as much as 30 per cent (Fig. 91).

Much the same result will flow from the intelligent use of lawns and dense ground covers: *Temperatures will be reduced.* Because of its rough texture and low color value, a grass surface will absorb more sunlight and re-radiate less heat than any paved or masonry surface. Because of transpiration, a lawn converts a large portion of the heat it absorbs into other forms of energy. In general, both air and radiant temperatures will be much lower above a grass plot than over a paved area of similar exposure. Observations in Texas, at 2 P.M. of an August day, revealed a temperature immediately above an unshaded asphalt pavement of 124.7° F: above a shaded grass plot thirty feet away the temperature was 98° F — a differential of almost 27 degrees.[8]

Geiger cites significant temperature differentials of various surfacing materials, made under similar conditions of exposure on a day in June.[9] He finds asphalt paving twice as hot as the grass it replaced. The microclimatic consequences of such local overheating are significant, as the measurements cited by Jeffrey Aronin[10] clearly demonstrate (Fig. 93). In view of the enormous expansion of paved surfaces (and especially asphalt and blacktop surfaces), the importance of data like these is obvious. They suggest the importance of shading the paved surfaces which surround most buildings — and shading them, where at all possible, with either trees or vines.

Fig. 92. Reduction of atmospheric and sonic pollution by trees and turf. All foliage acts as an impingement filter, trapping airborne particulates until washed away by rain. Trees, shrubs and turf are also highly effective absorbers of airborne sound.

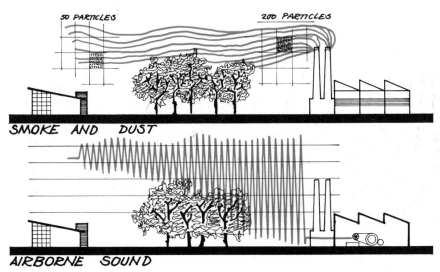

Glare will be eliminated. Grass presents a glare-proof texture. Despite immensely higher illumination levels out-of-doors, glare on a natural landscape will occur only over water, snow, or sheets of rock.

Dust will be reduced. Obviously a healthy lawn can be the source of very little dust; in addition, its grass blades will catch and hold a large amount of airborne dust.

Noise will be reduced. A grass surface offers an ideal surface for the absorption of airborne sound.

From facts such as these it is apparent that the landscape is an immensely important factor in building design — a factor which no architect can intelligently ignore. Trees, shrubs, sod, and ground cover must be viewed not as luxuries, not as ornaments, but as actual items of equipment, as essential to the efficient operation of the building as its furnace or lighting system. Their selection, disposition, feeding, and watering need not be charged off to overhead or justified as pleasant hobbies: they become serious matters of maintenance. Such an evaluation of the landscape implies new concepts for the landscape designer as well: his designs must recognize new disciplines. Purely visual considerations of composition, proportion, vista, and balance will be subjected to the acid test of environmental control. Landscaped areas will then be judged by their actual performance as well as by their beauty. No more than in architecture are the two contradictory; on the contrary, such an integration will yield new and higher esthetic standards.

Fig. 93. Turf as a thermal modifier. Both ambient and radiant temperatures are reduced by turf in two important ways: (1) it acts as an evaporative cooler as a side effect of the process of suspiration; and (2) in the process of photosynthesis it absorbs solar energy, reflecting much less heat or light than any masonry surface.

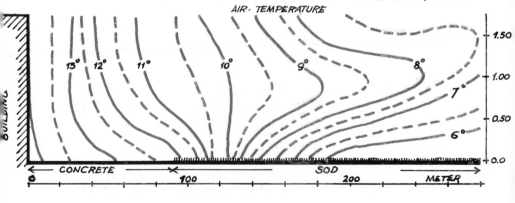

TOWARD A NEW AND HIGHER LEVEL OF SYNTHESIS

The meteorological features of the natural environment — the path of the sun, of prevailing breezes, the patterns of rain and snowfall — are, however, not subject to facile manipulation. Of course, in any densely built-up area even these forces are modified, sometimes importantly and almost always fortuitously. The way in which the sun falls upon a given building will be dependent upon the size, shape and proximity of its nearest neighbors. Similarly, the play of wind or the drifting of snow will be modified by the actual topography of the built-up area, just as drainage patterns will be radically altered by grading, earth-moving and paving.

More often than not, however, the consequences of such meteorological manipulation are unfortunate precisely because they have not been anticipated and hence not controlled. We have already seen the need for much more intensive outside studies of the aerodynamic behavior and surface-solar response of individual buildings. But it is obvious that, in any urban situation, the isolated individual building can seldom achieve even tolerable control in such matters. What is urgently required is a new sort of "environmental zoning" which would establish area-wide or city-wide norms of orientation, density and height. Such norms would establish an overall topology to which the individual building could conform. They would give the fabric of the city as a whole the type of surface response dictated by the actual climate of the area. In a region of overheating (e.g., Miami, Tucson), this topology would aim at minimizing solar heat gain and maximizing natural ventilation. In an underheated area (e.g., Fairbanks, Calgary), the surface response would be designed for maximum protection from winter winds and maximum exposure to winter sun.

The potential economies of such environmental zoning would be real, in terms of both capital and operating costs. It would certainly yield a far higher general level of amenity than is common in most built-up areas today, where the negative climatic factors are exaggerated and the positive ones canceled out. Nor need such environmental norms impose any great restrictions on the design of individual buildings — no greater, certainly, than those of normal American land-platting practices in which the arbitrary gridiron is the normal

pattern. On the contrary, the esthetic quality of the whole townscape would be enhanced, if we are to judge from folk practices in
such matters around the world.[11] Thus in the loess lands of western
China, where bitter winter cold is aggravated by high winds, the
peasants build entire villages below ground. Literally carved out
of the loess, each house consists of submerged rooms opening into a
sunken courtyard (Fig. 94). This environmental response has two
great virtues: it takes advantage of relatively high sub-surface soil
temperatures while at the same time escaping the chilling effect of
the wind. In addition, the courtyards are shaped, sized and oriented
to permit penetration of low winter sun. Such an urban topology
would be eminently appropriate for residential communities in the
Great Plains of the U.S. and Canada. And modern technology could
easily solve problems in waterproofing, daylighting and drainage
which are beyond the technical capacity of the peasant.

In the deserts of Northern Africa and the Middle East one can
observe another instance of canny folkloristic response to thermal
overloading. Here an architecture of mud brick masonry — ideal for
the great diurnal fluctuations of hot days and cold nights — is combined with a dense urban texture of narrow streets, inward-facing
buildings and highly compartmentalized courts and gardens. Often
the streets are continuously shaded with awnings and vines; and
often the entire village is shielded from the sun by a high, continuous
canopy of nut palms. Such principles of environmental response
could well be applied to the American Southwest, where real savings
in air-conditioning costs would be matched by a real increase in
amenity for the townscape as a whole (Fig. 95).

Precisely because of the spectacular development of environmental technologies in heating, cooling and illumination, we have tended
toward an extravagant reliance upon them, to the almost total neglect
of other possibilities. Contemporary architects and urbanists have
shown little interest in a systematic exploration of such problems.
Some years ago, under the editorship of the present author, the
climates of fifteen American cities were analyzed and a series of
climatic specifications for domestic architecture were evolved and
published.[12] The architects Viktor Olgyay and his brother, the late

Fig. 94. Troglodyte village, Honan Province, China. These settlements represent adroit response to environmental stress. To combat high winds and low temperatures of the steppe winter they build subterraneously: they thus minimize wind chilling of inhabited spaces and utilize comparatively high temperatures of subsoil.

Fig. 95. Mud masonry megastructures, in Moroccan desert. Here village is built to act as metabolic unit; high heat capacity of mud masonry plus self-shading effect of intricately subdivided ground plan acts to ameliorate intense heat and glare of daytime. Same configuration acts to cushion abrupt temperature drop after sunset.

Aladar Olgyay have published a series of papers and books dealing with architectural climatology, especially the manipulation of sunlight.[13] And, as we have seen in Chapter 3, an adequate technical literature has been developed on solar orientation, calculation of solar heat gain through various wall materials, etc. But most of these studies dealt with the design of individual buildings and not with that of neighborhoods or towns as a whole.

We have already seen that even with freestanding houses on narrow lots, it was still possible to locate the houses in such a fashion that each would have an optimal orientation with respect to winter sun and summer breezes (Fig. 27). This was a simple illustration of a profoundly important principle — namely, that the "empty" voids between buildings are just as important to the overall amenity of built-up areas as are the enclosed volumes of the buildings themselves. In his most recent theoretical works,[14] Knowles has extended his research on surface responses of individual buildings to a study of the metabolic response of whole neighborhoods to the environmental forces which play upon them. These studies emphasize the obvious but often forgotten fact that topography, whether accepted as given or radically altered by the designer, becomes a critically important factor in the viability of the completed settlement. With modern capabilities in mechanized earth-moving, it is no longer necessary to fit a new development to existing contours; if necessary, the landscape can be remolded to act as a new element in the final urban fabric. But the ultimate consequences of such radical interventions must be carefully studied if ecological disaster is to be avoided.

THE VIABILITY OF PREINDUSTRIAL PRACTICE

An understanding of folk and primitive practice is of more than academic interest to today's architect because, with the growing industrialization and urbanization of the Western world, he displays an increasing tendency to ignore or minimize the importance of the natural world and the precariousness of man's position in it. Not only is this modern architect largely insulated against any direct exposure to climatic and geographic cause-and-effect; he also seems persuaded that it no longer affects him. We have seen the disastrous consequences of this attitude in the preceding chapters. The central reason for this failure is lack of an adequate theoretical — one might properly say, philosophical — apparatus. It is expressed in his consistent underestimation of the magnitude of the environmental forces which play upon him, his buildings and his cities; in his failure to grasp their ineluctable unity; and in his persistent tendency to overestimate his own technological capacities for overriding or ignoring them.

The primitive builder never works under such misapprehensions.* In all his structures, he always faces one supreme and absolute limitation: the impact of the environment in which he finds himself must be met by his own efforts, using the building materials which that environment affords. The environment itself is scarcely ever genial; and the building materials available would seem to modern man appallingly meager in quantity or restricted in kind. The Eskimo has only snow and ice; the Sudanese, mud and reeds; the Siberian herdsman, hides and felted hair; the Melanesian, palm leaves and bamboo. Yet the architecture of these peoples reveals a very sophisticated grasp of the problem, not only within its own terms but even when analyzed in the light of modern scientific knowledge. Primitive practice reflects a precise and detailed understanding of local climate, on the one hand; and a remarkable grasp of the performance characteristics of local building materials, on the other.

It happens, coincidentally, that the forms of primitive architecture, like those of primitive artifacts in general, have esthetic qualities which make them attractive to modern urban man. House or totem pole, war canoe or wooden bowl, these artifacts display a harmony, a clarity, an integrity of form and function which represent high levels of artistic accomplishment. But it would be a serious error to assume that these forms can simply be appropriated, imported like tea or nutmeg. One must not oversimplify the cultural processes which endow primitive art with its attractive qualities. Spiritually and psychologically, a primitive culture is no less complex than our

---

* As used here, the term "primitive" describes a preliterate culture, whether historical or contemporaneous. In such cultures knowledge is transferred verbally, training is by apprenticeship, industry is handicraft, tools pre–Iron Age.

own. The exact path of the primitive artist, from aspiration to artifact, is equally obscure and mysterious. Primitive architecture, like primitive agriculture or medicine, will often have a magico-religious rationale which only anthropologists or psychologists can understand. But primitive practice — i.e., *how things are done as opposed to the reasons given for doing them* — is often astonishingly sensible and perceptive.

The primitive builder is the captive of an economy of scarcity, his resources in energy, time and materials being severely limited. At the same time, his conditions of life allow him little margin for error in coping with environmental stresses: disaster lurks behind even small miscalculations. Both his theory and his practice are strictly disciplined by these circumstances. Without the formal knowledge of literate civilization to rely upon, his practice is always subject to check and modification by direct, sensual experience. Thus primitive practice will offer many examples which contemporary architects can study with profit, but two will suffice — the Eskimo igloo and the mud-walled houses of the American and African deserts.

Of all environmental components, heat and cold are the two which confront the primitive architect with his most difficult structural problems. Since (as we have seen in Chapter 3) thermal comfort is a function of four separate factors — ambient and radiant temperatures, air movement and humidity — and since all four are in constant flux, any precise manipulation requires a real analytic ability on the part of the designer. And the Eskimo displays it in his design for the igloo: from a purely theoretical point of view, it would be difficult to formulate a better scheme for protection against the Arctic winters. Its performance is excellent: with no mechanical equipment, it achieves a performance which modern engineers might envy (Fig. 96); and this performance is a function of both its geometry and its material. The hemispherical dome offers maximum resistance to winter gales from all points of the compass, while at the same time exposing the minimum surface to their chilling effect. The dome as a form has the further merit of enclosing the largest volume with the least material; and it also yields that shape which is

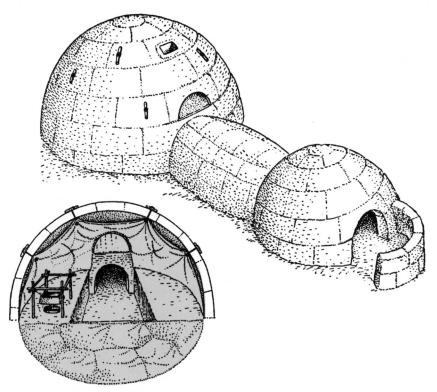

Fig. 96a. Eskimo igloo, Baffin Island, Canada. In shape and material, igloo represents high-level environmental response. Shape offers maximum resistance and minimum exposed surface to wind, while also enclosing most volume with least material. Thermal efficacy of snow wall is increased by draft-reducing inner glaze of ice. Draped furs act as insulation against radiant heat loss from bodies of family.

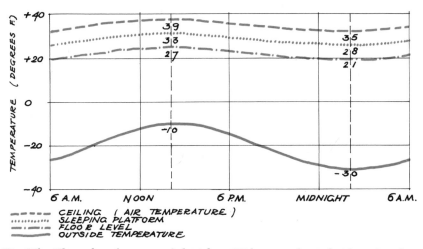

Fig. 96b. Thermal performance of the igloo. With no mechanical aids and no heat source beyond small blubber stove, internal air temperatures are held at tolerable levels. But chart plots only air temperatures: radiation from stove and bodies keeps effective temperature so high that family needs to wear few if any clothes for comfort.

most effectively heated by the radiant point source of a blubber lamp.

In terms of thermal response, the intense and steady cold of the Arctic dictates a wall of the lowest possible heat-transfer capacity. Dry snow meets this criterion most admirably, though at first glance it might seem the least likely structural material imaginable. The Eskimo unlocks the paradox by constructing a dome of snow blocks (18 inches thick, 36 inches long and 6 inches high), laid up in one continuous in-sloping spiral. The finished dome is made both stronger and more windproof by a glaze of ice on the interior surface. When, finally, he drapes the interior with skins and furs, thereby preventing body chill from either radiant or conductive heat loss to cold floor and walls, the Eskimo architect has completed a most admirable instrument for thermal control.

For the civilized nostril, olfactory conditions are said to be less than optimum; but odors are highly subjective in their impact; and ventilation inside the igloo is entirely adequate to supply oxygen needs of family and fire alike. Space inside the dome is certainly limited; but the Baffin Island Eskimos build igloos of several units, connected by barrel-vaulted tunnels and air locks, to house dog teams, extra food and equipment. The igloo has a short life, collapsing when outside temperatures rise above freezing. Like most primitive building, it sacrifices durability in favor of performance, and it lasts exactly as long as the Eskimo requires it.

If we turn to another thermal regime, that of the great deserts of the lower latitudes, we find another type of architectural response, equally appropriate to radically different conditions. Here the problem confronting the primitive designer is one of extremely high daytime temperatures and intense insolation, alternating with much lower temperatures at night. Sometimes, as in the Algerian mountains or the American Southwest, the diurnal fluctuations are superimposed upon comparably severe seasonal ones. The main requirement for thermal comfort in this situation would be a building material with a very high heat-holding capacity — i.e., one which could absorb solar radiation all day and release it slowly all night. The mud-walled, mud-roofed constructions which desert peoples all

Fig. 97a. Mud masonry Indian house, American Southwest. High heat capacity of mud masonry, well suited to great temperature fluctuations of desert, is cannily exploited in primitive housing. Since air, though dry, is very hot, ventilation is not desirable. Indians build freestanding brush-covered arbors for daytime shade, using houses for storage, cold-weather sleeping. Rooftops are used for summer sleeping.

over the world have evolved accomplish this task most admirably (Fig. 97). Since humidities are very low, cross-ventilation is not mandatory: indeed, at midday in midsummer, air temperatures are so high that a breeze passing across the skin would add more heat by conduction than perspiration could dissipate. Thus, the typical desert form is closed, centripetal, uses a very limited number of small openings to cut down heat and glare. In some arid areas, like those around the Persian Gulf, where diurnal fluctuations are reduced by water bodies, nighttime temperatures do not fall appreciably and ventilation becomes necessary. To meet such a contin-

Fig. 97b. Thermal performance of mud masonry house. High heat capacity of thick adobe walls and mud roof acts to flatten out stressful thermal curve of desert climate.

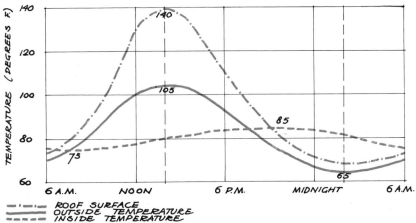

Fig. 98. Rooftop wind scoops, Hyderabad, Sind. A rare climatic paradox — high humidities superimposed on Arabian Desert temperatures — makes ventilation mandatory. These wind scoops are oriented to prevailing breezes.

gency, the native architects have evolved a fantastic family of wind scoops, as handsome as they are effective, to force night breezes down into the interiors (Fig. 98). Thus two quite contradictory tasks are accomplished: a closed vessel with a high capacity to resist intense insolation at one time of day is combined with a forced ventilation system with a high capacity for admitting the breeze at another.

We have already seen how this principle of controlled surface response, as a means of governing the building's metabolic relationship with its environment, has been demonstrated by Knowles (Fig. 32). But the same principle can be applied to the design of entire human settlements — villages, cities, whole regions — as the more advanced architectural theoreticians are coming to realize. Indeed, we will be compelled to apply this principle if current metabolic dysfunctions are to be corrected — especially in stressful climates where there is either an absolute deficiency of solar energy (Canada, Siberia); or an absolute surplus (the Arizona Sahara).

Environmental pollution is, to a very large extent, due to the misapplication of enormous amounts of energy required to *maintain* our cities — to heat and cool, ventilate and illuminate them at even minimal levels of amenity. This energy is largely derived from the combustion of fossil fuels and — more recently — nuclear fission. (Hydroelectric power plays a minor, and apparently diminishing, role in the energy chain.) Both methods of energy conversion produce large quantities of noxious wastes which, when discharged, lead directly to pollution of air, land, and water masses. It is technically possible, of course, to improve the efficiency of both conversion and waste disposal methods and thereby reduce the soaring rates of environmental attrition.

Ultimately, however, Western technology will be compelled to face the fact that much of this pollution is the consequence of a fundamental misunderstanding of the proper allocation of energies of all sorts to the problem of environmental manipulation. These consequences are especially significant for architecture, since most contemporary buildings employ walling membranes which are highly transparent to most forms of energy. Complex and delicate mechanical systems for compensating for this high energy exchange across the interface then become mandatory. The amounts of energy required to maintain this balance are exorbitant. Moreover, most buildings are designed as discrete, free-standing structures whose ratio of enclosing surface to enclosed volume is very high.* Obviously, very important reductions in energy input and pollutant output would result if this ratio were reversed.

Here again, the folk practice of preindustrial societies offers some astonishingly effective paradigms. The pre-Columbian builders of the great pueblos of the American Southwest built in a climate with very high insolation but with great diurnal and seasonal variations in ambient temperature. They employed the mud-masonry house (Fig. 97) but they used it as *the basic module of a megastructure.* Exterior walls per unit were thus reduced by some 60 per cent, and these exposed walls were very carefully oriented. Thus the overall heat exchange is manipulated to minimize summer surpluses and maximize winter deficiencies. The high energy costs of constructing the settlement are offset by very low energy requirements for maintaining it. Such allocation of available energy (whether animal or solar) is characteristic of folk practice. It yields a far more favorable "balance of trade" than such putatively modern cities as Albuquerque or Phoenix.

---

* This reaches unprecedented proportions in the typical middle-class American suburb of single-family detached houses standing in large lots. Never before in history have as many units of energy been required to supply a family life-support system.

NEW THEORETICAL APPROACHES TO
ARCHITECTURAL FORM

These are some instances, out of hundreds around the world, of the brilliant ways in which indigenous builders, whether primitive or folk, have responded to environmental stimuli. The body of conventional wisdom which such practice represents should be carefully scrutinized by architectural science; not brutally plowed under, as is so often the case, only to be replaced by some "international" methodology which is often grotesque in the coarseness and insensitivity with which it responds to local, micro-environmental conditions. Fortunately, there is growing recognition of this fact in the urban cultures of the West. Two remarkable recent studies by American architects — *Architecture Without Architects* by Bernard Rudolfsky[15] and *The Significance of Primitive Architecture* by Ernest Schweibert[16] — are symptomatic of this interest.

Rudolfsky's study (the by-product of his spectacular exhibition of the same name at New York's Museum of Modern Art in 1965) approaches the subject from a frankly "esthetic" point of view. He is interested in demonstrating the enormous range of beautiful solutions which illiterate craftsmen are able to produce without benefit of any body of formal literary tradition or academic training. He has selected his examples with an eye to their visual effect; but he recognizes that the effect itself is not, could not be, an arbitrary act like that of the contemporary "avant-garde" artist in search of novel forms. Schweibert, in an eloquent foreword, gives his reasons for a study of the primitives: his dissatisfaction with the formalism of current architectural theory and his dismay at the dysfunction it leads to in some of our most prestigious buildings. His material is similar to Rudolfsky's but his approach is from a functional point of view — i.e., analyzing the derivation of the forms in terms of response to climate, materials, techniques. But the inescapable conclusion of both studies is that, *for architecture, the solution of experiential problems is the only source of valid form.*

Such works as those of the American architect Ralph Knowles[17] or the Anglo-Swedish architect Ralph Erskine[18] fully confirm the rich possibilities of this approach to structural design. Even where there may be no indigenous folkloric prototypes (as in Knowles's studies on the skyscraper), or where the existing prototypes are only obliquely applicable (as in Erskine's new towns north of the Arctic Circle) — the environment becomes, for them as for their primitive predecessors, the fundamental generator of the building form.

Of course, the demands of modern urban life are much more rigorous and complex than any which preindustrial builders confronted. Study and analysis cannot remain purely pragmatic, learning can no longer be transmitted by apprenticeship nor design carried on by sheer intuition. Indeed, as Christopher Alexander has pointed out,[19] the many variables involved in contemporary architectural decision-making simply outrun the capacities of even the finest minds. Under such circumstances, the electronic computer has inevitably become an important new tool. It is already being widely used in purely structural computations; but Knowles's work indicates a much broader, and possibly even more significant, application. Describing his method as being "the mathematical derivation of surface response to selected environmental forces," Knowles says that "while it is true that design depends on imagination, imagination itself depends on the terms of reference given to it. These should be in the form of the most reliable knowledge available."[20]

It is apparent that Knowles, employing the resources of a most sophisticated technology, has arrived at substantially the same conclusion as the Eskimo designer. The parameters of the experiential problem remain the same; only the methods of analyzing them and the technical means of resolving them have been enormously expanded. It should also be apparent that this is no vulgar proposal for "instant" or "automatic" design. To the contrary, it aims at a methodology for establishing objectively valid reference frames for esthetic decision — i.e., for describing the variables in any given problem; for isolating the acceptable alternatives; and for assigning them a hierarchy of objective values. Such a reference frame, far from restricting the freedom or independence of the architect, affords him a greatly broadened field of choice across which his creative capacities can play, secure in the knowledge that the risks of frivolous or idiosyncratic solutions have been eliminated.

There are, of course, more pragmatic ways of approaching the same problem; and the work of Ralph Erskine is significant in this connection. An architect who has done both town planning and architecture in the Swedish Arctic, he has been projected into an extraordinary environment at two distinct levels of design. As a town planner he has been compelled to study the problems of founding modern urban communities in an environment which had never before supported any society more complex than the reindeer economy of the Laplanders. This has led him to formulate some far-reaching propositions for a long-range solution to the problem of civilizing the Arctic.

As Erskine sees it, the long, dark, severe winters of the far north subject human societies to quite severe stress, with psychological and social consequences that have never been fully explored. He

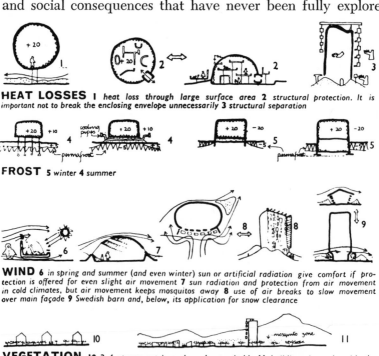

HEAT LOSSES I *heat loss through large surface area* **2** *structural protection. It is important not to break the enclosing envelope unnecessarily* **3** *structural separation*

FROST 5 *winter* 4 *summer*

WIND 6 *in spring and summer (and even winter) sun or artificial radiation give comfort if protection is offered for even slight air movement* **7** *sun radiation and protection from air movement in cold climates, but air movement keeps mosquitos away* **8** *use of air breaks to slow movement over main façade* **9** *Swedish barn and, below, its application for snow clearance*

VEGETATION 10 *3–4 storeys not in scale and not suitable* 11 *buildings in scale with the low vegetation or with an extensive or mountainous landscape— the monumental situation of man*

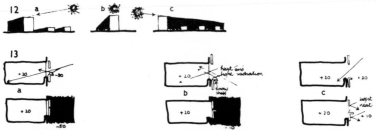

SUNLIGHT 12 a *winter* b *summer day* c *summer night* 13 *the need for a variable window: examples day and night* a *winter* b *equinoxes* c *summer*

thinks that the notorious alienation of many Swedes may well be related (culturally, not genetically) to the physical isolation which the northern winters impose upon the Swedish countryside and, to some extent, even the towns. This environmental load is so enormous in extent, so pervasive in psychosomatic effect, that it cannot be successfully ameliorated with individual buildings, no matter how well designed or built. What is needed in addition is a kind of town-wide megastructure specifically designed to handle the grossest environmental stresses — intense, steady cold, high winds, heavy snow cover, long periods of darkness. By thus lightening the environmental load, such a megastructure would make possible the year-round continuity of social life at optimal levels. It would guarantee that pedestrian circulation, for example, would be no more inhibited in January than in June.

Fig. 99a. Ralph Erskine's analysis (facing page) of environmental problems and indicated architectural responses in Arctic form basis for his novel solutions.

Fig. 99b. Apartment house, Lulea, Sweden. Ralph Erskine, architect. Any discontinuity in material or change in direction increases vulnerability of wall to attack by ferocious Arctic cold (below, left). Hence Erskine holds recesses and protuberances in wall plane to minimum. Triple-glazed windows have no sills or reveals. Exterior corners are rounded to equalize temperature gradient through wall, prevent cracks.

K POINTS
FROST DAMAGE

Fig. 100a. Town is conceived as a south-facing megastructure rimmed by housing.

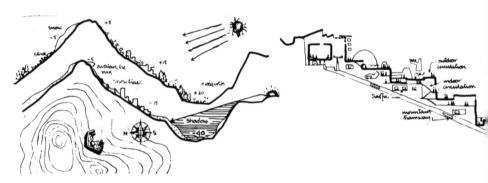

One of his prototypal designs for the Arctic represents a rigorous application of conventional orientational theories: here the entire town is built as a series of concentric interlocking terraces to form a south-facing hemacycle. Interior pedestrian streets, both concentric and radial, would facilitate movement in very bad weather. Another, more radical proposal goes further: here the entire town would be built inside a great dome (Fig. 100c). The function of this dome would be to absorb only the most severe meteorological forces — primarily wind and snow — in order to create a sort of meso-environment for the town as a whole. Within this context of ameliorated conditions, individual buildings of more normal design could provide the more precise environmental control required. Both Erskine variants employ a wide range of communalized facilities — car-wash stations, laundries and drying yards, kindergartens and parklets — which would at once facilitate and compel a wide movement of all family members outside the individual dwelling unit.

Fig. 100b. Microclimatic analysis leads to two levels of circulation, open (above) and closed (below).

Fig. 100. Studies for a town in the Swedish Arctic, Ralph Erskine, architect. Conceived as a single organism to lighten environmental load of a difficult climate, the town is a shallow bowl, tilted toward south and protected to the north by a continuous wall of multistory housing. Circulation is at two levels — above ground for good weather, below ground for bad. Traffic pattern combines circumferential and radial, with mountain tramways for all-weather transit.

Fig. 100c. Schematic design for an Arctic center. Ralph Erskine, architect. To facilitate social life, Erskine suggests a great enclosure to lift grossest environmental loads — low temperatures, high winds, heavy snow and darkness — off entire urban tissue. Within this meso-environment, streets, buildings, open and closed spaces can have normal configuration. Environmental conditions within individual buildings can be maintained to meet requirements of activities housed. Thus the town can act as a unit to support life styles such as those of lower latitudes where stress is lower.

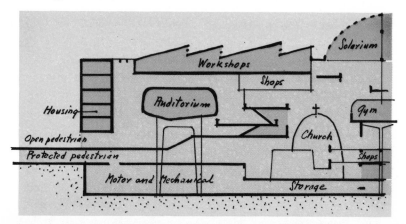

In one of the British New Towns, Cumbernauld near Glasgow, we can see something of the same philosophy of environmental response. The climate is, of course, less stressful than the Swedish far north, though the winters are characterized by much wind, rain, fog, and short days (it lies at the 56° N latitude). Only the town center employs the mega-structure principle, the residential quarters based on a conventional cul-de-sac layout. This large articulated structure is organized along a multi-level east-west spine of vehicular and pedestrian traffic ways. It incorporates a full range of activities normal for a town of its size — department stores, cinema, shops, pubs, a hotel, garages, an elementary school and a range of apartments. All living units face south, overlooking a series of landscaped areas whose microclimates are importantly modified by the sheer mass of the center behind them to the north. The result is a new kind of experience for Scottish townspeople — a dry, all-weather promenade which is rain-, snow- and wind-free with a small-scale coziness so welcome in this kind of climate (Fig. 101).

Fig. 101a. New Town, Cumbernauld, Scotland, designed by Office of the City Architect. Completed portion of Town Centre, seen below from south, is multi-level megastructure along an east-west circulation spine. Main environmental problems — long, wet, windy winters; cool summers with clouds, fog and rain — dictated all-weather enclosed pedestrian circulation along multi-level malls; all vehicular traffic is confined to lowest level. The levels serve stores, shops, pubs, library, meeting halls, cinema, schools and hotel. Ultimately Centre will serve population of 25,000.

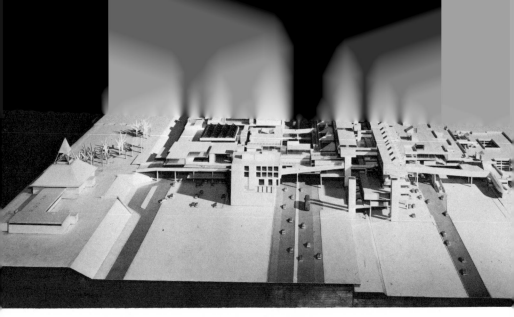

Fig. 101b. Model of Town Centre seen from east. Private cars, buses and trucks serve parking lots, garages and bus station at lower level. Pedestrians enter complex on transverse ramps leading to residential sections to north and south of Centre.

Fig. 101c. Two views of all-weather shopping mall on main level of Town Centre.

On the other side of the world, across the Nile from the ancient city of Luxor, the Cairene architect Hassan Fathy has employed this same environmental-response approach in the model town of Gourna.[21] The climatic and cultural conditions are about as far removed as possible from Sweden and Scotland; and the technical means available to Fathy (himself a thoroughly cosmopolitan architect) were both primitive in kind and limited in extent. But he deliberately used traditional building methods (load-bearing masonry of sun-baked brick) and village planning principles (narrow, curving streets, walled yards, rooftop sleeping terraces) to demonstrate the continuing viability of folkloristic practice. Gourna was built by the local peasantry, using only materials at hand and employing techniques that are millennia old. Yet the overall level of environmental amenity is qualitatively higher than the modern centers of most Egyptian cities. Its striking appearance is obvious.

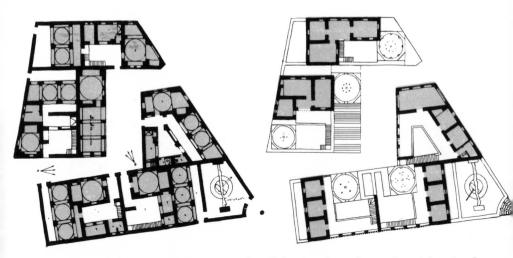

Fig. 102a. Gourna, Egypt. Town plan (below) and unit house plans (above) reflect desert climate and Moslem population of peasantry organized into extended families.

Fig. 102b. Typical village street.

Fig. 102c. Roof deck of peasant house.

Fig. 102d. Courtyard of boys' school.

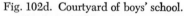

Fig. 102. Gourna, Egypt. Hassan Fathy, architect. Located across the Nile from Luxor, this village was planned by the architect as a demonstration of the continuing validity of the traditional theories and techniques of town planning, architecture and construction of the Egyptian peasant. Using mud masonry both because its thermal performance makes it ideal for desert climates and because it required no cash outlay, Fathy taught peasants ancient techniques of mud-brick vaulting without scaffolding. House plans provide walled living quarters at street level for cool weather and roof decks for hot-weather sleeping. Street layout is aimed at creating shade and privacy, discouraging outside traffic through extended family enclaves.

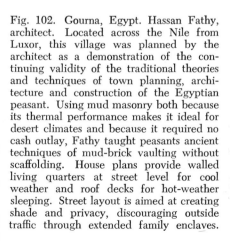

The most suggestive American demonstration of environmental manipulation on a town-wide scale is currently under way at Sea Ranch, California, a new residential community up the coast from San Francisco.[22] Designed by the landscape architect Lawrence Halprin, this new town is being built on a great natural meadow atop a range of bluffs overlooking the Pacific Ocean. Its natural assets are magnificent scenery, luxuriant flora, a moderate thermal regime (no frost or excessive heat), above-average number of days of sunshine. The single meteorological liability is the wind — so strong and so persistent that they have sculpted the native cedars into the typical "Monterey deformation."

The problem facing Halprin was: how to intervene urbanistically and architecturally in such a way as to create a truly pleasant environment. The central issue was the wind. To have developed the area with conventional detached single-family houses or isolated high-rise apartments would not only *not* have improved matters, it would have made a bad aerodynamic situation much worse. Taking his clue from the great cedar windbreaks used by the sheepmen who had grazed the meadows for a century, Halprin decided to cluster his houses in much the same fashion. By massing them as windbreaks (with, incidentally, much the same cross section as the cedar hedges), he created microclimates in their lee: since these areas faced south, they made possible warm, sunny, wind-free patios in a landscape which had previously resembled a Scottish moor.

Fig. 103a. Bioclimatic analysis of microclimate at Sea Ranch.

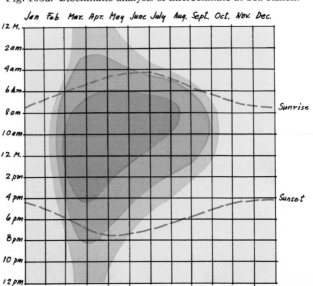

Fig. 103b. Panoramic view of site looking north shows existing cedar windbreaks.

Fig. 103c. View of house cluster shows how profiles conform to cedar windbreaks.

Fig. 103. Sea Ranch, Calif. Lawrence Halprin and Associates, planners and landscape architects. Design of this community of "second homes" on the Pacific Coast 75 miles north of San Francisco is based on an unusually comprehensive ecological and climatic analysis of the site. A spectacular landscape with many attractions, including the mild temperature regime of the Bay Region, it has one serious environmental drawback: strong, persistent winds from the north-northwest. To meet bioclimatic requirements for outdoor comfort (chart at left), outdoor living areas must be shielded from winds and exposed to sun. Halprin profile of existing cedar windbreaks, planted by ranchers a century ago, as aerodynamic prototype for new housing units.

Thus was confirmed Rudolph Geiger's prescient observation of forty years before that when the architect builds a house

he makes a number of separate climates out of the single one pre-existing near the ground above the building site. On the south wall, the microclimate will be so favorable that fruit, perhaps even grapes, can be grown. This gain is at the expense of the north side, which will be dark, cold, damp and raw. Still different will be [the microclimates] of the east and west sides. The climates of the various rooms are modifications of these four outdoor climates. In addition, there is the climate of the cellar and of the attic.[23]

Fig. 103d. Houses at Sea Ranch, Calif., are shaped and sited volumetrically in clusters to make their own wind-free microclimates in their lee. Since winds are from north, this permits full exploitation of sun. Result: small semi-tropic gardens like the shores of Lake Como in an overall environment like the moors of Ireland. Framed of wood and sheathed in plank and shingle, the houses resemble buildings of earlier ranchers.

Limited and disparate as are these examples, they are enough to indicate the possibility of reaching quite new levels of environmental amenity in human settlements. Though they aim at exploiting a whole range of phenomena in the natural environment, they by no means imply a rejection of scientific method or modern technological systems. To the contrary: adequately to master these subtle and intricate interrelations between man, his buildings and the natural environment will require the highest levels of scientific thought. They involve such a bewildering array of variables that they will certainly depend upon the computer for solution. And rather than aiming at the elimination of such basic elements of modern architecture as air conditioning and artificial illumination, they aim at creating the environmental conditions in which such systems will be able to operate at optimal levels of efficiency, economy and safety.

In view of the depletion of energy resources to power our cities, on the one hand, and the rising tide of environmental pollution from the waste products of this application of energy on the other, the question of a new environmental policy is no longer hypothetical. It is a matter of burning immediacy, as figures on the metabolism of cities clearly prove.[24]

		input (fuel)		per day	*output* (waste)	
water			625,000 tons	sewage	500,000	tons
food			2000 "	solid wastes	2000	"
	coal		3000 "	particles	150	"
fuel	oil		2800 "	sulfur dioxide	150	"
	gas		2700 "	nitrogen oxides	100	"
	motor		1000 "	hydrocarbons	100	"
				carbon monoxide	450	"

Table 8. Abel Wolman's formulation of the energy input-output of modern cities. Wastes are of two sorts: organic and inorganic. Organic wastes should be reclaimed for reuse as heat, electric energy or fertilizer; inorganic wastes should be contained in closed-cycle systems for recycling — not dumped into the environment.

When described in such quantitative terms as these, it becomes apparent that human settlements can only be thought of as complete organisms. Designs that fail to take this into account, with piecemeal decisions and patchwork actions, can only place their survival increasingly in jeopardy.

10.
PLAN, THE INSTRUMENT
OF POLICY

A plan is many things, depending upon how you look at it. From the point of view of society as a whole, a plan is an instrument of policy, a means of facilitating a certain line of action. Thus the plan of an American city may be regarded as an instrument of socio-economic policy for the production and exchange of goods and ideas. And the plans of individual buildings of which the city is composed are likewise expressions of smaller, individual policies. From the standpoint of the architect or physical planner, however, a plan is a representation of a horizontal plane passed through a building or a city. In such a sense, a plan is a *solution* for a given line of action. It inevitably reflects the designer's concept of how — within the limits given — a certain amount of space may be best organized for the specific operation to be housed. For the people who live or work in the completed building or city, a plan is something else again. It is the *schema* of a control mechanism which will, to a large extent, determine how happily they live or how well they work together.

Planning may therefore be analyzed at many different levels and from many points of view. Our concern in this book is with physical planning — the system of spatial relationships created by real buildings in actual cities. Here again, the most illuminating approach is from the point of view of the health of both the individual and society as a whole. The primary function of all plans — architectural, urban and regional — is to produce that specific organization of space which will simultaneously elicit and support the specific modes of behavior desired. (See pp. 160 ff.) A successful plan will maximize the social productivity and individual well-being of the people whose energies it channels.

In a limited, technical sense, to plan is to manipulate space. A set of blueprints has only, so to speak, a potential energy; but once the building is up and people are using it, its plan ceases to be an abstraction and becomes instead a very real and dynamic force. It modifies importantly the social relationships of the people who use it. Thus it may be said that planning is the manipulation of physical relationships for the purpose of facilitating social relationships. There is, of course, no metaphysical significance to what a plan can accomplish. You can force a family to live in a school or a church or a factory instead of in a house. Its relationships will be adversely affected, its well-being and productivity diminished, if it is forced to operate in a plan not designed for it. But as a social unit it will remain recognizably a family. It will not become either a history class, a church congregation, or a trade union. From this it is apparent that each social unit (class, congregation, work crew) and each social operation (study, worship, industry) has its own private set of spatial requirements.

THE CLASSIFICATION OF PLAN TYPES

It is characteristic of the emergence of any field of human endeavor into an independent status that it attempts two things — to define its area and to classify its content. It is ironic that John Ruskin should have been one of the first to do this in the field of planning. He was the first to recognize the growing specialization of Victorian building and to attempt to set up a system of categories for its planning. Said he:

Architecture proper naturally arranges itself under five heads:
Devotional — including all buildings raised for God's service or honor.
Memorial — including both monuments and tombs.
Civil — including every edifice raised by nations or societies for purposes of common business or pleasure.
Military — including all private and public architecture of defense.
Domestic — including every rank and kind of dwelling place.[1]

This was an ethical critique of English building — a sermon on what he thought it should be rather than a description of what it actually was. He established a separate category for monuments and tombs while blandly ignoring all the new plan types which were so important a part of contemporary life. He saw no distinction between the plan of the Crystal Palace and that of the Houses of Parliament, and nothing which distinguished both of them from the great railway stations designed by Phillip Hardwick at Euston Square (1839) and by Francis Thompson at Derby (1839). The factories which had already made England the leading manufacturing nation in the world cannot anywhere be crowded into Ruskin's list. Clearly, when he provided for "private military architecture of defense," he had in mind the England of Walter Scott's novels and not that of Darwin's essays.

The truth is that an accurate classification of the buildings of a given era is determined not by abstract systems of ethics but by the character of the society itself. The more advanced the society, the more numerous and specialized becomes the range of plan types required to house it. (It has been estimated that American society today requires some 270 distinct types). And no juggling of types according to some preconceived scale of ethical values can conceal the fact that *social process is the determinant of plan.* Moreover, it must also be observed that there is an internal relationship between each process and the others. These relationships mesh and interlock to form a closed cyclical system. In theory, this cycle may be entered at any point, but since industrial production is the most decisive of all contemporary processes, it seems logical to classify plan types in relation to it. The factory is the crucial building of our society It is the factory which at once makes possible and necessary all the rich variety of modern American building. If old types such as the livery stable disappear, it is because of the factory; and if new ones like the airport appear, this is also due to the factory. It is the factory again which is responsible for the astonishing specialization in the dwelling houses — the self-contained suburban cottage, the towering apartment houses and hotels, the tourist motels, the trailer parks and the resort hotels. There is not a single building type which does not — in its structure, equipment, and plan — reveal the impact of the factory and its products. Indeed, our very history would be unintelligible without an understanding of this relation-

Social Process or Operation	Corresponding Plan Types to Facilitate It
1. Production	Smelters, mills, mines, factories, etc.: farms, dairies, greenhouses, canneries, abattoirs, etc.
2. Power	Dams, hydroelectric and steam generation plants, electrical distribution systems, etc.
3. Transportation and communication	Airports, railroad and highways systems, marine terminals, etc.; telephone, telegraph, radio, television, and postal systems; and newspaper and publishing plants, etc.
4. Storage	Warehouses, refrigeration plants, grain elevators, oil tanks, vaults, etc.
5. Exchange	Shops, stores, markets, warehouses; banks, stock exchanges, etc.
6. Administration	Capitols, courthouses, city halls, etc.; offices, headquarters, etc.
7. Protection	Jails, fire halls, etc.
8. Dwelling	Houses, apartments, hotels, resorts, tourist and trailer camps, dormitories, etc.
9. Education and research	Nurseries, schools, universities; laboratories, libraries, museums; zoos, botanical gardens, experimental stations, etc.
10. Recreation	Stadiums, natatoriums, gymnasiums; theaters, cinemas; race tracks, ball grounds, parks, playgrounds, beaches, etc.
11. Repair and reconstruction	Clinics, health centers, hospitals, sanatoriums; rest and old-age homes; orphanages, reformatories and asylums, penitentiaries, etc.
12. Religious worship	Churches, synagogues, chapels, etc.
13. Elimination and conservation of waste	Cemeteries, crematoriums, etc.; water systems, sewerage systems, incinerators, etc.
14. War	Military installations of all sorts (there are few buildings which do not automatically become military under total war).

Table 9. Classification of plan types relative to six-phase production; formulated by Knud Lönberg-Holm and C. Theodore Larson. Six phases are (1) research; (2) production; (3) distribution; (4) consumption; (5) obsolescence; (6) elimination.

ship. Industrial production is the nodal point of our society. Thus, any classification of modern American plan types must be of the order given above.*

* This classification is based upon that set forth by K. Lonberg-Holm and C. Theodore Larson in their pioneering study, *Planning for Productivity* (New York: International Industrial Relations Institute, 1940).

There is, naturally, some deviation from such a schematic classification as this in real life. Some of the simpler building types may serve more than one process or operation without adversely affecting it. A movie theater built for entertainment may be used for certain types of visual education, an auditorium may serve for both a church service and a bingo game. Again, a given plan type may in one situation form a complete building while in another and more complex project it may be only a small unit. From biological necessity, some types are more or less constant in all buildings. Washrooms and toilets which require only a small corner of an airplane will grow into large and complex buildings at the pithead of a mine.

Functionally, each of these specialized plan types can be viewed as a unit in a subsystem which, in turn, is a component of larger local, regional and national systems. Locked together vertically in hierarchical order, each system supports some social processes — e.g., communications, health, education, etc. Of course, each of these systems coexists and intermeshes with other types of systems on a horizontal basis to form villages, towns and cities. This leads to the necessity for the development of two distinct scales of planning: (1) architectural (the design of the discrete building or complex); (2) urbanistic (the design of districts, communities, whole towns).

EVOLUTIONARY PROCESS AND ARCHITECTURAL PLAN

A formal classification which groups buildings according to type and relates them to social process is necessary to an understanding of the planning field. But building activity is in constant flux, subject to the impact of social, economic and technical developments. Our society is very fertile in invention and architecture is quick to reflect each innovation. Thus the automobile made obsolete the horse-drawn buggy: coincidentally, the garage replaced the feed store and blacksmith and the giant traffic interchange replaced the dusty crossroads and the regional shopping center replaced the crossroads' general store. Movies and radio supplanted the legitimate theater and vaudeville house; sound stage and broadcast stage appeared in their stead. Then television appeared — and under its remorseless advance, all other theatrical forms began to decline.

With such an interplay of forces, the individual plan type is anything but static. There is a steady obsolescence in all types so that no plan of thirty years ago is apt to be satisfactory today. Sometimes, the very life cycle of a plan is very brief. Thus a scant four decades encompasses the rise, dominance, and decline of the tuberculosis sanatorium. It appeared in response to a certain theory of combating the disease by sunshine, fresh air, and quiet. It flourished in the desert and the mountains. Now that surgery and chemotherapy are becoming the accepted treatment, the sanatorium is slipping back and seems destined for abandonment.

These movements are not so aimless or unpredictable as they might seem at first. They appear as surface disturbances, so to speak, and long periods may elapse between the first wave and a deep-going tide of change. Such lags are especially characteristic of the building field, for buildings are hard things to liquidate, either physically or financially. Some types respond to changes much more readily than others: thus the backwardness of housing is notorious while the rate of change in commercial building types is quite rapid. This unevenness of development is even more noticeable in city planning than in individual buildings, for here the lag is cumulative in both time and space. Nevertheless, standards in planning do change and along fairly definite lines. At the present time, several characteristics are notable in most building types:

1. Multiple use of space
2. Flexibility
3. Mechanization

The multiple use of space is characteristic of many modern plans. One has only to compare contemporary plan types to those of a century ago to realize the extent to which we have intensified the use of enclosed space. Though by no means the most spectacular example of this trend, the steady compression of the American home is the most familiar example. A century ago the parlor was used only for company, weddings, and funerals: if the home had any pretensions, it boasted two parlors, the front one being opened only for the most formal occasions. Today, at the same socioeconomic level, there is likely to be only a living room, and this space is used all the time, by all the family, every day in the week. One corner is often used for eating, another as often as not for sleeping. The dining room of a century ago has all but disappeared; and despite the fact that the kitchen has absorbed this function also, it is apt to be only a fraction as large as its early Victorian progenitor. This compression of a given range of activities into smaller and smaller spaces has occurred in most building types. While it is a form of overcrowding, it differs from the procrustean congestion of the slums in this important respect: it is a designed compression, with the introduction of all sorts of structural and mechanical devices aimed at compensating for the lost space.

A multiple use of space may flow from physical or mechanical necessity, as in the case of a trailer or an airliner. Here weight and bulk must be held within fixed limits, yet the resulting space must provide facilities for a fixed number of operations (lounging, sleeping, cooking, eating, defecation). Since these cannot occupy the same space at the same time, the areas allotted to each must be compressed to the minimum and the space — wherever possible — organized so as to permit different uses at different times.

The same tendency appears in buildings, but usually as the result of economic forces. Rising land values, construction costs and taxes, and a demand for high return on capital investment also tend inexorably toward compression of plan. In commercial buildings, where street frontage is at a premium, shops which thirty years ago would have been cramped with fifty feet are today able to manage with ten. In office buildings, the cubic space per clerical worker has been reduced by perhaps two-thirds since the days of H. H. Richardson. In theaters and auditoriums of all sorts another expression of the same tendency is apparent. A movie theater may occupy a relatively large amount of expensive space but this space is used twelve hours a day, seven days a week. A legitimate theater will occupy the same amount of space and yet be used only twenty-four hours a week, seldom as much as twenty-six weeks per year. This uneconomic use of space has already forced the disappearance of most legitimate theaters. But there is another possibility, one which is increasingly apparent in auditoriums, and that is the tendency to extend the working day of the building by providing for a greater range of activities. This leads to large auditoriums which can be subdivided into smaller ones; to seating which can be shifted or removed altogether; to floors which can tilt to create proper sight lines, rise to form platforms, or sink to form pools. Here, the intense use of time is made to compensate for the comparatively lavish use of space.

It is, of course, in the "efficiency apartment" that most Americans have become acquainted with the multiple use of space. Here, because of economic (not physical or mechanical) limitations, the processes of living have been compressed into steadily dwindling areas. A multiplicity of devices and equipment make it possible and simultaneously make it tolerable. Tables fold out of the walls, sofas pull out to become beds, kitchens fit into ventilated closets, and beds drop out of other closets. Soundproofing, lighting, and elevators are added to compensate for increased densities. Because there is less space for the housewife to dust, clean, and mop, because there is a place provided for everything, these apartments are often economically organized in terms of space: but it does not necessarily follow, as is so often assumed, that they are also efficiently organized from the standpoint of the human user.

An economical organization of space may result in a plan which, objectively, makes work easier — in other words, channelizes the energies of its tenants effectively. But an *economical* plan will only be truly *efficient* if the internal requirements of both the process and the worker involved in the process are carefully considered and substantially met. Modern kitchens are marvels of compression. Old equipment has been radically improved, new labor-saving equipment has been added (dishwashers, deep freezers, powered egg-beaters), and all of it has been organized into a space only a fraction as large as its prototype of fifty years ago. Insofar as the new model cuts down waste motion on the part of the housewife, economy may coincide with efficiency. But there is a point beyond which a multiple use of the same space makes work harder and not easier. If the family eats in a small kitchen with limited counter space, the chances are that more energy is required to prepare the meal, serve it, and clean up afterward than would be required in an old-time layout of large kitchen, pantry, and eighteen-foot dining room.

The same paradox holds true for much more complex social operations and much larger buildings. It holds true for the city as a whole. For example, the compression of a range of cultural and entertainment activities into a single building might give a community a more satisfactory solution than a whole series of single-purpose buildings. There is no merit to wasting space. But generally speaking, the tendency to scrimp on urban space, inspired as it is by economic pressure, should not be raised to the level of a principle. The criterion of physical planning must be: what space does the process require for its fullest development, not merely how much of such-and-such process can be crammed into a given area?

Flexibility is the natural result of the rapid rate of change which obtains in industry, commerce, and all urban institutions in general. In some production fields, the rate of change in technique is very rapid. Industrial processes and operations are being constantly revised in the light of rapidly broadening knowledge. New ones appear and old ones drop out; and the ones which persist undergo steady modification. This flux exerts great pressure upon both structure and plan. The total amount of enclosed space necessary to house a given operation is changing; and the fashion in which this space is subdivided and organized by the plan changes likewise. Buildings designed along conventional lines, built of conventional materials, are thus apt to be technologically obsolete before they are completed. Unpredictable changes in production techniques will occur, rendering all but the most flexible and far-sighted plans prematurely out-of-date. Thus there is real point to the apocryphal tale of the manufacturer who, when asked to describe the best type of building for his needs, responded: "None at all." He meant by this that changes in his manufacturing processes were so continuous and so profound that any layout would be soon out-of-date. He meant that most buildings are so planned as to make any radical spatial reorganization both time-consuming and expensive. And he meant that most structural systems are so unsalvageable as to make it more economical to build a completely new structure than to try to re-use the old components.

The multiple use and flexible organization of space are, at the contemporary scale, inconceivable without a high degree of building mechanization. If space is at such a premium that it must be intensively used, then it must be flexibly organized, readily convertible from one use to another. To make conversion easy or at least tolerable, the process must be mechanized. The municipal auditorium of the average town offers a typical illustration of this problem. To be of maximum effectiveness, it must be adaptable to a wide range of uses. To be economically operated, it must be intensively used. Thus, an auditorium seating five thousand will be desirable for large political rallies, whereas a room seating only seven hundred and fifty might be needed for chamber music. A level floor is essential to basketball, while a sloping one is desirable for stage performances. For a boxing match, a raised platform is required; a swimming meet would imply a pool at the same spot. For dancing, a waxed hardwood floor must be furnished; for hockey, a sheet of smooth ice. And each of these activities will have its own requirements in terms of illumination, acoustics, ventilation, temperature, etc.

Fifty years ago, separate structures would have been required for most of these activities. And since it takes a comparatively large group of people to support most of them, adequate provisions were seldom found anywhere but in the largest cities. Thanks to our technical development, all such facilities can now be housed in a single building. The changes they imply can no longer be made manually, however. The scale of the elements is too large, the time available for change too short, the cost of manual labor too high. Hence the structure is mechanized. Motor-operated walls, floors, seating and partitions rise, drop, slide or fold at the touch of a button. Lighting, sound, and air-conditioning systems can be designed to serve the large cheering crowd of a basketball game or the smaller sedate group at a lecture.

Such mechanization of buildings is today quite feasible: there is scarcely a conceivable problem that is not technically soluble, as the recent moon walks have demonstrated. Nor is there any doubt that mechanization can greatly increase the productivity of enclosed space. But mechanization has its own problems. It is very expensive to install and to operate. And, the more sophisticated the apparatus, the more vulnerable it is to systemic dysfunction and to external exigencies such as regional power failures. Moreover, the social desirability of highly mechanized buildings should be measured against a larger reference frame. Such intensively exploited spaces may lead to needless congestion, wasteful travel for the users, a concentration of facilities in locations which are detrimental to the overall well-being of the community.

DIALECTICS OF CITY PLANNING

City planning in the Western world has been the exclusive province of architects and civil or military engineers from the Renaissance until the very recent past. This fact has had important consequences for the development of both theory and practice. Few urban designers had any background in what today would be called the environmental sciences: the Frenchman André Lenôtre and the American Frederick Law Olmsted, with their backgrounds in horticulture, were very much the exception. Because of this tradition, it was easy for the city to come to be regarded as a sculptural or stereometric construct. Added to this was the fact that most urban designers would have come from upper-class backgrounds and hence indoctrinated with academic preconceptions of formal order and monumental form. Given these two tendencies, the city could be considered as a work of art.

The great era of urban expansion in both Europe and the United States was dominated by such conceptions. Baron Georges Eugène Haussmann, the military engineer, was responsible for the reconstruction of central Paris between 1853 and 1870. Here, a geometry of radial and intersecting boulevards was dropped like a cookie cutter upon the medieval street pattern. Onto the exposed faces of the intersected tissue was grafted a new streetscape of standardized Renaissance façades. This conception was imported into America, with the Chicago Columbian Exposition of 1893, by a triumvirate of powerful designers — the architect Daniel Burnham; the landscape architect Olmsted; and the sculptor Augustus St. Gaudens. Their astonishing popular success with this project led to their being named as the planners of the national capital by the McMillan Commission of 1901. They thereby established the "City Beautiful" movement which was to dominate American city planning almost until World War II.

Given such an historical background, it is not surprising that urbanistic theory developed in isolation from environmental and ecological considerations, on the one hand, and from social and economic theory, on the other. Nevertheless, in the period between the two World Wars, many new movements growing out of the crisis of the rapidly expanding cities were gaining great momentum. The new field of social work was symbolized by the pioneer Jane Addams; the slum clearance and housing movement was led by such figures as Edith Elmer Wood; and the Garden City concept was imported from England by Clarence Stein, Charles Harris Whitaker and the elder Henry Wright. By the time of the Great Depression and the New Deal, the theoretical propositions of these movements had been fairly well absorbed into academic city-planning theory. But, unlike the physical planners with their Beaux Arts idiom, these new social forces were without any special interest in esthetics. They were generally content to accept the Roman-Renaissance vocabulary of the architects or the English Cottage bias of the British town planners.

But, beginning with the New Deal, architects and city planners became more and more anxious to give their theory an esthetic dimension commensurate with their changing social and political goals. This new esthetic idiom they were to derive from two main sources — the utopian schemes of Le Corbusier for rebuilding Paris as a skyscraper-studded park (1921–25); and the utopian decentralist plans which Frank Lloyd Wright set forth in his Broad-acre City (1935). Although they occupied opposite poles of urban theory — Le Corbusier for urban concentration, Wright for decentralization — both men discarded the discredited eclectic idiom in favor of their own private vocabulary of form. Since in visual terms they were so radically new, it was easy to assume that all necessary modifications had been made to American planning theory to bring it into line with contemporary reality.

Opportunity to apply these new theories on any wide scale did not occur until after the end of World War II. But immediately thereafter, a series of huge federal programs for housing and slum clearance and for urban renewal and redevelopment gave planners their first wide-scale opportunities. The following quarter of a century has afforded ample opportunity to measure the efficacy of our city-planning theory and to demonstrate that, even with the additional input from the economists and social scientists, it shows deficiencies which lead to serious dysfunction in completed projects.

The most devastating critique of orthodox city-planning theory came in 1959 with the publication by Jane Jacobs of her book, *The Death and Life of Great American Cities.*[2] The arguments in this epochal work are too dense and intricate to permit any easy summary. But her thesis was, in substance, that the architects and planners were actually killing the cities that they were in the process of "renewing" and "redeveloping." And this was the inevitable consequence, she argued, of the middle-class origins and formalistic education of the planners themselves. They might have relinquished the neoclassic iconography of the City Beautiful for the avant-garde idioms of Le Corbusier and the Bauhaus. They might even be liberal in their attitudes toward the explosive social and political issues which were convulsing American cities. But they still clung to a fundamental fallacy — that the city was a work of art and that their task was to make the city beautiful.

It was not that beauty was "bad," it was that it was completely irrelevant. Mrs. Jacobs's model of the city was of a living organism responding to its own ineluctable requirements in both its form and its development. The true measure of urban success was therefore *viability,* the quality of the life the city elicited and supported, and not mere surface appearances. Moreover, her book challenged the competence of middle-class white professionals even to conceptualize, much less adequately to house, the varied life styles of all the ethnographic components of the American city: European immigrants like the Jews, Italians and Middle Europeans; native displaced populations like the Negroes, Puerto Ricans, Indians, and Mexican Americans.

As the planning field attracted specialists from the social sciences, they began to scrutinize the city from vantage points quite outside the scope of architects, landscape architects and civil engineers.

The critique of the economists was especially relevant; and no one has analyzed the economic functions of the city more eloquently than Louis Winnick in a remarkable paper of 1961, "The Economic Functions of the City Today and Tomorrow." He saw the city as

a mammoth labor-saving innovation for which no patent has been issued and no inventor honored. The primary economic function of the city is to lighten the toil of mankind, to make more effective use of its productive capacity.[3]

Mankind, Winnick went on to point out, is the victim of two inherent limitations: the "friction of distance" and the "affliction of uncertainty." The city overcomes these two disadvantages by the physical organization of space in such a way that

people are placed close to other people, workers to employers, producers to consumers, establishments to establishments.[4]

The city thereby afforded economic man three advantages, critically important and nowhere else available: proximity, predictability and hence option of choice.

Viewed as an economic invention, the city constituted a common reservoir of raw materials and finished goods, of manual and intellectual skills, upon which everyone engaged in production could draw. This reservoir was of absolutely incalculable value, one which no single individual could conceivably afford to maintain alone. Its concentration in space guaranteed that every producer had *proximity* to all the goods and services upon which he depended, as well as to those which, in turn, depended upon him. Because there was always duplication of every type of skill, goods and service, there was always *predictability* of supply. And finally, because of the above factors, the city offered that last essential ingredient of the marketplace: *option* — a range of choice within any given category.

Jane Jacobs continued her examination of the city in her second book, *The Economy of Cities.*[5] Essentially an investigation of urban morphology, her book is mainly an attempt to discover the laws that governed the growth and development of the cities. Why have some cities languished while others flourished? Her model of the economic city is like a kind of engine for the performance of work. It is a reciprocating engine, absorbing imports, turning out exports but in the process yielding an "awesome force," what she calls "new work." This latter by-product is the index of the city's health and viability. But if this is a general law that governs their development, each city must be studied as a living organism, bedded in a specific environment and always delicately balanced between growth and decay. To understand the city, Mrs. Jacobs argues, one must study it like a biologist who knows that, while all members of a given species display common characteristics, no two individuals are identical. Such a study will reveal unexpected (and, in her argument, almost *unexpectable*) possibilities inherent in each city: hence the danger of abstract formalistic plans. Manchester, the widely hailed model city of the nineteenth century, turned out to have far fewer developmental potentials than "inefficient" and "unplanned" Birmingham; and Los Angeles, so impractically located far from transportation centers and sources of raw materials, turns out to be far more viable than Detroit, ideally placed with reference to both.

Mrs. Jacobs argues that the city is uniquely valuable precisely because of its "inefficiencies" and "impracticalities":

Cities are indeed inefficient and impractical [when] compared to towns . . . but I propose to show that these grave and real deficiencies are necessary to economic development and are thus exactly what makes cities uniquely valuable to economic life.[6]

This being the nature of the city organism, its physical form must at all times allow for the fullest, freest interplay of economic forces. Its development must not be hampered by arbitrary or formalistic physical configurations imposed upon it by professionals who do not understand its inner, ineluctable demands. In essence, Jane Jacobs is arguing for the purest laissez faire, the socioeconomic Darwinism so popular earlier in the century.

It would be difficult to formulate a theory more directly contrary to most assumptions of orthodox planning theory or more outrageous to professional planners. And yet, as Christopher Alexander has pointed out in *A City Is Not a Tree,* another of the truly significant papers of the past decade,[7] contemporary experience in city building seems to confirm her diagnosis. What he calls "artificial cities" — Brasília, Chandigarh, the new towns of England and Sweden, as well as the Levittowns and Restons and Columbias of this country, have not lived up to expectations. Despite the fact that they often offer high levels of visual beauty and physical amenity, they have not succeeded in generating the self-supporting life expected of them.

Mrs. Jacobs's diagnosis of the organic complexity of the city may indeed be valid. But her proposed therapy overlooks a central fact: She is not dealing with living tissue, with its properties of cellular subdivision and genetic memory. All environmental manipulation is the consequence of deliberate human action. All city building proceeds according to someone's plan, whether it be that of a national government, a county school board or the corner grocer. Moreover, the complexity of modern life makes it impossible that the implementation of these plans not be in the hands of trained specialists — architects, planners, environmentalists.

Current failures in city building do imply that planning theory must be completely restructured to accommodate totally new levels of complexity. Moreover, there are serious students of the city who question the ability of the human mind to handle these problems unaided. Just as space travel became possible only with the appearance of advanced mathematical theory, and actually soluble only with computer technology, so too with the planning of the modern metropolis. Christopher Alexander has dealt with just this conceptual problem. Himself an architect and mathematician, Alexander points out that

The process of thought itself works in a treelike way, so that whenever a city is "thought out" instead of "grown," it is bound to get a tree-like structure . . . for the human mind, the tree is the easiest vehicle for complex thoughts. But the city is not, cannot and must not be a tree.[8]

What is the nature, the inner ordering principle, which distinguishes the "natural" cities (London, Boston, Istanbul) from the "artificial" cities of the world (Chandigarh, New Delhi, Canberra)? Alexander finds it in their fundamental structure: the natural city has the organization of a semi-lattice but the artificial city has the structure of a tree.

Within the treelike structure, no piece of any unit is ever connected to other units except through the medium of that unit as a whole.

The enormity of this restriction is difficult to grasp. It is a little as though the members of a family were not free to make friends outside the family, except when the family as a whole made a friendship.[9]

The greater structural complexity of the semi-lattice yields an enormously greater range of overlap, ambiguity, multiplicity of aspect. This is clear from the fact that

A tree based on 20 elements can contain at most 19 further subsets of the 20, while a semi lattice based on the same 20 elements can contain more than 1,000,000 subsets.[10]

Necessarily, the men who design and plan new cities or remodel old ones, manipulate a range of sets, subsystems and systems of material elements — "people, blades of grass, cars, bricks, molecules, houses, gardens, water pipes and the water that flows in them." But what they ultimately manipulate are invisible, immaterial relationships and processes. And the simplistic tree structure makes no physical provisions for this complex overlap.

In every city there are thousands, even millions, of times more systems at work whose physical residue does not appear as a unit in these tree structures. In the worst cases, the units which do appear fail to correspond to any living reality; and the real systems, whose existence actually makes the city live, have been provided with no physical receptacle.[11]

A city is a receptacle for life. But if the city has a treelike form, it severs the overlap of the multiple strands of life within it, "like a bowl full of razor blades on edge." Only the semi-lattice, Alexander argues, with its thicker, tougher, more subtle and more complex structure, can support life.

THE CITY AS A PROSTHETIC INSTRUMENT

Critiques of traditional city planning such as these by Jacobs, Winnick and Alexander cannot be lightly dismissed. The new levels of complexity they describe undoubtedly do run far beyond traditional parameters; new modes of mathematical logic and a new computerized technology are essential to meet them. But more is required than merely new techniques: planners must also resolve a number of internal contradictions in their own relations to society. Since they can, at best, only implement the social, economic and political policies of their society, it is obvious that their powers are strictly limited. Nevertheless, within the limits of a given policy, sheer professional competence plays an important role. Lack of it has too often vitiated many a valid project. Too often merely visual criteria have been applied to the solution of complex problems in which overall amenity is the desideratum. This amenity is a difficult quality to describe in positive terms. Although formal esthetic qualities — proportion, balance, harmony, rhythm, etc. — do play a role in achieving amenity, they are by no means decisive. We have had ample opportunity to see in this volume that architecture engages man at every level of his existence — psychic and somatic, subjective and objective, individual and social; and these levels have their own hierarchy of importance.

These hierarchies are very apparent in the behavior of city dwellers in response to various aspects of the city. Thus many visually "beautiful" areas — plazas, malls, civic centers — will be empty, neglected and unused while many areas nominally "ugly" and unkempt will support an active life. Pedestrians vote with their feet. Though the reasons for their behavior may often seem obscure (even, on occasion, to themselves) the controlling factors are very real. They are almost always experiential: a slight change in level; a better-lighted block; sun as against shade; a choice between mud and pavement; the visual interest of shop windows as against a blank wall. Such factors will often override a subjective opinion that the chosen path of movement or locus of action is "beautiful" or "ugly."

Certain street-side attractions or distractions — a political speaker, a traffic accident or an auction sale — can of course attract people to the sunny side of the street, even on a blistering day. But they will not stay there very long: all things being equal, they will return to the shade in hot weather or to the sunshine in cold. It takes a fairly strong motivation to draw a pedestrian up three steps into a shop, as any retailer can tell you. A climb of three or four flights is the upper limit of normal motivation and muscle power alike. In much the same fashion, it takes either an obstacle or a policeman to make pedestrians do a right-angle turn when a diagonal cutoff is possible.

The same behavior can be observed inside buildings. Almost every house has elements of which it is said: "We never use it — I don't know why"; or "People are *always* tripping over that step"; or "Don't sit there — there's a draft or something." These are judgments based upon observed experience. They outweigh formal value judgments as to the "beauty" of the stairway or chair. Yet they are seldom consciously analyzed by architects or urban designers.

Many amenities — and many nuisances and hazards, too — are the result of *relationships* between buildings rather than of the individual buildings themselves. They thus fall into a kind of *terra incognita*, for which the individual architect is not responsible and about which the urban planner is either unaware or unable to act. An active shopping street is one such construct. Smog is another. Both are the result of urban concentration: one is a major amenity of civilized life; the other a cause of lung cancer and emphysema. The cause-and-effect of one is immediately perceived; the other is never even sensed by the victim. Both phenomena are integral aspects of the urban experience yet neither are encompassed by conventional definitions of "beauty."

If the amenity of our cities is to be raised above the lamentably low current level, the vantage point from which architects and planners approach them must be radically altered. The required change in perspective is both technical and cultural. Technically, we must shift our attention to the actual city dweller in his life zone six feet above the earth. Culturally, professionals must recognize their middle-class mores and esthetic standards as being of limited validity for their own milieu and often ridiculous when applied to working-class groups and ethnic minorities.

Comprehensive planning, at a regional and metropolitan level, is obviously an indispensable step if we are to restructure our urban environment along more satisfactory lines. But such plans, even when completely elaborated, will be far from actual, human-scaled designs. These will have to be developed on a micro-environmental scale, where a six-inch change in level, or a ten-degree change in temperature, or a difference of a few foot-candles of illumination are important considerations.

This does not mean the abandonment of larger-sized (or smaller-scaled) concepts. It does mean that, once clearly formulated, these concepts ought to be temporarily put to one side while subplans are developed for the micro-environment. At this stage, we should proceed from the bottom up, from the particular to the general. Most large models of small scale (e.g., 1 inch equals 100 feet) are not only of limited informational value; they can actually be dangerous to the design process. Decisions affecting 68-inch people are, in effect, made from an altitude of 3500 feet — a distance too great to permit any real discrimination in matters of great experiential significance. Whether a mother is to be separated from her three-year-old child in his sandbox by a horizontal distance of 30 feet or a vertical distance of 10 floors is a spatial decision of vital importance to the well-being of both. But, at the scale of most architectural models, such distances will seem merely matters of formal composition.

The time scale of the pedestrian's movement, no less than his actual size, is crucial to truly satisfactory urban spaces. Few modern streetscapes or traffic schemes recognize this: hence they do not hesitate to introduce into the micro-environment scales of movement and rates of speed that are literally hostile to urban life, not to mention urban well-being and amenity. Yet conflicts of this sort can never be discovered, much less resolved, at the scale at which most urbanistic studies are carried on.

Most architects and planners are, by definition, middle-class in origin. (The sheer cost of professional education has taken it beyond the reach of all but the most talented and lucky children from low-income and minority groups.) From this education, if not from their familial backgrounds, they develop characteristic modes of life and typical attitudes toward esthetic matters. Though they are apt to think of them as absolute and universal, these modes and attitudes are actually highly localized, even in American culture. Whether these are "better" or "higher" than mass taste is not at all established, either, though professionals would like to think so. In any case, the tendency to reorganize the urban scene along middle-class lines of "beauty," "tidiness," "order," etc., often creates tensions as serious as those it seeks to alleviate. Slum clearance and public housing, and now urban redevelopment projects, afford ample evidence of this danger. If the populations of "depressed" and "substandard" neighborhoods are going to be salvaged instead of simply bulldozed, designers are going to have to display more imagination than they have as yet. And this act of imagination can only come from an authentic shift in their conceptual vantage point.

For in modern America the *real* client of the environmental designer is less and less his *legal* client. The white-collar man in the big skyscraper, the worker in the big plant, the housewife in the big housing project, the child in the big consolidated school — these are the people for whom the architect works and to whom he is ultimately responsible. They are the "contained" for whom the building containers should be accurately and sensitively designed. Yet these are the people whom the architect or planner no longer sees. He deals instead with their agents — those corporate or institutional entities who commission the projects. Instead of firsthand observation of real people and their needs and aspirations, the architect is given statistical data with which to work — peak loads, median incomes, average family size, minimum floor areas, etc. These data, of course, may be essential for the establishment of the broad lines of policy, but they are no more a substitute for firsthand detailed knowledge of the actual "consumers" of the building than statistics on the incidence of cancer are to a physician with an actual patient.

Nor can it be assumed that these corporate or institutional clients, acting though they may be as agents for the consuming public, are always to be relied upon to represent its best interests or requirements. In a profit-motivated society, criteria for actual architectural projects are all too apt to drop to the minimums permitted by building codes or by the law of supply and demand. Of course this tendency will vary from field to field. The speculative builders of tract housing are notorious for the venality of their design and construction policies. On the other hand a life insurance company planning a big housing project for long-term investment purposes may — out of sheer self-interest — follow more enlightened policies. The demand for maximum economy in public projects can often prove quite as limiting a factor as the demand for maximum profit in a private one. Naturally many public builders with specialized requirements, such as hospitals or schools, must meet factual standards determined by the uses themselves. American public housing, on the other hand, has been permitted to slip to the lowest levels of mediocrity of any country in the West.

The current popularity among many young architects and planners of so-called "advocacy planning" is a response to this unhappy state of affairs. The advocacy concept abandons the idea of the planner as being a kind of Olympian agent, who accurately weighs the needs of all the diverse elements of his community and doles out environmental justice on an even-handed basis. The advocate planner recognizes that the Establishment has not met the burning needs of the nation's minorities — blacks, Latin Americans and Indians; the poor, the sick and the aged. He therefore argues the need to intervene directly in their behalf, arguing correctly that the better-off sections of any community will find adequate spokesmen for their needs. In a narrower, more technical sense, the advocate planner is also arguing that to work directly with his actual clients, instead of the usual legal surrogates, is the only way to improve the experiential quality of our cities.

Advocacy planning is thus the first professional recognition of this chain of cause and effect. The sheer complexity of modern technological society makes inescapable the development of comprehensive planning at all levels; but it also makes inevitable a bureaucratic apparatus to prepare and administer them; and this, in turn, raises the problem of democratic control over the inertia which all bureaucracies develop. Although confrontation politics are always distasteful to the bureaucrat, they often seem to the disadvantaged the only way of persuading him to respond effectively to their needs. In the process, better plans and better planners will appear.

11.
PROSPECTS FOR THE
DEMOCRATIC ESTHETIC

The crisis of architecture is worldwide and profound; but it is fundamentally no different from that which invests other fields of activity such as medicine or agriculture or art. The crisis is more advanced in the United States than elsewhere; but this is largely due to the fact that the historic process which we loosely term the "scientific-technological revolution" has flowered here earlier and more extensively than elsewhere. Symptoms of the same crisis are everywhere apparent — in the architecture of Western and Eastern Europe, in Asia, Africa and Latin America.

Quite literally, in both its scope and its profundity, this crisis is without historic precedent. For that very reason it will not be resolved by traditional means. New tools will be required: and it has been the fundamental thesis of this volume that these tools must be theoretical — in the fullest sense of the word, *philosophical.* Architecture today, no less than cosmology, needs a "unified theory," a system of postulates which can fully explicate the principles that cause, control or explain facts and events. Clearly, no such system is in common use today. The squalor and confusion which characterizes the American landscape is a clear expression of the ideological confusion which invests the entire building field. Nowhere are the evidences of this crisis more obvious than in today's debased levels of popular taste and in the more specialized esthetic controversies which this situation generates among professional designers of all categories.

The evolution of esthetic standards in American architecture over the three centuries of its history can be understood only when seen in relation to the underlying technical, economic and cultural forces which conditioned their development. Volume 1 of this book traced the main lines of development of these forces, indicating how they interacted to produce the significant stylistic patterns of the nation's architectural history. From such a survey, we are able to see esthetic standards as the end result of an enormously complex social process.

In this volume, we have studied in some detail the experiential relationships between man and his environment. We have concentrated upon the material aspects of these relationships because this is most urgently required. But this by no means implies that the esthetic experience is negligible. On the contrary, as was pointed out in the opening chapter of this book, esthetic judgment constitutes the quintessential level of human consciousness. Thus, it is obvious that a building can meet all objective criteria of physical performance and still be esthetically unsatisfactory to a given person or group of persons. It is likewise apparent that a building can be hopelessly obsolete when judged by such criteria and yet be esthetically satisfactory to many people. This is merely another way of saying that, to be genuinely effective, a building must conform to esthetic as well as physiological standards of performance.

But to formulate these esthetic standards we are forced to consider a whole range of social, cultural, and ideological phenomena. We are forced to examine not building but man. The whole tradition of architectural criticism in this country — like criticism in other fields — has been permeated with metaphysical abstraction. Consistently the attempt was made to divorce esthetics from life, to emphasize only its metaphysical aspects. This tradition led to a paradox: While consistently overemphasizing the importance of beauty in architecture, it stubbornly insisted at the same time that beauty was not and could not be subject to an orderly, scientific investigation. On the one hand we were told that "a thing of beauty is a joy forever"; on the other that "beauty lies in the eye of the beholder." According to dicta like these, beauty is thus simultaneously a property of (1) the object, and (2) the beholder. Yet the whole history of art exists to prove the fallacy of both propositions.

Most art forms once considered beautiful have outlived that prestige, to fall ultimately into disuse and obliquity: while disagreement in any mixed group as to the esthetic value of a given object is axiomatic.

CULTURE, CLASS, AND THE ESTHETIC PROCESS

The esthetic process in architecture must be discussed at two different levels: the *reaction* of the individual and the *standard* of the group. The reaction is not a property of either the individual or the building but of the relationship between the two. As a process, it is the result of the individual's intricate psychological and physiological response to external stimuli. It will vary with objective circumstances — whether he is hot or cold, rested or tired, hungry or well-fed. But, within these physiological restraints, the individual's evaluation of the reaction — his sense of satisfaction (beauty) or dissatisfaction (ugliness) — will be largely conditioned by his social and cultural background. Agreement between individuals as to the esthetic merit of a given building is therefore largely a matter of similar social and cultural background. From this it follows that esthetic standards are expressions of social agreement, of a common outlook or attitude toward this particular aspect of human experience. These standards will vary from one period to another. And in any given period they may vary somewhat between this class and that, although the relation between the popular taste and the dominant high style is intimate. The folk arts echo the idiom of the fine arts. The latter are, in turn, an expression of the outlook, ambitions and prejudices of the dominant social classes of the period.

The process is firmly rooted in social reality and operates in American architecture as in every other phase of American life. Yet in architecture the problem is complicated by special factors which prevent a mechanical comparison between buildings and other art forms or artifacts. The field as a whole is lethargic in responding to changes in esthetic standards. Because buildings are very large, expensive, and permanent things, the field will at any given time show strata upon strata of conflicting styles. Their sheer, physical persistence is reflected in subsequent standards, so that both high style and popular taste are full of echoes and repercussions of the past which, in any other medium, would have long since died away.

It is this confusion of cause and effect that has troubled every critic since Ruskin. The esthetic standards of architecture, when measured against the great periods of the past, were demonstrably low. What caused this? How could the process be reversed? In its most familiar form this problem was reduced to a hen-and-egg conundrum: which came first — bad design or low popular taste? Since the discussion has been almost exclusively the property of specialists in esthetics — architects, editors, and critics — it was perhaps not surprising to find that the verdict was against the people. Low popular taste was responsible for bad building design. Yet the question is actually meaningless, for it ignores both the *constant interaction* between popular taste and high style and their *joint subordination* to the exigencies of our society as a whole.

Under handicraft methods of production for use there is no such thing as bad taste; popular standards cannot be corrupted or debased. Modern scholarship has established this beyond question, both in the folk arts of preindustrial Western civilization and in the great primitive cultures of Africa, Asia, and the South Seas. This is not due to any moral or artistic superiority but rather to the simple fact that, in such societies, esthetic standards are constantly disciplined by the production method itself. Here design is so intimately linked to execution as to make any divergence between the two most difficult. Designer, producer, and consumer are one and the same person. There is consequently neither much incentive nor much opportunity for adulteration of workmanship or design. It would, of course, be absurd to hold that even in primitive cultures every individual is able to make every item he needs, or that everyone is equally skilled or gifted in making them. Even here there is specialization. Yet each member of the community remains close to actual production, can from his own experience judge what the craftsman or artist is trying to do and how well he has succeeded in doing it. This creates a situation in which the average level of esthetic judgment is extraordinarily high — a fruitful environment for both artist and consumer. It also makes possible the striking unity of primitive art wherein there is no qualitative difference between the design of a lowly wooden bowl and an important ceremonial canoe. It creates a situation in whch popular taste and high style are one and the same.

Much the same forces operated to create the folk arts of pre-capitalist, preindustrial Europe and America. Here too handicraft production — despite a relatively high degree of specialization — involved a large part of the community in the actual work of design and fabrication of buildings and artifacts. Here too was production for use with its inherent resistance to adulteration of workmanship and corruption of design. This folk art coexisted with the high style of the ruling classes, to which it loaned and from which it borrowed liberally. Despite this continuous interaction, however, folk art preserved a large measure of independence. It was slow to respond to the abrupt changes of upper-class taste. Indeed, until production relations were altered by the capitalists, it could not change. As a result, the folk arts were expressions of popular taste of an uncommonly high average level. They may never have reached the pinnacles of achievement of the high styles, but they always avoided their disastrous collapses. It is this quality which, beginning with Ruskin and Morris and continuing down to the present day, has held such fascination for modern artists and architects. They might, like Ruskin, fail to understand the material conditions which produced these esthetic standards. They might have romantic ideas as to how such conditions can be re-created. But they recognize that until the past century popular taste always proved itself sound.

Under modern industrial capitalism, this relationship is quite disrupted. The design process is separated from that of fabrication. It is put into the hands of a very small group of specialists who, by the same token, are isolated from the work and the workmen. Since production is no longer for use, the entire production process is subjected to the remorseless pressure of the profit motive. This makes possible an unprecedented advance in technical standards and increases in productivity. At the same time, however, it introduces the motive and the opportunity for deterioration — adulteration in workmanship and materials at the level of fabrication; artificiality, irresponsibility, and vulgarity at the level of design.

The paradox hinges upon the new position of the common man under the new system. For his taste is the product of his experience both as consumer and producer. The good taste he once displayed in what he bought under earlier systems of handicraft production was of a piece with the good sense required of him in what he made: indeed, the two are only different aspects of the same thing, as is clear enough in folk art. Here the confrontation of man the consumer with man the producer is of the most direct sort. The folk artist works by himself and for himself, on artifacts of his own design, intended for his own use.

The industrial system of serial production acts in precisely contrary fashion: the industrial worker labors with others, for others, on artifacts designed by professionals with whom he has no contact, for ultimate uses of which he often has no comprehension. Divided and particular production on the assembly line robs the work of either significance or intelligibility for the individual worker placed somewhere along it. That good sense which is the basis of good taste cannot derive, as it always had in the past, from the world of work. And any specialized knowledge or skills will have very little application to the act of consuming, in which the worker as consumer is forced to judge the values of artifacts of increasing complexity. The result for the common man has been a steadily declining capacity for mature and satisfying esthetic decisions.

THE CHANGED RELATIONSHIP BETWEEN ARCHITECT AND CLIENT

The consequences of this historic process can be clearly seen in the history of American architecture. For the first two hundred years or so, American architects and builders were guided by a fairly effective body of theoretical postulates, however unsophisticated or unformulated they may have often been. These principles derived in about equal parts, as I have shown in the first volume of this work, from folk experience and formal scholarly knowledge. They only began to collapse in the nineteenth century, under rapidly developing science and technology, on the one hand; and the unprecedented proliferation of new social, economic and industrial processes and institutions, on the other. At any time prior to the death of Thomas Jefferson in 1826, both the architect and his building would have been disciplined, structured, "held in shape," by a clear and comprehensible reference frame of needs and means. The size, shape and contours of this reference frame were established by two sets of complementary but opposing forces, endogenous and exogenous.

The endogenous forces, those representing the client's minimal requirements, pressed outward from the center. These minimums would have varied with culture and class. The ethical standards and ceremonial apparatus of the Roman emperor required quite different architectural accommodations from those of President Jefferson, just as Jefferson's minimal requirements as president were quite different from those of his slaves at Monticello. Both emperor and president had at their disposal the most advanced theories and technical means afforded by their respective societies. And they employed them architecturally to win optimal amenity, not mere physical survival.

Nevertheless, objective conditions sharply restricted the ambitions of even the mightiest, establishing the limits of satiety and survival alike. The exogenous, inward-pressing forces were six in number: (1) the impact of the climate; (2) a limited range of building materials; (3) a lack of mechanical prime movers; (4) limited means of transport and communication; (5) a slow rate of cultural change and technical invention; and (6) a well-informed but extremely conservative clientele.

The formal consequences of such an equilibrium of forces are obvious in the buildings of both folk and primitive cultures. Under such circumstances, the architect's margin of error was sharply curtailed; personal idiosyncrasy was disciplined by external limits upon his freedom of action; the possible solutions to any given problem were restricted in range and number. Under such pre-industrial conditions, an architect like Jefferson could encompass both the poetic and the practical requirements of his day by employing the formal and folk knowledge of the times. He could design

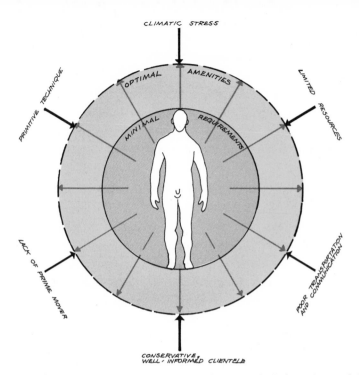

Fig. 104a. Preindustrial building developed with a strictly balanced set of forces, endogenous and exogenous. As a life-support system, it could not drop below fixed experiential thresholds; it did not often reach optimal levels of amenity; but it did produce furnishings, buildings and communities of great esthetic consistency.

Fig. 104b. Modern science and technology have disrupted this balance of forces by reducing magnitude of exogenous forces and increasing man's capacity for environmental manipulation. Paradoxically, no new equilibrium has appeared. Western technology is producing few buildings and even fewer communities which yield optimal amenity while it is producing millions of buildings and thousands of communities which fall below minimal standards of efficiency, health and safety.

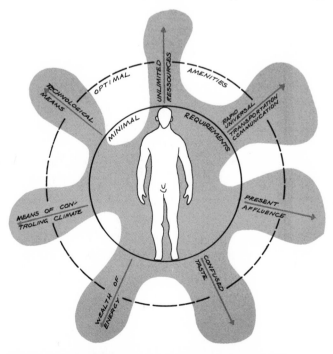

both the curriculum and the campus of his beloved university and then move on to supervise the making of the bricks and nails required to build it. Concept and campus display an elegance and balance, in both formal and functional terms, which we must still admire today.

But the balance of forces which established the reference frame of Charlottesville has been radically altered by the intervention of science and technology. Either by removing or by greatly reducing the magnitude of the inward-pressing limitations upon building, a complementary expansion of the outward-pressing demands of appetite and ambition has been encouraged. Technology has enormously extended our capacity to manipulate the natural environment, so that habitable structures *anywhere* become a reality, not only at the poles but in outer space as well. This has been accomplished by an unparalleled fluorescense of new methods and materials, of new prime movers and sources of energy. The cultural expression of all this has been an accelerated rate of invention whose consequences none can predict but whose negative impact upon the esthetic standards and inherent good sense of both the architect and his client is all too clear to see.

This crisis in architectural esthetics did not appear — indeed, could not appear — until around the last century. It was not until industrialization had successfully infiltrated the major fields of production that design began to be removed from the hands of millions of anonymous, independent artisans and put into the control of a handful of specialized designers. Whatever else it accomplished, this process of centralization automatically isolated design from the healthy democratic base of popular participation. A new esthetic idiom began to emerge, leaving its subtle imprint upon every article of daily use — art forms, buildings, clothes, china, furniture, and trains. It was the idiom of the Victorian mill and factory: Whether it was better or worse than its predecessors might have been subject to some argument, but there was no need for confusion as to the responsibility for the change. It was the Victorian *entrepreneur*, not the consumer, who brought it about.

Under this new system, the *entrepreneur* took over some of the functions of the earlier consumer — that of ordering and paying for production. The independent master craftsman became a professional designer, whose orders came from a faceless management, not a specific customer. And the customer, who could only accept or reject the finished product, was reduced to the truncated function of simple consumption. Both architect and client suffered under this new arrangement.

As a result, the nation's physical plant, whether analyzed from a functional or from an esthetic point of view, falls grotesquely short of national capacities. This is in large part due to the inability of the building consumer to understand or implement his demands, requirements, expectations. And the result of the architect's isolation from his real client is the increasing prevalence of the abstract, the formal and the platitudinous in architectural and urban design. This changed relationship is not only expressed in the architect's personal life, whose fortunate position in J. K. Galbraith's economy of abundance has served to insulate him against the squalor and discomfort of Michael Harrington's culture of poverty. It is also expressed in subtle but definite changes in his cultural orientation. It is true, of course, that from the very nature of his work, the architect has always stood closer to the upper classes than to the common man. For ordinary people his services were always much more rare and much less imperatively required than those of lawyer or doctor. Nevertheless the tradition of the socially conscious, intellectually committed architect has a long history in the United States. One might say indeed that the leading spokesmen of the profession in each generation were of this persuasion: Jefferson, Latrobe, Greenough; Sullivan, Wright, Gropius, Neutra. This tradition reached its apex during the days of the Great Depression and the New Deal, when unemployment in normal channels forced approximately three-quarters of the architectural and engineering professions into government-sponsored projects of one sort or another. This switch from the private to the social client gave the architect an exhilarating sense of identification with society. It served to shift his attention, if not his allegiance, toward social architecture.

To a certain extent the afterglow of this Rooseveltian liberalism still diffuses the profession, giving a more liberal aspect to its posture, perhaps, than to those of the American Medical Association or the American Bar Association. But increasingly since the 1950s the profession has returned to "normal." Architects have been reabsorbed into the world of private enterprise. Some of them have themselves become men of big business: in 1964 there were 25 firms *each of which* had over $60,000,000 worth of work on their boards. Ironically, this general prosperity has led to the impoverishment of intellectual speculation and invention. The utopian element in architectural thinking has largely disappeared; theory itself is in disrepute. The men whose polemics (whether in print or in stone) once galvanized the Western world — Wright, Mies van der Rohe, Le Corbusier and Gropius — are gone. Few younger men aspire to their prophetic role. The dominant attitude is one of complacent laissez faire whose esthetic expression is a genial eclecticism. The result is a body of work as antipopular and aristocratic in its general impact as anything ordered by Frederick the Great or Louis XV.

This aristocratic esthetic is very evident in all the most prestigious buildings of the day. It is dismayingly apparent in the urban redevelopment schemes which are currently convulsing the centers of many American cities. Aimed at radically altering the social character of the central city, these projects almost without exception end by evicting the poorer worker, the racial minority, the small merchant and tradesman, and replacing them with what are euphemistically called "upper-middle-income" groups. The result is some of the most candid class planning since Baron Haussmann remade central Paris to correspond to the imperial pretensions of Napoleon III. Designed in the self-styled avant-garde manner, these projects are often handsome from a purely formal point of view. But this should not blind us to the fact that this particular mode of expression has been largely emptied of its original functional-democratic connotations. Its main components were formulated decades ago, under conditions quite different from those which obtain today. The spacious and humane iconography of Roosevelt is today being put to quite other uses. It will not be the first time, of course, that the same style has been the vehicle of different points of view. Jefferson and Napoleon alike turned to the Romans for a language of figurative expression; and two such antithetical figures as Emerson and

Calhoun could both feel comfortable with the Greek Revival. Whatever one's personal estimate of this aristocratic esthetic, it remains the outward evidence of an internal involution: the abdication by the profession of its claim to be the architect of the whole people, to become instead the agent and spokesman for the elite.

How the profession will extricate itself from this cul-de-sac is a knotty problem. Because of its default, it probably faces that sort of "socialization" that has frightened the medical profession, and for many of the same reasons: for just as millions of Americans lack good medical care, so are the same millions deprived of good housing, good schools, good hospitals. The satisfaction of this need undoubtedly implies the increased intervention of governmental agencies; and this probably implies an increase in the bureaucratic architecture so abhorred by the profession. But — aside from the fact that big private firms are quite as bureaucratic as any counterpart in local or national agencies of government — this "socialization" of architecture will not, of itself, guarantee qualitatively superior architecture and town planning. Only a greatly improved system of education and training, together with a new kind of functional rapport with the building consumer, can accomplish this goal.

TRAINING TOMORROW'S ARCHITECTS

The historical origins of architectural education lie much closer to engineering or dentistry than to those of medicine or law. This was due to the fact that competence in the former *could* be acquired through apprenticeship exclusively, whereas theoretical training was of critical importance to the latter. Thus, until the opening of the present century, the vast majority of building was in the hands of men whose origins were closer to the craftsmanship of millwright and mason than to academic scholarship. Professional education at the university level has been a commonplace requirement in medicine and law for centuries. But the first professional school of architecture in the United States was established only in 1865, at the Massachusetts Institute of Technology. The American Institute of Architects itself had been formed only eight years before in an effort to establish professional standards of training and competence.

And it was to be decades before the various state governments, acting under the public health and welfare clause of the Constitution, could be persuaded to pass legislation establishing a system of examination and licensing procedures (Illinois was the first in 1897, Vermont the last in 1951). Only in the last few decades, then, has the training of architects been put upon an equal footing with the older professions.

But preindustrial architecture had one anomaly which it shared with no other profession — the presence in its midst of the amateur and the connoisseur. (Both terms, in those days, had the very favorable connotation of a disinterested love of the field.) From the Renaissance onward, the architect's patron often crossed the line to become, in actuality, an architect himself. But whether these amateurs remained passionate and tireless patrons, like Horace Walpole or the Earl of Burlington, or became the actual designers of buildings, like Jefferson at Charlottesville, they established the other polarity of preindustrial architecture. As opposed to the direct economic incentive of the craftsman, they entered the arena from many other lines of approach: from an enthusiasm for literature, especially the classics; from antiquarianism; from political commitments (Jefferson saw the Roman basilica as the only fit container for his new Republic); even from religious conviction (the Gothic Revival was above all the vehicle for nineteenth-century religiosity).

In view, then, of their widely divergent cultural milieus and their disparate motivations, it must be reckoned as extraordinary that these early architects managed to resolve the contradictions between craftsmanship and scholarship, poesy and practicality — in short, the contradictions between the formal and the functional — to the extent that they did. Nevertheless, the fundamental tensions remained; in fact, they grew steadily sharper with the rise of industrialism, and they are accurately reflected in the curriculums of our schools today. The effort of the schools to resolve this contradiction has been, generally speaking, to move toward increased emphasis on the academic, always at the expense of the craft elements of the field. From one point of view this has been both inevitable and desirable. Modern architectural problems can no more be solved by carpentry than can spacecraft be built by village blacksmiths. However, the shift in training away from craftsmanship has been more toward mere technology than a truly scientific investigation of architecture as a whole.

But there can be no denying that the price paid for this new professionalism has been high. It has played an important role in the complete extinction of the conventional wisdom of the entire preindustrial field. Few contemporary architects have any firsthand knowledge of actual construction methods and techniques. Simultaneously, by the same process, the craftsmen themselves are being robbed of their historic competence and wisdom. What with the factory production of building components and the mechanization of the construction industry itself, there is less and less need for the intelligent, well-trained craftsman. Indeed, the modern working drawings from the architect's office objectively tend to *discourage* good workmanship. More and more, as they reduce building to a process of mere assembly, they imply the "headless hand" of the assembly line. The result is the further lowering of the taste and literacy of the workmen, a situation which the old apprenticeship system made impossible. And this disastrous process of impoverishment is then reinforced by the disappearance of the individual patron of architecture and his replacement by the faceless consumer who has no real voice in, or control of, the buildings in which he is born, lives and dies.

Both the incentive to, and the opportunity for, adulteration of material quality and debasement of design appear to increase in direct proportion to the increasing centralization, mechanization and automation of design. This specialization of the worker and the parallel atomization of the work; this isolation of the policy-making from product-making; this dwindling of the power and authority of the designer himself — all of these seem to be corollaries of modern production. All of them inhibit the creativity of the worker, whether manual or intellectual: of him is demanded a precocious knowledge of his chosen field while he is permitted sheer illiteracy in other fields of knowledge or experience. One sector of his capacities will be enormously developed while the others are permitted to shrink or ossify. The very conditions of modern work act to limit any generalized experience, to inhibit spontaneity, to restrict the play of intuition. The result is that esthetic standards, like those in other areas of judgment, are stultified.

Artifacts themselves become increasingly complex, involving a constantly expanding range of processes and materials. Less and less able to encompass the complexity of modern technology, the architect's function is truncated. His designing becomes more and more a process of assemblage, more removed from functional necessity and therefore more susceptible to the pressures of fad and fashion.

Meanwhile, the consumers of the architect's production, the actual inhabitants of his buildings, are removed by this same process from any possibility of firsthand knowledge of what they are buying (or renting). The consumer can only express his satisfaction (or dissatisfaction) by buying (or refusing to buy) from among the range of artifacts offered by mass production. In real life, it is difficult for this consumer to refuse for long to buy essentials — a house, a bed, a car. So he is compelled, ultimately, to make his choice from a range of products, some or all of which may be unworthy or unsuitable for his precise requirements. In accepting this new relationship, he largely abdicates his power — first his voice in the design process, then his capacity for coherent judgment of design.

It is true, of course, that this same consumer can sometimes drive a given product off the market by simply refusing to buy it. (The quick demise of the Edsel automobile, produced with such fanfare by the Ford Motor Company some years ago, is the most notorious demonstration of this power.) But this is a clumsy and socially extravagant method. Since the consumer can never tell the designer which features he objects to, the designer cannot profit from the experience. Instead, the rejected model is abandoned and another one — also based on statistical data — is rolled out onto the market in its stead. Only the fantastic fertility of modern technology conceals the fundamental wastefulness of this process. And while it may succeed in meeting our gross material needs, it does so with artifacts whose esthetic quality is ordinarily quite low.

Under such circumstances, a broad and fundamental educational program in both architectural and environmental design is urgently required. Such a program would have to include both architect and layman, since no professional field can reach a higher level of competence than that demanded by its clientele. Where the formal education of architects is concerned, their entire curriculum should be infused with a truly scientific (as opposed to a merely technical) approach to environmental and ecological problems. Such enriched and reoriented curriculums should be supplemented by internships in three distinct areas:

1. construction work on actual building projects (e.g., carpentry, masonry, mechanical equipment, etc.)
2. staff and maintenance work in functioning institutions (e.g., housing projects, hospitals, schools, etc.)
3. drafting room and office experience in architectural firms

These kinds of experience would be of help in giving the young architect a multidimensional grasp of how buildings are actually designed, how they are put together and how they affect the people who ultimately inhabit them.

At the same time, the layman requires a broad program of consumer-oriented education in architecture and environmental design. It should be a structural part of his primary and secondary education, like physical education, sex and personal hygiene or home economics. While the traditional art history and art appreciation courses for laymen are useful, they should be considered as supplementary to a factual, concrete and user-oriented curriculum. This should aim at giving the individual a clear understanding of his experiential requirements as a human being; a general concept of what levels of amenity and well-being he is entitled to expect as a citizen in a democracy; and a grasp of what standards of performance and appearance he is entitled to demand as a consumer in the world's most advanced technology.

American building as it stands today is far too broad in scope, complex in function and rapidly changing in both form and material to be easily encompassed by any private set of esthetic standards. It may well be true, as is often charged, that the average American has a low level of taste. But there are historic reasons for this situation, one of them being the architect himself. For it is also true, as we have had occasion to see, that the esthetic standards which the architect is advancing are all too often incorrect in the light of experiential reality. In the last analysis, the current dichotomy between esthetic and technique, between high art and popular art, is an expression of deeper conflicts in society itself. To free American building from the contradictions which stultify it today, building designer and building consumer must join with all Americans of good will, to build a society of peace, freedom and plenty. Thus perhaps will they lay the objective basis for a new flowering, both rich and wide, of a truly democratic esthetic.

NOTES

CREDITS FOR ILLUSTRATIONS

INDEX

NOTES

CHAPTER 1
EXPERIENTIAL BASES FOR ESTHETIC DECISION (pages 1–26)

1. Walter B. Cannon, *Science and Man* (New York: Harcourt Brace, 1942), p. 290.
2. Edward T. Hall, *The Hidden Dimension* (New York: Doubleday, 1966).
3. George E. Ruff, "Psychological Stress," *Program*, Journal of the School of Architecture of Columbia University (Spring 1962), pp. 66–79.
4. Philip Solomon, "Sensory Deprivation and Psychological Stress," lecture, School of Architecture of Columbia University (November 12, 1963).
5. Woodburn Heron, "The Pathology of Boredom," *Scientific American*, vol. 196 (January 1957), p. 56.
6. Ibid.
7. Hannah Arendt, *The Human Condition* (New York: Doubleday, 1959).
8. Turpin C. Bannister, ed., *The Architect at Mid-Century: Evaluation and Achievement* (New York: Reinhold, 1954), Table #57, Appendix.
9. Ernst Fischer, *The Necessity of Art* (Baltimore: Penguin Books, 1963), p. 17.

CHAPTER 2
THE SOCIAL CONSEQUENCES OF ARCHITECTURAL INTERVENTION (pages 27–37)

1. U.S. Department of Health, Education and Welfare, *Accident Fatalities: 1959*, Washington, D.C., vol. 54, no. 8, December 15, 1961, p. 205.
2. U.S. Department of Health, Education and Welfare, *Health Statistics: 1959–1961*, Washington, D.C., series B, no. 39, p. 1.
3. Britten, Brown and Altman, *Certain Characteristics of Urban Housing and Their Relation to Illness and Accident* (New York: American Public Health Association, 1941), p. 93.
4. Ibid., p. 178.

CHAPTER 3

FAIR AND WARMER: CONTROL OF THE THERMAL
ENVIRONMENT (pages 38–59)

1. C. E. A. Winslow and L. P. Herrington, *Temperature and Human Life* (Princeton, N. J.: Princeton University Press, 1949), p. 255.
2. Ibid., p. 251.

CHAPTER 4

PURE AS THE AIR YOU BREATHE: CONTROL OF
THE ATMOSPHERIC ENVIRONMENT (pages 60–82)

1. F. W. Wendt, David B. Slemmons and Hugo N. Mozingo, "The Organic Nature of Atmospheric Condensation Nuclei," proceedings, National Academy of Sciences, vol. 58, no. 1, p. 71.
2. See papers read at Smithsonian Institution Symposium, *Quality of Man's Environment*, Washington, D.C., February 17–19, 1967. Especially relevant: René Dubos, "Destructive and Creative Consequences of Adaptation"; Baron Bertrand de Jouvenal and Ian L. McHarg, "Values, Process and Form"; Leo Marx, "Pastoral Ideals and City Troubles."
3. This change in perspective is readily apparent in the first edition of this book, *American Building: The Forces That Shape It* (Boston: Houghton Mifflin, 1947), pp. 219–222.
4. Leonard Greenberg, *Technical paper no. 65–4*, read at the Air Pollution Control Association, Toronto, Canada, 1965.
5. James G. Townsend, "Investigation of the Smog Incident in Donora, Pa., and Vicinity," *American Journal of Public Health*, vol. 40 (February 1950), pp. 183–189.
   See also Berton Roueche, "Eleven Blue Men," *The New Yorker*, vol. 26, September 30, 1950, p. 33 ff.
6. The epidemiological character of London's smog-related deaths has been investigated at length. See, among others, J. Pemberton and C. Goldberg, *British Medical Journal*, vol. 2 (1954), p. 567; R. E. Waller and P. J. Lawther, ibid., vol. 2 (1955), p. 1356; D. J. B. Ashley, *British Journal of Cancer*, vol. 21 (1967), p. 243.
7. Leonard Greenberg, "Air Pollution, Influenza and Mortality in New York City: January–February 1963," *Archives of Environmental Health*, vol. 15 (October 1967), pp. 430–438.
8. Study developed jointly by Division of Air Pollution, U.S. Public Health Service and School of Medicine, Vanderbilt University, Nashville. (Reported by Walter Sullivan, *New York Times*, November 12, 1968.)
9. Gladwyn Hill, "Los Angeles: A Model for the Nation," *New York Times*, September 26, 1966, p. 36.
10. Ibid.
11. A recent attempt to present an overall view of environmental pollution is *Waste Management and Control*, National Academy of Sciences, Washington, D.C., 1966.
12. 1966 *Guide*, American Society of Heating and Ventilating Engineers, New York, p. 123 ff.
   See also William F. Wells, "Sanitary Significance of Ventilation," ASHVE *Transactions*, vol. 54 (1948), pp. 275–290.

13. C. P. McCord and W. W. Witheridge, *Odors: Physiology and Control* (New York: McGraw Hill, 1949), p. 15.
14. John E. Amoore, James W. Johnston and Martin Rubin, "The Stereochemical Theory of Odors," *Scientific American,* vol. 210 (February 1964), p. 42.
15. Hall, *The Hidden Dimension.*
16. Roy Bedichek, *The Sense of Smell* (New York: Doubleday, 1960).
17. Hans Kalmus, "The Chemical Senses," *Scientific American,* vol. 198 (April 1958), p. 97 ff.
18. McCord and Witheridge, p. 15.

CHAPTER 5
"OH, SAY CAN YOU SEE . . .": CONTROL OF THE
LUMINOUS ENVIRONMENT (pages 83–130)

1. Hans Blumenfeld, "Integration of Natural and Artificial Lighting," *Architectural Record,* vol. 85 (December 1940), p. 49 ff.
2. Hall, *The Hidden Dimension,* p. 40.
3. H. Richard Blackwell, "Specifications of Interior Illumination Levels," *Illuminating Engineering,* vol. 54 (June 1959), p. 320.
4. John Lott Brown, "Afterimages," in *Vision and Visual Perception,* ed. Clarence H. Graham (New York: Wiley, 1965), p. 497.
5. H. C. Weston, *Illuminating Engineering Society Transactions* (London: 1953), vol. 18, pp. 39–66.
6. Samuel H. Bartley and Eloise Chute, *Fatigue and Impairment in Man* (New York: McGraw-Hill, 1947), p. 34.
7. Ralph Knowles, "The Derivation of Surface Responses to Selected Environmental Forces," *California Arts and Architecture,* June 1964, pp. 21–24.
8. Ralph Knowles, "Form and Stability," paper read to the Building Research Institute, National Academy of Sciences, Washington, D.C., April 23, 1968.
9. H. Richard Blackwell, "Visual Benefits of Polarized Light," *Journal* of the American Institute of Architects, vol. 40 (November 1963), pp. 87–92.
10. Ibid.
11. Ibid., p. 92.
12. Robert M. Gerard, "Differential Effects of Colored Lights on Psychophysiological Functions" (thesis, University of California, Los Angeles, 1958).

CHAPTER 6
SILENCE — MEN AT WORK: CONTROL OF THE
SONIC ENVIRONMENT (pages 131–157)

1. The large and growing body of literature on the health hazards of noise has been most recently summarized by the Committee on Environmental Quality, Federal Council for Science and Technology, Washington, D.C., 1968.
2. Paul E. Sabine, "Control of Sound in Buildings," *Architectural Record,* vol. 85 (January, 1940), p. 69.
3. Van Bergeijk, Pierce and David, *Waves and the Ear* (New York: Doubleday, 1960), p. 74.

4. Cf. John D. Dougherty and Oliver L. Welsh, "Community Noise and Hearing Loss," *New England Journal of Medicine,* vol. 275 (October 6, 1966), pp. 759–765.
5. Lewis Goodfriend, "Sound or Fury: Man's Response to Noise," *Architectural and Engineering News,* vol. 7 (April 1965), p. 43.
6. Gilbert Seldes, "Communication," *Columbia University Forum,* vol. 6 (Fall 1963), p. 44.
7. Harold C. Schonberg, "The House That Roared," *New York Times,* November 20, 1966, p. 34.
8. Ada Louise Huxtable, *New York Times,* September 17, 1966, p. 17.
9. Harold C. Schonberg, "Music: Good Acoustics," *New York Times,* September 12, 1966, p. 36.
10. Ibid.
11. Cf. R. S. Lanier, "What Happened at Philharmonic Hall?" *Architectural Forum,* December 1963, pp. 119–123, and Harold C. Schonberg, "New Philharmonic Sound Glows," *New York Times,* September 24, 1969, p. 1 ff.
12. Alexander Cohen, "Noise Effects on Health, Productivity and Well-Being," *Transactions of the New York Academy of Sciences,* series II, vol. 30, no. 7, p. 911.
13. In Jones and Cohen, "Noise as a Health Hazard at Work, in the Community, and in the Home," *Public Health Reports,* vol. 83 (July 1968), p. 533.
14. Ibid., p. 535.
15. Dougherty and Welsh, p. 761.
16. Dr. Samuel Rosen, College of Physicians and Surgeons, Columbia University, as quoted by *New York Times,* March 19, 1967, p. 42.
17. Committee on Environmental Quality.
18. Samuel Rosen et al., "Presbycusis Study of a Relatively Noise-free Population in the Sudan," *Annals of Otology, Rhinology and Laryngology,* vol. 71, no. 3, pp. 732–733.
19. Ibid. See also Samuel Rosen et al., "Relation of Hearing Loss to Cardiovascular Disease," *Transactions of the American Academy of Opthamology and Otolaryngology,* May–June 1964, pp. 433–444; and Samuel Rosen and Pekka Olin, "Hearing Loss and Coronary Heart Disease," *Archives of Otolaryngology,* vol. 82 (September 1965), pp. 236–243.
20. Rosen et al., *Transactions,* pp. 436–437.
21. Ibid.
22. Rosen and Olin, *Archives,* p. 236.
23. See Andrew D. Hosey and Charles H. Powell, eds., *Industrial Noise: A Guide to Its Evaluation and Control,* and Alexander Cohen, *Location-Design Noise Control of Transportation Systems,* both from U.S. Department of Health, Education and Welfare, Washington, D.C., 1967.

CHAPTER 7

THE ARCHITECTURAL MANIPULATION OF SPACE,

TIME AND GRAVITY (pages 158–198)

1. Raymond G. Studer, "The Dynamics of Behavior-contingent Physical Systems," *Proceedings of the Symposium on Design Methods,* Portsmouth College of Technology, England, December 1967.

2. James J. Gibson, *The Senses Considered as Perceptual Systems* (Boston: Houghton Mifflin, 1966), p. 111.
3. Christopher Alexander, *Notes on the Synthesis of Form* (Cambridge: Harvard University Press, 1964), p. 3.
4. Winslow and Herrington.
5. Ibid., p. 178.
6. Bartley and Chute, p. 39.
7. Hans Selye, *The Stress of Life* (New York: McGraw-Hill, 1956).
8. Tillisch and Walsch as cited by Bartley and Chute, p. 39.
9. Stanley Schacter et al., *Social Pressures in Informal Groups* (Berkeley: University of California Press, 1962).
10. Hall, *The Hidden Dimension.*
11. Robert Sommer, "The Ecology of Privacy," *Library Quarterly,* vol. 36 (July 1966), p. 236.
12. Ibid., p. 248.
13. Ibid., p. 244.
14. Humphry Osmond, "The Relationship between Architect and Psychiatrist," in *Psychiatric Architecture* (Washington, D.C.: American Psychiatric Association, 1949).
15. Humphry Osmond, "The Psychological Dimension of Architectural Space," *Progressive Architecture,* vol. 46 (April 1965), p. 160.
16. Alexander Kira, *The Bathroom* (New York: Grosset & Dunlap, 1967), p. 202.
17. W. T. Dempster, "The Anthropometry of Body Action," *Annals of the New York Academy of Sciences,* vol. 63 (1955), pp. 564–565.
18. Jane Callaghan and Catherine Palmer, *Measuring Space and Motion* (New York: John B. Pierce Foundation, 1944).
19. Mary Heiner and Helen McCullough, "A New Look at the Kitchen," *Architectural Forum,* vol. 84 (February 1946), pp. 155–158; (March 1946), pp. 187–190.
20. Francis Schroeder, *Anatomy for Interior Designers* (New York: Whitney Publications, 1951).
21. In *Architectural Record,* vol. 86 (September 1939), pp. 60–75.
22. Kira, p. 12

CHAPTER 8

SKELETON AND SKIN

THE MORPHOLOGICAL DEVELOPMENT OF

STRUCTURAL SYSTEMS (pages 199–234)

1. *A Decent Home: The Report of the President's Committee on Urban Housing* (Washington: U.S. Government Printing Office, 1968), p. 40.
2. Clay L. Cochran, "The Scandal of Rural Housing," *Architectural Forum,* vol. 134 (March 1971), p. 52.
3. *1968 Yearbook,* Department of Housing and Urban Development (Washington: U.S. Government Printing Office, 1968), p. 52.
4. *A Decent Home,* p. 40.
5. Ibid., p. 42.

CHAPTER 9

THE INTEGRATION OF ENVIRONMENTAL

CONTROL SYSTEMS (pages 235–285)

1. E. R. Biel, "Microclimate, Bioclimatology and Notes on Comparable Dynamic Climatology," *American Scientist,* vol. 49, no. 3 (1961), p. 330.
2. Cited by Helmut Landsberg in "Microclimatology," *Architectural Forum,* vol. 86 (March 1947), p. 115.
3. Abel Wolman, "Metabolism of Cities," *Scientific American,* vol. 213 (September 1965), pp. 179–190.
4. James Marston Fitch with Daniel P. Branch, "Primitive Architecture," *Scientific American,* vol. 203 (December 1960), pp. 133–144.
5. Fitch, "The Aesthetics of Function," *Annals of the New York Academy of Sciences,* vol. 128 (1965), pp. 706–714.
6. Paul A. Siple, "Regional Climate Analyses and Design Data," *Bulletin of the American Institute of Architects,* September 1949, p. 17.
7. Rudolph Geiger, *The Climate near the Ground* (Cambridge: Harvard University Press, 1959).
8. Charles F. Brooks, "Parade-Ground Temperatures at College Station, Texas," *Monthly Weather Review,* November 1919, p. 801.
9. Geiger, p. 213.
10. Jeffrey Aronin, *Climate and Architecture* (New York: Reinhold, 1943).
11. Cf. Bernard Rudofsky, *Architecture Without Architects* (New York: Museum of Modern Art, 1964), especially Figs. 15–18.
12. *Climate Control Project of House Beautiful:* the meteorological data and architectural performance analyses were published in monograph form by the *Bulletin of the A.I.A.* between the years 1949 and 1953.
13. Aladar and Viktor Olgyay, *Solar Control and Shading Devices* (Princeton, N. J.: Princeton University Press, 1957) and Viktor Olgyay, *Design with Climate* (Princeton, N. J.: Princeton University Press, 1963).
14. Ralph Knowles, "Form and Stability;" and Knowles, *Owens Valley Study: A Natural Ecological Framework for Settlement* (Los Angeles, Calif.: University of Southern California, 1969).
15. Rudofsky.
16. Ernest Schweibert, "The Significance of Primitive Architecture" (unpublished dissertation, Princeton University, 1965).
17. Knowles, "Derivation of Surface Response," pp. 21–23.
18. Ralph Erskine, "Building in the Arctic," *Architectural Design,* vol. 30 (May 1960), pp. 194–197; "Two Lectures," *Journal,* Royal Institute of Canadian Architects, vol. 41 (January 1964), pp. 194–197; "Indigenous Architecture: Building in the Sub-Arctic Region," *Perspecta,* vol. 8, pp. 59–62; "Construire dans le Nord," *Architecture d'aujourd'hui,* 38, no. 134 (October–November 1967), pp. 96–97; "Restructuration de Kiruna, Ville de Laponie," ibid., pp. 98–99; "Turistation i Borgafjall," *Byggmasparen Arkitektur,* vol. 3 (March 5, 1955), pp. 82–86.
19. Christopher Alexander, *Notes on the Synthesis of Form.*
20. Knowles, "Derivation of Surface Response," p. 21.
21. Hassan Fathy, *Gourna: A Tale of Two Villages* (Cairo: Ministry of Culture, 1969).

22. "Ecological Architecture: Planning the Organic Environment," *Progressive Architecture*, May 1966, pp. 120–137.
23. Geiger, p. 377.
24. Wolman, p. 180.

CHAPTER 10

PLAN, THE INSTRUMENT OF POLICY (pages 286–307)

1. John Ruskin, *Seven Lamps of Architecture* (New York: John W. Lovell, 1885), p. 17.
2. Jane Jacobs, *The Death and Life of Great American Cities* (New York: Random House, 1959).
3. Louis Winnick, "The Economic Functions of the City Today and Tomorrow," in *Urban Problems*, ed. Thomas P. Peardon, 28th Proceedings of the Academy of Political Science, April 29, 1960 (New York: Academy of Political Science), p. 12.
4. Ibid., p. 13.
5. Jane Jacobs, *The Economy of Cities* (New York: Random House, 1969).
6. Ibid., p. 83.
7. Christopher Alexander, "A City Is Not a Tree," *Architectural Forum*, April (part I) and May (part II), 1965.
8. Ibid., part II, p. 61.
9. Ibid., part II, p. 58.
10. Ibid., part I, p. 60.
11. Ibid., part I, p. 62.

CREDITS FOR ILLUSTRATIONS

INDEX